Demanding Child Care

WOMEN IN
AMERICAN HISTORY

Series Editors
Anne Firor Scott
Susan Armitage
Susan K. Cahn
Deborah Gray White

*A list of books in the series appears
at the end of this book.*

Demanding Child Care

Women's Activism and the Politics of Welfare, 1940–71

NATALIE M. FOUSEKIS

UNIVERSITY OF
ILLINOIS PRESS
Urbana, Chicago,
and Springfield

Publication supported by a grant from the
History Department and an award from the
College of Humanities and Social Sciences
at California State University, Fullerton.

Library of Congress Cataloging-in-Publication Data
Fousekis, Natalie Marie.
Demanding child care : women's activism and the
politics of welfare, 1940–71 / Natalie M. Fousekis.
p.   cm. — (Women in American history)
Includes bibliographical references and index.
ISBN 978-0-252-03625-5 (cloth)
1. Child care—California—History—20th century.
2. Child care—United States—History—20th century.
3. Women political activists—California—History—20th century.
4. Women political activists—United States—History—20th century.
5. Public welfare—California—History—20th century.
6. Public welfare—United States—History—20th century.
I. Title.
HQ778.65.C2F667   2011
362.709794—dc22   2011006824

For my father, James T. Fousekis,
and in memory of my mother,
Susana Cox Fousekis

Contents

Acknowledgments

A project this long in the making could not have been completed without much assistance and support.

This book (and the child care movement it chronicles) relied on the generosity of the women who invited me into their homes and lives to share their memories of the battle for child care in California. I am thankful to Lynne Beeson, Barbara Gach, Sharon Godske, Loretta Juhas, Jeanne Miller, Tillie Olsen, Virginia Rose, Debbie Young, Mary Young Arnold, Faye Love Williams, Winona Sample, and Docia Zavitovsky. In particular, I am grateful I located Mary Young Arnold, who not only shared with me her recollections as legislative chairman of the California Parents' Association for Child Care (CPACC), but also unearthed her personal collection of documents on CPACC. Moreover, on two separate occasions, I had the pleasure of enjoying lunch and dessert with Mary and her charming husband, Bruce. I cherish those afternoons we spent together. Unfortunately, Mary did not live to see this project completed, but during one of our last conversations even as dementia had begun to take her mind, she smiled and talked about the book I was writing about her. Additional thanks go to Jeanne Miller who spent an afternoon showing me photographs of her mother, Theresa Mahler, shedding light on the Mahler family history, and providing details about her mother's life that were absent from the archives. I feel fortunate to have found Lynne Beeson and Faye Love Williams near the end of my research and writing. My interviews with them transformed my final chapter. Moreover, I am grateful for the friendship I have formed with Lynne. While retired and no longer in the field of child care, Lynne's passion about the public policy issues important to our communities and our families remains.

Many librarians and archivists provided me with invaluable assistance. I want to give special thanks to: Robert Marshall at the Urban Archives Center, California State University at Northridge; Jennifer Schaffner (now a Program Officer with OCLC Research and the RLG Partnership) and Patricia Keats at the California Historical Society; Robert Haynes at the African American Museum and Library at Oakland; Tim Gregory and the staff at the Pacific Oaks College Library; Kristie French at the Special Collections, California State University at Long Beach; the staff at the California State Archives, especially Melodi Andersen, Genevieve Troka, and Lucy Barber (now Deputy Executive Director at the National Historical Publications and Records Commission); and, finally, David Kessler and the staff at the Bancroft Library who helped me locate one last photograph for the book. I also appreciate the generosity of Irene Byrne, Executive Director of the Golden Gate Kindergarten Association, who allowed me to spend a week in the basement of the Phoebe Hearst Preschool Learning Center looking at the unprocessed papers of the Kindergarten Association, as well as its longtime director, Rhoda Kellogg, for letting me monopolize their copy machine on more than one occasion. I can think of no better place to conduct research on child care than sitting on a toddler-sized chair surrounded by the sounds of preschoolers learning and playing.

This book would have never been completed without a year-long fellowship from the American Council for Learned Societies. Time away from teaching allowed me to conduct additional research, write, and revise the entire manuscript. Additional important financial assistance for travel came from a State Special Fund for Research, Scholarship, and Creative Activity, Summer Stipend and a Carl Albert Congressional Research and Studies Center, Visiting Scholars Grant.

Over the course of writing this book, which began as my dissertation in the late 1990s, I have been fortunate to be surrounded by a supportive group of friends, colleagues, and family. Barbara Boxer inspired my interest in women and politics. I had the privilege of working briefly for Boxer in the House of Representatives as she was running for the U.S. Senate against Bruce Herschensohn, a race close enough in the spring of 1992 that I chose to go to graduate school instead of taking a chance to work for Boxer in the Senate. While Boxer is now one of the most powerful women in the U.S. Senate, like the women in this book Boxer got her political start at the grassroots, organizing neighbors and friends to improve the community where she was raising her children.

In my years as a graduate student at the University of North Carolina at Chapel Hill, I benefited from the friendship and exceptional talents of my classmates and the faculty. In particular, the women in my dissertation writing group—Kirsten Delegard, Ginny Noble, Kathy Newfont, Stacy Braukman, Eve Duffy and D'Arcy Brissman—read every early draft of this project. For their encouragement, valuable critiques, and good food and drink during those years of writing, I am deeply grateful. Joe Mosnier helped me tally and develop categories for the letters written to Governor Earl Warren in 1947. He had no investment in this project except as my good friend. A special thank you goes to Sherry Honeycutt Everett for providing transcription and detailed tape logs for the interviews I conducted during this phase of the project.

My greatest debts among the faculty at UNC go to Peter Filene and Jacquelyn Hall (more about Jacquelyn later). In the early years, Peter encouraged me, particularly when I was having a difficult time remembering what I liked about being a historian. I am thankful for all the times he allowed me to walk into his office or to lunch and talk through the difficulties I was having with a particular chapter. Often he sent me home with a piece of paper scribbled with his notes summarizing our conversation. Most of all, I am grateful for the way Peter supported me both as an advisor and a friend, particularly during the early years of my mother's battles with Alzheimer's disease. Thanks are also due to Judith Bennett, Nancy Hewitt, Lucie White, Jerma Jackson, Sonya Michel, and Eileen Boris who provided thoughtful critiques in this project's early stages. Ann Dunbar, a close friend of my mothers from Wellesley College and a faculty member at UNC, provided moral support and warm conversation from the first day I set foot in Chapel Hill until the moving truck arrived to take me back west. I am deeply saddened by her recent passing.

My participation in and interaction with other members and guest speakers in the year-long seminar "Think Globally, Act Locally: Women's Leadership and Grassroots Activism," sponsored by the Andrew W. Mellon Foundation and the Duke University-University of North Carolina-Chapel Hill Center for Research on Women, dramatically altered the trajectory of my research. As a project coordinator and interviewer for the Southern Oral History Program's related Women's Leadership and Grassroots Activism Project, my thinking on grassroots politics developed further. As part of the research team, the questions we posed and the conversations we shared about leadership and activism shaped many of the questions I asked the women in California's child care movement.

I am grateful for the trenchant comments and crucial suggestions for revision made by Eileen Boris and an anonymous reader for the University of Illinois Press. Their proposed changes helped me hone my argument in key places, simplify some of my more complicated discussions of the welfare state, and provide additional context about the political terrain of California. The University of Illinois Press has demonstrated an interest and commitment to this project from my early conversations with Anne Scott to my initial meeting with Laurie Matheson. Since that first meeting Laurie has encouraged and remained enthusiastic despite the length of time that passed between reader's reports to the finished product. As the project neared its completion, I had the good fortune of working with Grey Osterud who brought a fresh eye, her historical insight, and editorial talents to the manuscript.

Good friendships have sustained me throughout. Friends outside academia helped me remain grounded in the real world and reminded me of my life away from work. Special thanks go to Sheryl Bracken, Kelly Manno, Vanessa Kaylor, Andy Petesch and Treena Hall. Claudia Lopez provided me with critical moral support and much needed distraction during the final push to submit my manuscript to the University of Illinois Press in 2006. My "Tri buddies"—Krisi Raymond, Sarah Gott, and Monique Davies—helped me stay sane by pushing myself physically on the race course, kept me in good wine throughout this long journey, and, most importantly, made me laugh so hard it hurt.

The fabulous members of history department at California State University, Fullerton, have constantly reminded me how lucky I am to work surrounded by such a collegial bunch. Some of the department's long-time members, in particular Gayle Brunelle and Gordon Bakken, as well as its young leader, Clark Davis, provided examples of an active research agenda. Unfortunately, Clark passed away only six months after I arrived at Fullerton, but his stamp on the department remains in those of us who had the pleasure of being his colleague. Cora Granata and Kristine Dennehy, both recent hires with me, read pieces of this work during our short-lived writing group, but also provided me with critical emotional support. Mindy Mechanic, whom I met during my first week on the job at CSUF, has encouraged and listened as well as shared stimulating conversation. I am also thankful for the dedicated staff at the Center for Oral and Public History who have had to endure an absent administrator for weeks here and there as I made the final revisions to this work. Other local scholars have provided me with a wonderful intellectual community in this big, dispersed urban setting. My 20th Century U.S. reading group members—Mark Wild, Chris Endy, Doug Smith, and Laura McEnaney exposed me to literature I might not have read and, most importantly, provided me with a space to talk and laugh about life as an academic. A special thanks to Laura for her insightful comments on chapter 2 and to Chris for his last minute editorial suggestions on the introduction and chapter 6 as I prepared the manuscript for submission. Others who deserve special thanks are Cheryl Koos and Carla Bittel. Robert Self, whom I met while he had a fellowship at the Huntington Library, has become a very close friend and deserves credit for helping me come up with the book title. My colleague and friend, Lynn Sharp, whom I met during my one-year job at Whitman College spent a critical month with me at my family's house in the Sierras working on our books. We wrote, we hiked, and we talked about our research. Some of my earliest ideas for revision developed during this summer retreat.

As I completed the last phase of research for this project I was fortunate to have research and transcription assistance from two extremely capable history graduate students, Julie Davis and Maria Hernandez-Figueroa. Both provided me with invaluable assistance tracking down sources and narrators. Maria transcribed almost all of my recent interviews.

During various stages of this project friends have taken me into their homes, providing me both with a place to stay and a welcome distraction once the archives were closed. Tommy and Tracey Hinkley took me in for multiple weeks during my research trips to southern California in 1998. Those weeks in 1998 changed my opinion about the Los Angeles basin (of course, I was staying in the Hollywood Hills). Krisi Raymond and Kirk Wrede generously allowed me to stay with them for weeks at a time while I was doing research in Sacramento in the fall of 2005.

Jacquelyn Hall and Bob Korstad provided me with a place to do my most focused and in-depth thinking and writing. Their house became my writing retreat on multiple occasions. Not many friends would let me invade their space for so many weeks at a time. Leaving behind the hustle and bustle of southern California, the responsibilities of my growing administrative work, and escaping to the pristine and serene setting of their beautiful house overlooking the forest in Chapel Hill, allowed me the clarity to write and re-write efficiently. The setting was ideal, but having such good friends to share wine and conversation with at the end of the day made those weeks some of my fondest memories. Jacquelyn and Bob are my North Carolina family.

My deepest scholarly gratitude goes to Jacquelyn Hall for her guidance and unwavering support. Her careful reading of my work and rigorous questions over the years have helped me sharpen my analysis and encouraged me to be bold. Her diligent editing has helped me become a better writer. Evidence of her insight and thoughtful editorial suggestions can be found throughout the narrative. Her genuine kindness, warm encouragement, and sharp wit have kept my spirits high throughout this long process.

Finally, my family has always given me their love and support. I would like to thank my parents, James and Susana Fousekis, for raising me in an environment that encouraged intellectual thought and political debate. My father has always made it clear he is proud of my accomplishments and has tried hard over the past few years to not ask about the book. My greatest disappointment is that my mother is not able to share the completion of this project with me. Unfortunately, my mother's fourteen-year battle with Alzheimer's disease took her away from my family a little bit at a time. She passed away in 2008, but much of her strength, intellectual curiosity, and empathy will live with me forever. My sister Sara has been with me through it all and provided critical emotional support as I worked to complete this book while our mother faced some of the most debilitating aspects of her disease. I am also thankful to my aunt and uncle, Lou and Penny Rosso, and for the newer members of my family—Alice,

Winnie, Joe, and Cross Creason as well as Greg Derelian, and my new nephew, Milo. Family time has always been filled with laughter and love.

It is appropriate that I completed this book in California while living across the street from an original Lanham Act child center. I wrote and revised portions of the manuscript as I looked at children playing in the same spot as the daughters and sons of some who advocated for child care sixty years ago.

When I began this project, I never thought my life would resemble that of the women I am writing about, but it has in one important way. In September 2008, I became a single mother by choice. My son Henry has changed my life in ways I never imagined, and I am thankful to him for reminding me of what's important in my life and for all the smiles he brings to me daily. Like the mothers in this book, my most important concern now is finding quality and safe care for my son. I was fortunate to have the assistance early on of Joey Taylor, who helped me get much needed sleep during Henry's early months. Joey introduced me to her sister, Yvonne Bryant, who became Henry's child care provider for the first two years of his life. Knowing Henry was safe and well cared for gave me "peace of mind," a term frequently used by mothers who placed their children in California's Child Care/Children's Centers. Henry is now in the care of the wonderful teachers and staff of the Early Childhood Education Department at the Alpert Jewish Community Center in Long Beach. As I complete this book and my son enters his third year of life, I am now more than ever amazed at what it took for the mothers who sustained California's child care movement to accomplish what they did. Their dedication to write letters, organize others, and lobby the legislature all while being the sole earners and sole parents in their families has my respect and admiration.

Introduction

In 1947, a recently divorced mother, whose two young children were enrolled in a publicly supported child care program that had its funding threatened, penned a letter to California Governor Earl Warren: "If there were fewer children affected by this action, I would not be writing to you. Because while this is a personal letter, it is *not* a personal program. There are so many of these children. Adequate care of children is the basis of things—the home, the government—even civilization itself. We cannot let the extended day care measure fall through. We must have your help."[1] Maurine Jorgensen of Sherman Oaks explained how her former husband had stopped paying child support and how the state's child care center had enabled her to survive as a wage-earning mother. Her letter expressed a sense of solidarity with women facing similar circumstances. She understood child care not as a special circumstance but as the key to mothers' participation in the labor force and as a social need that the government must address.

I discovered Jorgensen's letter and the letters of hundreds of mothers like her on a spring day in 1997 at the California State Archives in Sacramento. As I waited in the bustling reading room for the reference librarian to bring me the 1947 folders on child care in Governor Warren's papers, I had no inkling of what I would find. To my surprise, the archivist delivered not just one box, but three filled with petitions signed by thousands of Californians and hundreds of personal letters written by concerned citizens, most of them mothers with children in the state's centers. As I turned the pages, I read the dignified, determined, and forceful words of one working mother after another. Their heartfelt letters allow a rare glimpse into the lives of California's working mothers. They reveal not only their views on child care but also their individual stories. Taken together, their words document the network of parents and educators that sustained a movement for publicly sponsored child care in California from World War II into the 1970s.

The letters inspired me to tell the story of women's activism for child care in California. I undertook a decade-long search to reconstruct the history of the women who conducted letter-writing campaigns, traveled to the capital to lobby their representatives and public officials, and coordinated statewide political action. These women acted on the conviction that they had authority as mothers and advanced a vision of their rights as citizens to social programs.[2] They spoke on behalf of themselves and other working-class women, gaining a new sense of collective identity that included a commitment to making their voices count in the political process. In their campaigns, working mothers had the support and guidance of a group of female educators who supervised and taught in the state's centers. These educators spoke passionately in defense of the program, emphasizing the benefits of education-based care to the children of working mothers and to society at large. The efforts of mothers and educators to save child care in California put them at the center of state and local politics, and their struggle illuminates the nationwide contest after World War II over the contours of the social welfare state.

Thanks to these women, for almost thirty years California maintained a vision of how the liberal state could serve the working poor. Unlike other states, California put education-based child care at the core of that service. Although the program these women upheld did not offer a comprehensive alternative to the federal government's main welfare program, Aid to Dependent Children (ADC), their efforts ensured the autonomy of California's low-income mothers by caring and providing education for their children while they earned money to support their families. In the end, their efforts prevented tens of thousands of the working poor from dropping into the ranks of the underclass.[3]

Although the letters at the state archives constituted the paper trail left by this movement, the story told in *Demanding Child Care* came to life as I conducted oral histories with the mothers and educators who animated this network of publicly sponsored centers.[4] Many of the movement's main players, especially in the parents' groups, have been forgotten by history until now—Mary Young, Winona Sample, Virginia Rose, Ellen Hall, Sharon Godske, Barbara Gach, Willie Mae Addison, Fay Williams, and Lynne Beeson, to name a few. Without capturing these women's memories, I would have been unable to tell this story. One contact led to another. In July 1998, after a year of searching for and writing letters to more than a dozen Mary Youngs in California, I finally located the former legislative advocate of the California Parents' Association for Child Care (CPACC). Before our first meeting Young unearthed a box of documents from her garage that gave me evidence on the Parents' Association during her tenure in the organization from the late 1940s to the mid-1960s.[5] These papers provided me with names of additional women who joined the movement. Eight years later, when I interviewed Lynne Monti (now Beeson), she lent me a box of her material, which provided critical details about the Parents' Association's later years. Despite all these discoveries, the picture offered here remains incomplete. Many women vanished from the historical record, threw away their papers, or died before I could contact them. What follows is my reconstruction of this remarkable movement, with all of its successes and failures, in hopes of capturing what it meant to the women who participated in it and what it reveals about the kinds of services the government should provide for its low-income citizens.

In this book, I use the term *working poor* when discussing the mostly female-headed households that benefitted from California's child care program. By working poor, I mean those who held full-time jobs but made only enough money to hover just above the poverty line. These working mothers earned enough to avoid Aid to Dependent Children and its successor, Aid to Families with Dependent Children, but with a small pay cut, illness or injury, or the loss of a wage-earning spouse, some were forced onto welfare. These were families with little or no savings and who rented rather than owned their houses. Most of their heads of household earned a woman's wage.[6]

This is a story about improved lives and better opportunities for California's working poor. Glenda Gilmore argues that historians too often focus on the outcome of a struggle, forgetting that "what is past to them was future to their subjects. Too often [what] they lose in the telling is what made their subjects' lives worth living: hope."[7] State-sponsored child care provided hope for working mothers, early childhood educators, and teachers in California from the 1940s to the 1970s. From the perspective of the twenty-first century, the services they won appear paltry because they were available to only a small number of California's families. Yet, to early childhood educators and California's working mothers, their initial victories seemed to portend a better future. They presented working mothers with a "real opportunity" to become independent wage-earners, elevating their families' income and status in the community.[8] For California's nursery educators, the state centers represented the seeds from which a universal state-sponsored preschool program could grow. If they had been able to realize their vision, education-based care would have become available to all.

The passage of the Lanham Act during World War II marked the first and only time in U.S. history that the federal government supported child care for any mother who worked, regardless of her income level. This federal program, however, was short-lived. When Harry Truman announced his plan to close the centers only weeks after Japan's surrender, women in California rose up in protest. Together, a cross-class and cross-race coalition of mothers and educators, initially aided by labor unionists, mainstream women's organizations,

New Deal liberals, and left feminists, helped make California the only state to convert wartime centers into a permanent program. Were it not for the coalition's efforts, the ideal of universal, education-based care would have vanished from the political landscape after World War II.

What began in a simple desire to preserve a child care program turned into twenty-five plus years of attending community meetings, testifying at hearings, organizing letter-writing campaigns and petition drives, and lobbying legislators at the state capital. As they set out to convince the state of their child care needs, mothers and educators were drawn into the world of politics and policymaking. Over time an ad hoc, emergency-inspired organization coalesced into a cadre of politically savvy activists who put firm and consistent pressure on the government.

They did so in the face of widespread resistance to universal public child care provisions, which many saw as an unwarranted intervention into family matters. Their success suggests what a coalition of dedicated women—in this case mothers, teachers, and early childhood educators—can do. Motivated by their desire to secure education-based care for California's working families, activists obtained publicly funded child care at a time when it existed only on a small scale elsewhere.

The struggle for these services introduced an entirely new group of women to politics and taught them to how to assert authority in the public realm. For some, becoming politically active marked a sea change in their identities as citizens and mothers. While operating under the constraints of the Cold War, the women marshaled arguments for child care based on traditional values, in part out of genuine concern as mothers and in part to gain credibility in a hostile political environment.[9] They described independent working mothers' need for child care as synonymous with the "greater good of society" and countered conservative resistance to maternal employment by arguing that child care allowed them to remain self-sufficient and stay off welfare. At the center of their political actions, however, were the radical notions that women could be workers and mothers and live independently from men and that the state should support them in this endeavor. Both their political activism and their arguments for child care had the potential to transform American society.

The women featured in this story expanded the possibility of democratic action well beyond the confines of the halls and hearing rooms of the state capitol. Their political actions and claims for child care played a critical role in shaping public debate.[10] Their activism forced the government to respond to their basic needs as mothers and as workers. In 1957, the immediate result was a permanent child care program for some of California's working families. Beyond that, they launched a child care movement that continues to this day.

This network of activists learned to operate within the world of California state politics. During the war and for much of the early Cold War period, that meant convincing moderate Republican governors Earl Warren and Goodwin Knight that funding child care was in the state's interest. Warren and Knight, political moderates, were followed by Edmund Brown, a Democrat who espoused "responsible liberalism" and then by Ronald Reagan, an ideological conservative. The rhetorical differences between them were not always translated into policy. Although the governor's position mattered, especially when it came to securing a permanent program, the larger hurdle was convincing the state's conservative rural legislators to support child care services that primarily benefited the state's urban areas. Senators representing rural areas held powerful positions on the budget committee and many of the social welfare committees over the years.

California women succeeded where those in other states failed for three major reasons. First, California had a remarkable number of progressive preschool educators committed to establishing public nursery schools. Most had taught in or directed wartime centers, and some had experience stretching back to the New Deal's WPA Nursery Schools.[11] They saw the Lanham Act centers as the first step in bringing nursery schools to children of all economic and social backgrounds. These preschool teachers provided the institutional support and the professional expertise for the state's education-based program and had the organizational skills and resources to pursue their ideals and aspirations in the political arena. Second, California's centers could count on a large constituency of mothers who knew firsthand the benefits of this new public service.[12] Because of the many defense industries already established in the state, the war multiplied the demand for laborers. Consequently, California claimed one-quarter of the nation's wartime centers, serving approximately twenty-five thousand children at the program's peak in 1945. Finally, in addition to a population explosion, California experienced a wrenching transformation in social relations during the war, with the arrival of migrants without local kin networks, the rapid sprawl of urban areas, and a rising number of single mothers in need of child care services.[13]

California's unique child care program, however, did not develop in a vacuum. Child care activists had to navigate a national climate that promoted the ideal American family with a male breadwinner and a stay-at-home wife whose primary responsibility was to care for the children and home. This family ideal minimized and ignored differences among Americans and promoted a lifestyle rooted in the suburbs and epitomized by the white middle-class family. While this model was not available to all Americans—race prevented some and economic opportunities prohibited others—the nation claimed the ideal as available for all citizens.[14]

California's child care movement also grew up alongside a growing postwar hostility toward welfare, especially Aid to Dependent Children, a federally funded program that provided an income to needy children in families without a male breadwinner. Established in 1935 as part of Franklin Roosevelt's New Deal, ADC was modeled on the mother's pension programs of the Progressive Era, which had been used mostly by white widows, being that requirements stipulated that only "worthy" mothers could receive assistance; unmarried mothers and divorced women were regarded as morally suspect. With an increase in funding and new federal eligibility standards, ADC expanded dramatically the number of poor children who received aid. Welfare rolls grew during the 1940s and 1950s, and so did the number of African American families on public assistance. By 1960, ADC had become a racialized and stigmatized welfare program. California's centers provided an alternative to public assistance for generations of the state's poor mothers and their children.

Mothers who worked outside their homes or received public assistance had reason for optimism when Lyndon Johnson went before the nation and declared an "all-out war on human poverty" on January 8, 1964.[15] In one of the most ambitious federal initiatives of the twentieth century, rivaled only by the New Deal, the federal government funded new programs for the nation's poorest communities. Unfortunately, as Annelise Orleck points out in her work on the efforts of black welfare mothers in Las Vegas to establish their own antipoverty program, accepting War on Poverty funds "was a double-edged sword."[16] In the case of California's child care program, federal funds meant the eventual destruction of a locally controlled, education-based child care program for the state's working poor. The alternative vision that had developed in California as a result of the political actions and innovations of activist women was subsumed and transformed by federal welfare laws. The War on Poverty's compensatory education funds initially led to an expansion of California's centers, but expansion came at a price. It obligated the state's program to adhere to the federal government's welfare-oriented goals and subjected the families it served to caseworkers' supervision. In the end, it reinforced what many already believed: child care was not a basic right but a grudging service to the dependent and undeserving poor.

Demanding Child Care focuses on a unique coalition of women, most of whom became politically engaged for the first time after the war. The Southern California Association for Nursery Education (SCANE) and Northern California Association for Nursery Education (NCANE) had roots in the turn-of-the-century progressive education movement. The mothers, whose activism grew out of their experiences with the Lanham Act centers, established the California Parents' Association for Child Care Centers (CPACC). As many had before them, educators and mothers depended on separate women's institutions as well as strategic alliances with men. This coalition stepped forward to lead the battle for child care in California as the political repression of the Cold War demolished the political strength of the left.[17]

The politicization of the working-class mothers who depended on California's centers stands at the heart of this story.[18] They took their first political steps in the name of their socially valued roles as mothers.[19] Drawing on the "embedded identities" that "inform[ed] their routine social lives," they demanded safe care of good quality for their children. In doing so, they could be good mothers, fulfilling their responsibilities to their children while working to support their families.[20] Over time, their demands began to reflect a collective awareness of the needs of other mothers in their centers, their cities, and throughout the nation. These women operated under the assumption that it was the responsibility of legislators and the governor to respond to their shared needs. They saw government-supported care as a collective means of enabling mothers to provide for their families.

The women's organizations that spearheaded the battle contributed not only to the building of the modern welfare state but also to the expansion of American democracy. Parents' associations and nursery school associations were vital in securing a state-sponsored child care system. Their actions influenced political leaders and helped maintain public child care at a time when programs disappeared completely in most parts of the country. These groups encouraged members to inform themselves and gave them tools with which to fight for political change. As a result, rank-and-file women learned the skills and values fundamental to sustaining effective participation in civic life.[21] The struggle of women in California for child care demands that historians develop a more expansive view of democratic participation and continue to widen the definition of politics to include the organizing and advocacy of ordinary women. The active participation of these women, very few of whom ever became well known, exemplifies the importance of including parents' voices in current debates and discussions over public child care provisions.[22]

Demanding Child Care furthers a new understanding of the years between World War II and the emergence of the women's movement in the 1960s, a period once known as the "doldrums" of women's reform. Historians no longer assume a fifty-year hiatus in women's activism between suffrage and the second wave of the women's movement.[23] What used to be a story dominated by the National Women's Party as the lone feminist voice and the passage of the Equal Rights Amendment as the main goal has become a story of many voices and diverse forms of feminist reform.[24] As scholars have shed light on the efforts of labor feminists, women in the civil rights movement, and both liberal and conservative suburban homemakers, a more complex picture of women's activism in the postwar period has emerged, extending well beyond elite, professional women to those in the middle and working classes who organized around a wide range of work and family issues.[25] This study shows that mothers, teachers, and early childhood educators in California, the majority of whom had little or no political experience, took inspiration from a federally sponsored program and used it as the framework for a grassroots political agenda. By funding child care under the Lanham Act, the federal government inadvertently created a space that politicized a new group of women, and their activism was sustained and reproduced across multiple generations.[26]

This cross-class and cross-race coalition of reformers advocated publicly funded child care in a political climate in which demanding these services as a woman's right would have undermined their cause, so they couched appeals to policymakers in less provocative terms. Because they made these claims on the basis of what now sounds like traditional "family values," their voices and actions have been overlooked as part of the history of the modern feminist movement. Yet, affordable quality child care is fundamental to women's liberation. Although these women did not identify themselves as feminists, their story represents a critical chapter in the history of modern feminism.[27] Parents' groups as well as the Child Care Directors and Supervisors' Association served as consciousness-raising groups; they advocated for a liberating social policy, and, especially in the case of the working mothers, asserted themselves in the political realm on behalf of their children.[28] They would not have embraced the label feminist, but, as Stephanie Gilmore puts it, child care activists "did the work of feminism."[29]

In the late 1960s and 1970s, California's child care activists grappled with the new opportunities and challenges presented by the second wave of feminism. More recent scholarship has extended the scope of this uprising beyond the two groups featured in the media at the time: the mostly white and middle-class liberal feminists epitomized by the National Organization for Women and the women's liberation movement made up of loosely affiliated groups with a more radical agenda. The addition of labor feminists, black feminists, welfare rights activists, and Chicana feminists has, in turn, led to a rethinking of the liberal/radical divide in the modern women's movement.[30] Child care activists add a new cast of characters: poor mothers and early childhood educators. With these women at the center of the story, it becomes even clearer that categorizing women activists as either liberal reformists or radical "women's libbers" does little to help make sense of the diverse group of women who pushed for feminist policies in the 1960s and 1970s.[31]

In addition to furthering a more expansive understanding of the women's movement, this study complements and modifies scholarship on child care policy on the national level. It builds especially on work that addresses the question of why, despite great need and a long history of employed mothers, the United States has failed to provide child care as a basic entitlement similar to public schooling. Beginning in the 1990s, scholars turned their attention to the history of child care in the United States for the first time, producing a thorough and comprehensive history from 1790 to the present. These studies argue that the nation's failure to develop services resulted from the widely shared belief that a mother's proper place is at home with her children rather than in the workplace.[32] Each time policymakers and educators debated and rejected public child care provisions, they reinforced the assumption that mothering is women's primary responsibility and projected an ideal of what a "good mother" should be and do.[33] Finally, this body of work shows how gendered notions of citizenship have shaped the possibilities for child care as a social provision and probes the varying arguments mothers offered in defense of this service.[34]

This book adds a new dimension to these policy studies by featuring informal networks, grassroots organizing, and personal experiences of mothers and educators. For assistance in helping me formulate my approach to these policies, I initially turned to the legal scholar Lucie White and the historian Nancy MacLean. White, who has written about women with children in Head Start, maintains that the program's legal mandate to promote "the maximum feasible participation of the poor" led to the creation of new public spaces, in the centers and their policy councils, where Head Start mothers influenced and shaped how the centers were administered.[35] MacLean maintains that we cannot understand the evolution of public policies that affect women's status without exploring women's agency in shaping those policies.[36] It is essential, then, to understand what encouraged women to take political action for child care and explore the sites where these actions were carried out. The state's child care centers provided political training and awareness for wave after wave of working mothers and allowed social learning to take place as one generation of activists passed its wisdom to the next. Civic engagement and involvement in the political process emerged from the face-to-face interactions that took place in the buildings, on playgrounds, and at other spaces offered by California's child care centers.[37] By closely examining women's letters to governors and legislators, and by considering such spaces as sites of political activity, we can track the development of a group identity, growth of a sophisticated political strategy, and intergenerational transmission of a struggle that still continues.[38]

This study spans three distinct political periods that provided challenges and opportunities for California's child care advocates. It begins with the programs created during and immediately after World War II, then follows the child care struggle through the repressive political environment of the Cold War to the War on Poverty and the social protests of the 1960s.[39]

Correspondingly, the book is divided into three parts. Part 1, "War and Its Aftermath," begins by revisiting the Lanham Act program established by the federal government during World War II. Rather than looking at public policy from the perspective of Washington, D.C., however, it focusses on the main centers of war industry in California: Los Angeles, the San Francisco Bay Area, and San Diego. The move to establish child care during the war was fueled by the grassroots political activism of local child care committees and political organizations, many of which were dominated by women. It was the initiative of people far removed from Washington that resulted in the planning, implementation, and promotion of Lanham Act centers.

Federally funded centers did not last long. Chapter 2 examines the protests that erupted in California when the federal government threatened to close the Lanham Act centers and the broad-based coalition that pushed for a permanent program in California. That year, 1946, marked a moment of possibility for advocates of state-supported child care for working mothers. Many in the progressive coalition insisted that wartime child care should be the basis for a universal nursery school program on the state level. While these citizens saw child care as social service the government should provide, political leaders had a different view. In the eyes of most politicians the centers represented a temporary service only for the state's neediest residents.

Part 2, "Mobilizing during the Cold War," focuses on the mothers and educators who emerged in the late 1940s as the leaders and core activists in legislative battles at a time when the coalitions' most radical members—labor activists, left feminists, and current and former Communist Party members—were being driven out of politics. Chapter 3 examines the politicization of these women and the strategies they employed to fight for child care in an era of conservatism and fiscal constraints. Once mothers and educators had cut their teeth on these early political battles, they stepped to the front of the movement. Chapter 4 focuses on two rather different women leaders, Theresa Mahler and Mary Young, and describes how they helped the coalition navigate female networks, create alliances with men inside and outside the legislature, and, finally, secure a permanent public child care program, even if only for California's low-income working mothers.

Part 3, "The War on Poverty and the Age of Protest," explores what happened to the child care coalition when the federal government provided new child care funds. Child care did not have the same meaning for federal officials that it did for the early childhood educators and mothers. The federal government's goal was to provide compensatory education to poor children through programs such as Head Start and to reduce welfare rolls with the Public Welfare amendments to the Social Security Act. Unfortunately, these programs symbolically and practically linked child care to "welfare mothers" and their children. Advocates, who by this time had confidence in their influence, effectiveness, and place in the democratic process, encountered a federal government that considered child care an appropriate service only for the poorest Americans. New voices began speaking for child care in this era as well, both in California and across the nation: black mothers in the welfare rights movement and white middle-class women in the feminist movement. In the greatest tragedy of this story, despite the diverse groups advocating for child care and a government focused on programs for the poor, the California public welfare vision did not become the model for the nation. Rather, its universal, education-based program was subsumed under a poorly funded and stigmatized federal welfare program.

This denouement suggests that *Demanding Child Care* can be read as a cautionary tale about the dangers of even the most well-meaning top-down social welfare reforms. But this is also a story about the promise of democracy, for it demonstrates what can happen when ordinary people make their voices heard in public policy debates. At a time when more than 50 percent of women with young children are in the workforce and the need for child care is more pressing than ever, it is important to heed the voices of California's child care movement and continue pushing their demands for affordable, quality care.

PART 1

War and
Its Aftermath

1

Californians Secure
Wartime Child Care

At 7 A.M. on June 18, 1943, fourteen children between the ages of five and eleven walked through the doors of San Francisco's first public child care center, located in the McKinley School. The children played with dolls, stacked blocks, and read books. At noon they became members of the "clean plate club" by finishing their lunch of macaroni and cheese, coleslaw, bread, milk, and Jell-o.[1] By the time the last mother came to pick up her child at 7 P.M., thirty-five more children had been enrolled. The opening of the McKinley center was the culmination of four months of intense activity on behalf of working mothers. The city had first requested federal Lanham Act funds in February. Determined not to let their children roam the streets of San Francisco, parents refused to wait any longer. After documenting child care needs in a survey, a coalition of mothers, educators, and labor representatives convinced the Community Chest to appropriate $5,000 to open the center at the beginning of the schools' summer vacation. The agency agreed, knowing that when federal funds became available, it could withdraw support.[2] A month later, federal funds arrived, allowing the McKinley center to expand and care for sixty children of working mothers. Tillie Olsen, who later became known as a working-class feminist writer, was the president of the California Congress of Industrial Organizations (CIO) Women's Auxiliary, a member of the San Francisco Board of Education Child Care Committee, and active in the local Parent-Teachers Association. She told a newspaper that "only by actual down-to-earth work such as this survey can we . . . win-the-war for child care." Indeed, the grassroots activism of the coalition Olsen helped lead was critical in bringing about "this unique and unheralded move": the establishment of public child care centers in San Francisco to meet the needs of a rapidly increasing population of working mothers.[3]

This historic shift to public support for day care during World War II has been described primarily as the result of a high-level debate in the nation's capital featuring Congress, policymakers in government agencies, the president, and Eleanor Roosevelt.[4] The federal government, backed by major corporations, took the unprecedented step of offering funds to local communities to establish child care centers for mothers entering the workforce. By 1943 it was clear that without the help of women workers, many of whom had young children, the country would face a potentially debilitating labor shortage. With this crisis looming large in their thinking, politicians and policymakers suspended briefly the dominant cultural presumption that mothers with young children should not work outside their homes. For the first time, the federal government, through the Lanham Act, sponsored child care for any employed mother regardless of her income level. In so doing it transformed child care from a service reserved for poor women to one that assisted working mothers from all socioeconomic groups. Although federal funding was terminated at the end of the war, this was the most comprehensive public child care program in the nation's history.

In fact, local child care committees and political organizations far removed from Washington planned, implemented, and sustained wartime child care. As a result of grassroots activism, Lanham Act child care centers flourished in the San Francisco Bay Area, Los Angeles, and San Diego. Women, who historically have had greater political involvement in and influence on local and state policy than at the national level, played a key role in establishing child care centers.[5] These activists came from a variety of backgrounds, bringing many different skills and giving the coalition a wide base. They were members of CIO auxiliaries, heads of private nonprofit day nurseries, members of middle-class women's groups, mothers employed outside their homes and early childhood educators. Out of these actions emerged a new network of female reformers led by single working mothers and teachers. The wartime experiences of employed mothers and educators in California prompted them not to accept the termination of this program at war's end. Wartime child care is significant as the first time the federal government provided day care for the children of working mothers, but the centers existed because of the political initiative, exhaustive research, and vocal demands of average women.

Wartime Labor and Child Care Policy

As Europe was consumed by war, the United States prepared to aid its allies on the continent and braced for direct involvement in the hostilities through an increase in war-related production and the expansion of the draft. Masses of Americans rushed to areas rich in defense industry work, but many communities were ill-prepared to receive them. Housing, health care, and child care were essential to support industrial expansion. People who relocated could not fall back on networks of family and friends, so they scrambled to find these services on the market and from the government.

Defense was a national priority, and many Americans believed that the federal government should address the domestic social problems created by the war. Policymakers in Washington initially shied away from assuming this responsibility, especially when it came to an issue as contentious as child care. Acknowledging the need for day care centers for the children of women war workers meant rethinking deeply held beliefs about young children being cared for at home and public policy upholding the primacy of women's role as wife and mother. Long-standing uneasiness over women's changing social and economic position, coupled with agency infighting and the fear of setting a precedent for federally funded day care, led to the establishment of a program intended to facilitate the employment of women with young children for the duration of the emergency. Child care was available to working mothers of all classes, but only a limited number of families were served. The contradiction between wartime necessity and conventional gender arrangements led to a federal child care policy fraught with conflict, confusion, and ambivalence.

The program's roots lay in New Deal efforts to employ Americans during the depression. In 1933 the Works Progress Administration (WPA) set up a nursery school program, primarily as a way to provide jobs for unemployed teachers, teachers' aides, cooks, and custodians. By 1942 the WPA had created 1,900 nursery schools throughout the country staffed by women who had degrees in teaching or backgrounds in social work. Half of the six to eight thousand employees of "Uncle Sam's nursery schools" were teachers, many of whom had been trained in child development. Operated by and located in public elementary schools, the centers were justified as providing "educational care" to preschool-aged children, not in merely custodial terms.[6] The National Association of Nursery Education (NANE), founded in 1925 when Patty Smith Hill called together a group of nursery school teachers, parent educators, and child psychologists, argued that the nation should move toward universal early childhood education. When the WPA moved to set up nursery schools, NANE urged its membership to take an active role to ensure their quality. According to Sadie Ginsberg, an expert in child development, "These depression nursery schools made the idea of group care of young children much more widely known all over the country; and they brought hundreds of teachers into the early childhood education field."[7] The idea of child care centers gained legitimacy and a small corps of experienced advocates.

In July 1942, seven months after the United States entered the conflict, the first war-related child care funds came to the WPA at the request of one of the few female members of Congress, Representative Mary Norton of New Jersey.

Responding to the rising number of mothers working in defense industries and pressure from local communities, Norton asked for $6 million to expand the WPA's public child care program to include children whose mothers were employed in war plants. By the end of the year, the economy rebounding, President Roosevelt recommended that the WPA be discontinued by July 1943. Scores of letters and telephone calls came into WPA offices, begging that the centers be kept open. Precisely at the moment when demand for day care was highest, the federal government threatened to close the doors of its only public nursery school program. In response to these protests, the Federal Works Agency (FWA) stepped in and, with Lanham Act funding, took over administration of child care centers. The Lanham Act, passed in 1941 to provide social services to war-affected areas, was not originally intended to fund day care services. The decision to use Lanham money for child care meant that the government would support nursery schools and centers for school-aged children on a fifty-fifty basis with local communities. Most local governments, with few financial resources to spare, covered their share by charging parents fees.

The shift from WPA sponsorship to Lanham Act funding entailed substantial changes in child care centers' location and coverage. Almost one-third of the WPA nurseries closed because they were situated outside major war production areas. Thousands of low-income working mothers with young children who had benefited from the free child care provided by the WPA had to search for other arrangements, which were often unavailable or unaffordable. In war-affected areas where centers remained open, the Lanham Act stipulated that only the children of working mothers could be enrolled, so those whose mothers were unemployed were turned away from nursery schools they had previously attended.[8] For some parents, the fact that their child's nursery school was no longer free created new financial hardships.

The greatest resistance to developing a child care program during the war came from other federal government agencies. Neither the Children's Bureau nor the Office of Education embraced the idea of group care. Their leaders believed that if day care centers were absolutely necessary, they should be funded by the states. In July 1941, before U.S. entry into the war, the Children's Bureau held a National Day Care Conference, and experts from around the country and delegates from every state came to Washington to discuss ways of addressing the growing child care crisis. The position outlined at the conference and supported by other federal agencies encouraged women with young children to stay home rather than take jobs in defense industries. The social workers who led the Children's Bureau clung to the vain hope that mothers could be persuaded to forgo employment. Recognizing that women were responding to the rising demand for labor, they believed that a federal child care program should be a last resort limited to the duration of the crisis. Ironically, these women professionals upheld the long-standing belief that mothers and young children belong together at home.

Even when it became clear that women would be an essential part of the workforce, the War Manpower Commission issued a directive to limit the scope of their participation. Making the Children's Bureau position official policy, the commission stipulated that "no woman responsible for the care of young children should be encouraged or compelled to seek employment which deprives her children of her essential care until after all other sources of labor supply have been exhausted."[9] In the summer of 1942, Paul McNutt, director of the manpower commission, had assigned the task of coordinating child care to Community War Services Division and recommended that women who had to work place their children in foster homes rather than group care.[10] Yet, women continued to file into shipyards and airplane factories, operating blow torches and welding alongside men, and they brought their young children with them when they moved to find jobs in war plants. To keep war production at high levels, the federal government overlooked the opposition to group care and went forward with the plan to fund child care centers.

Federally funded day care centers were not immediately placed under the purview of the Lanham Act. Federal agencies, members of Congress, and the state departments of welfare and education held differing views about who should administer the program. For example, Senator Elbert D. Thomas (D.-Utah) introduced the War-Area Child-Care Act of 1943, which proposed funding child care through "grants to the states," giving the Children's Bureau and the Office of Education administrative roles in carrying out child care policy, pushing for more foster care, and limiting federal funding to $20 million. Those who favored this bill pointed to the inadequacies of the Lanham Act program. That law, they claimed, had no business offering child care services, given that it was intended to cover only the construction of school buildings.[11] State directors of education and welfare voiced strong support for the Thomas Bill, hoping to wrest control over child care services from the federal government.

The Thomas bill drew opposition from a variety of quarters. The FWA contended that the lag time involved in switching administrative agencies would cause suffering for the children of employed mothers. African Americans, represented at the hearing by Alpha Kappa Alpha, a black sorority, opposed the bill because it gave control to "states where segregation has been imposed upon one segment of the population and where past experiences have shown the distribution of public funds to be grossly inequitable and where the most glaring inequalities are made for Negroes."[12] Black children had benefited from the Lanham Act: in 1943, 259 "Negro" centers were operating primarily in the South but in the North and West as well, and hundreds of other black children attended integrated centers. The proposal would have allowed states where white supremacy reigned to exclude them. African American women had high rates of labor force participation even before the war, so the availability of child care was of particular importance to them.

The Senate approved the Thomas bill, but the House let it die in committee. The intervention of President Roosevelt ensured that the program would operate as a partnership between the Lanham Act and local communities rather than be placed under state control. Roosevelt characterized the agency infighting as "unfortunate" and requested that the FWA revise its procedures to incorporate child care.[13] That fall, Congress passed an amendment to continue Lanham Act funding for child care. The result was a federally sponsored child care program, controlled and carried out by local communities, which left power in the hands of school boards and city councils.

The Lanham Act placed the burden of proof for day care needs on local communities. Although the federal government funded the centers, administrators continually referred to them as "a community program of day care." Early on, Emma Lundberg of the Children's Bureau wrote that it was "the responsibility of the community to take such steps as may be needed to safeguard family life and to protect children from dangers which may threaten them."[14] Federal agencies set guidelines for exactly how local communities ought to ascertain the need for child care. They asked communities to hold conferences on day care and women's participation in the labor force, create committees composed of local organizations and individuals, and conduct surveys assessing present and future day care needs. The consequences of local control were threefold. First, it helped many communities build an infrastructure for considering child care needs that would last far beyond the duration of the war. Second, it helped bolster grassroots activism. Those cities and neighborhoods with the best infrastructure, which in turn depended on local organizing efforts, proved most successful in obtaining federal funds. Finally, placing the onus on local groups to implement child care inadvertently created an opening for California women to enter the policymaking process, a space they would occupy for the next three decades.

Nowhere in the nation was the wartime need for child care greater than in California. "Nice little American towns" along the West Coast were being transformed by the rapid growth of defense industries and the migration of thousands of workers to shipyards and aircraft plants.[15] Shipbuilding magnate Henry J. Kaiser labeled this era California's "second gold rush." His observation, echoed by many of his contemporaries, was no exaggeration: not since 1849 had California's economy and population experienced such dramatic growth.[16] Scholars have debated the extent and character of the changes California underwent during World War II, but those who lived and worked there during the war perceived this as a dramatic transformation.[17] California was responsible for 17 percent of the nation's wartime production. The state received $35 billion of the $360 billion spent by the federal government during the war. In 1942 alone, five new shipyards were constructed in the Bay Area.[18] Huge new aircraft plants transformed Los Angeles; by the end of the war, four of the nation's largest airplane producers had built their main plants in southern California.

These rapidly expanding industries attracted migrants from across the country. Families from the Midwest and the South flocked to California in search of higher-paying jobs. They responded to advertisements for jobs that paid workers while they trained, offered the "highest wages for comparable work anywhere in the world," and promised them a part of the "California dream."[19] Between 1940 and 1945 the state's population grew by 30 percent. Although migration affected the entire state, the majority of newcomers settled in California's three main urban areas: San Diego, greater Los Angeles, and the San Francisco Bay Area. Growth was particularly rapid in certain communities. On the eastern shore of San Francisco Bay, both Richmond and Vallejo exploded from approximately twenty thousand residents in 1940 to a hundred thousand five years later. San Diego, the "sleepy Navy town," gained 190,000 new residents during the war, an increase of 147 percent. Massive migration changed the racial and ethnic composition of California as well. In and around San Francisco, the proportion of African Americans grew from 1 percent to 14 percent. Los Angeles gained a hundred thousand black residents.[20] Northern and southern California communities experienced firsthand the strains of providing housing, transportation, schooling, and other services to the migrants.

California faced tough questions. Where would the newcomers live? How would they get medical care? Where would their children go to school? Where would they shop for food? John Miller reported on the growing pains of Richmond and Vallejo to the U.S. House Subcommittee on Congested Areas: "Shipyards required ship workers. Ship workers required homes in which to live. Homes were built. People came to live in homes, trailers, tents, tin houses, cardboard shacks, glass houses, barns, garages, in automobiles, in theaters, or just fenced off corners with stars for a roof."[21] Zelma Parker, supervisor of Child Welfare Services for the Richmond Public Schools, described the camps that appeared overnight outside Richmond. "Beyond the town limits lay a vast area of untilled fields. . . . Trailers are scattered in a haphazard fashion over the fields; they are overcrowded, usually housing four to six people."[22] Los Angeles, the country's "premier automobile city," faced serious traffic congestion as employees of growing shipbuilding and airplane factories made their way from federal housing projects and trailer camps to work.

Through the duration of the war, women were a substantial proportion of those who responded to the desperate labor shortage. As the draft pulled more and more men into the war, women became an increasing number of migrants to California, outnumbering male migrants for one of the first times in the state's history. Women also became particularly critical to the state's wartime economy.[23] The total number of women employed in industry in California rose from 634,000 in 1940 to approximately two million in 1944.[24] In San Francisco alone, the number of women workers increased from 138,000 to 275,000. In Los Angeles, women composed 45 percent of the workforce and held prominent places in the defense industry.[25] These women, many of whom were married, found it difficult to juggle raising children and maintaining their homes while working full time in an aircraft factory or shipyard.

Horror stories began to surface about employed mothers who could not find adequate care for their children. The *Saturday Evening Post* reported, "In a Southern California trailer camp nine children and four dogs were found chained to trailers while their parents worked all day in factories."[26] A social worker counted forty-five infants locked in cars in a single parking lot. Agnes Meyer, a reporter for the *Washington Post* who traveled the country making reports on the home front, described a thirteen-year-old girl sitting in the corner of a beer hall, waiting until her bed would be empty, and children spending all day at the movies and going "without having a mouthful of food, neither breakfast or lunch."[27]

Communities Mobilize

Local communities translated these vignettes into a well-documented plea for services, and almost immediately, coalitions in support of child care were organized in California's major industrial cities. At the urging of both federal and state policymakers, leaders in the San Francisco Bay Area, Los Angeles, and San Diego created two child care committees, one made up of local government officials and the other of citizens, which brought together representatives from labor councils, nursery school organizations, women's groups, welfare organizations and agencies, and school administrators and teachers. These committees and their member organizations were given the task of demonstrating working mothers' need for child care. As Elizabeth Hall, executive secretary of the Mental Hygiene Society of Northern California, put it, "Before San Francisco can obtain Federal or State funds for such care, it is necessary to prove the need for [child care] by facts and figures."[28]

Labor councils and union locals, particularly those affiliated with the CIO, played an active role in organizing local communities to make day care needs known to Washington and Sacramento. The more conservative trade unions in the AFL mostly paid lip service to women workers' need for day care, just as they did little to recruit women to their membership. Women in the AFL spoke in favor of child care at both national and state hearings but received little support from union leaders.[29] The CIO, however, especially its Women's Auxiliaries, actively lobbied, promoted, and publicized government-sponsored day care. Although the labor movement had been male-dominated, women who took jobs in war plants where unions held contracts were required to join. Some industrial unions provided a social space for women's collective action during the late 1930s and 1940s.[30] Since the 1930s CIO auxiliaries, made up of both employed women and wives of male union members, had promoted a wide-ranging legislative agenda that affected women's lives both on and off the job—maternity leave, abolishing the poll tax, and an end to job discrimination based on race. Women in the United Electrical Radio and Machine Workers (UE) and the United Auto Workers (UAW) led efforts to secure child care services. A UAW women's regional conference held in Detroit in 1943 encouraged the union to push for day care.[31] Male union leaders relegated the issue to women union organizers, who had quickly become one of the most vocal and persuasive voices for child care. The women seized the opportunity to mobilize their communities to secure necessary funds.

The California CIO's male leadership took the increase in women's union membership seriously.[32] Union leaders spent considerable time trying to educate the male rank-and-file to view female counterparts as necessary wartime laborers and valuable union members. At a statewide conference on Women in Industry in Los Angeles in June 1942, the CIO highlighted issues on its political agenda that were relevant to women workers. Second on the list of recommendations was the "immediate establishment of Nursery Schools," followed by support for "an overall program for child care with government supplying facilities and supervision; food at nominal cost to parents."[33]

Harry Bridges, the left-leaning president of the California CIO Council, wrote a pamphlet entitled *We Must Change Our Thinking: Women in the War*, and in a speech before the state convention told union members not to fear women workers. Because so many men had gone off to fight, the only solution to the labor shortage was "drawing into industry those large groups of people who have heretofore been outside of industry. That is the minority groups and women." CIO men, Bridges urged, had to change their thinking. Women belonged "right alongside the men in working and helping to win the war."[34]

The CIO pushed ardently for federally funded child care. On a national level, the CIO Women's Auxiliary, along with UE and to a lesser extent the UAW, took the lead in advocating for child care services during the war. At its annual convention in September 1943 the UE Committee on Women maintained that "a mother coming into industry . . . cannot do a full job on the production line and certainly finds it impossible to be active in the organization when she is constantly worrying about the care her child may or may not be receiving."[35] The group articulated a distinctly feminist position by asking the government to address women's double burden. The CIO Women's Auxiliaries, led by the director, Eleanor Fowler, aggressively campaigned in Washington, D.C., for child care. Fowler's articles in both the *CIO News* and *U.E. News* pressed for urgent action throughout the war. In 1932, she wrote that "home responsibilities" constituted the primary reason women hesitated to enter the workforce. "Many of them," she added, "have children—and there isn't a community in the country now where adequate facilities exist for the children of working mothers."[36]

On the state and local level, the CIO and its women's auxiliaries participated in all aspects of child care organizing. Unions and their women leaders employed many established networks in the campaign: statewide and local newspapers, training courses in political organizing, and access to large numbers of workers. CIO Council members held positions on the Los Angeles Committee on Children in Wartime and had representatives on the Bay Area Council on Child Care. In 1942 and 1943, the CIO, along with a handful of other organizations, took the lead in pushing school boards to apply for Lanham Act funds.

Responding to the L.A. school board's failure to act, the CIO women's auxiliary organized child care committees in every school district and called on members to "write to the school board insisting that it make provision for the mothers."[37] When it came time to apply for Lanham Act funds, the CIO "presented the board with clear-cut, well-substantiated facts proving the need for at least ten times" the number of child care centers that the board had planned to request—250 instead of twenty-five. As a result, local governments and school boards saw the CIO and its women's auxiliaries as experts in defining working mothers' child care needs. In San Francisco, after the city had received less funding than it requested, the superintendent, Curtis E. Warren, turned to the CIO for help in developing the program, particularly to help the city conduct a survey in North Beach and the outer Mission. The CIO passed out questionnaires to union women who lived in these neighborhoods to discover how many would use child care.[38] CIO women, who had unequaled experience pounding the pavement, calculated the child care needs of San Francisco's working mothers. Then, once they had completed the survey, leaders in the auxiliary, led by its president, Tillie Olsen, presented their findings to school officials and the community.

The Northern California Mental Hygiene Society, with the help of the San Francisco Labor Council, spearheaded one of the many community surveys of women's day care needs. In July 1942, immediately following the announcement that Lanham Act funds would be available for child care, the nonprofit organization made up of physicians, surgeons, psychiatrists, and "others interested in the welfare of children" distributed questionnaires about the child care needs of working mothers.[39] Elizabeth Hall, the group's executive secretary, wrote to the president of the San Francisco Labor Council "asking [for] the endorsement" and "requesting the cooperation" of the Council for the survey.[40] She suggested that unions pass out the questionnaires at their meetings. Without collecting facts about working mothers, San Franciscans would not secure federal preschool and after-school care for their children.

To get the best assessment of families' child care needs, Hall suggested the surveys be placed directly in the hands of working mothers, who could "give us the necessary facts and figures." Only women struggling to hold jobs and raise children could define their child care needs. The Child Care Committee of the San Francisco Labor Council suggested that "if there are no mothers in the Union, let the fathers furnish the facts instead, as in all probability their wives will be in some War industry before very long."[41] When it came to child care, however, advocates preferred to hear directly from women. The questionnaire asked mothers to describe their work situations and family sizes as well as their current child care arrangements. With these statistics, the committee could determine how many centers were needed, where they should be located, and what age groups should be served.

Communities throughout California conducted similar surveys. Groups fanned out into neighborhoods, walking door to door with questionnaires to solicit information from thousands and thousands of mothers. In Los Angeles, reports and studies appeared every month. The Southern California Committee on Care and Training of Preschool Groups, led by Susan Moore, canvassed neighborhoods and trailer camps to determine the number of preschool children and what kinds of care mothers wanted. In Los Angeles, "the distance of all camps to established nursery school care was too far for many parents." They had no services of their own, not even a playground. In northern California, the Alameda County Welfare Commission found similar conditions. As of June 1943, it identified 2,500 "uncared for and unsupervised" children of employed mothers; by October the figure had climbed to almost four thousand.[42] These surveys carried the political debates over child care literally into the homes and neighborhoods of California's working mothers.

Drawing on their longtime commitment to care for poor children, nonprofit nursery schools and day nurseries stepped in to address the wartime crisis. In San Francisco the Golden Gate Kindergarten Association (GGKA), which operated five nursery schools for children from age two to five, discussed in its monthly board meetings methods for helping working mothers. The association provided care and education for San Francisco's "poor and needy" children since 1879.[43] Before the earthquake and fire ravaged the city in 1906, the association had operated forty kindergartens serving 3,588 children. These services were cosponsored by the Community Chest and by grants from California's leading female philanthropists. Once public schools took over kindergarten education, the organization dedicated its programs to preschool education.

During the war the Kindergarten Association did its best to care for the children of mothers who worked in war industries. At its board meeting in

September 1943, for example, the group discussed working with the San Francisco Board of Education to ensure that "more children could be taken [into their schools] if certain changes and improvements are made."[44] In early 1943, when the need for child care services had begun to approach crisis level, the association announced that it would extend its hours at two preschools, opening early and closing late to accommodate working mothers' schedules. Later, the association implemented a program to assist with other responsibilities, maintaining that "to try to shop and cook at the end of the day is too much for the working mother." The GGKA started a dinner program and two nights a week offered a "tempting nourishing dish ready and packed in cartons for mothers to buy and take home for dinner" when they picked up their children.[45]

Across the bay, the Berkeley Day Nursery (BDN) debated its role during the wartime crisis. Founded in 1908 by a group of female philanthropists to aid families displaced by the San Francisco earthquake and fire, the nursery had made the care of working mother's children its main goal. As its brochure explained, the nursery looked after "the children of the poor whose mothers had to work, for one reason or another, to support them, and who were otherwise left to incompetents or virtually on the streets."[46] From 1926 on, the BDN enjoyed Community Chest sponsorship to serve children in low-income families. When war broke out, the nursery participated in meetings on child care, offered advice on obtaining Lanham Act funds, and altered its enrollment policies to accommodate the increased demand. As an unofficial member of the Committee on Children in Emergencies, Gertrude Middleton, superintendent of the BDN, was kept informed about the government's child care plans. In her monthly reports to the board, Middleton considered the day nursery's role in the wartime crisis. In February 1942 she had been told that "we should start making plans for taking care of the children of women in defense work, perhaps establishing other nurseries if it became necessary."[47] The Berkeley Day Nursery did not open another nursery school because the board believed that the government had the primary responsibility to care for the children of female industrial workers and that mothers who did not have to work out of financial necessity should stay home. But for women who could not find government-sponsored care, she wondered, "shall we stick to our peace time rules or shall we accept those children at a rate commensurate with their income so long as we have room without interfering with the lower income group, which is our basic responsibility?" Middleton informed the board that unless she heard otherwise she would move forward, admitting children in this fashion.[48] Day nurseries played a critical role in accommodating the rising numbers of children whose mothers were employed.

Middle-class women's organizations took an interest in the wartime child care needs of California's working mothers. The American Association of University

Women (AAUW) and the National Federation of Business and Professional Women (BPW) endorsed the Lanham Act child care centers. By 1942, sixty AAUW branches across the country had helped establish centers.[49] In California, the most vocal women's organization on behalf of child care services was the California League of Women Voters (CALWV). Successor to the National American Woman Suffrage Association, the LWV devoted itself to educating women so they could take full advantage of their citizenship. While advancing a wide-ranging reform agenda, the LWV became a "significant factor" in California's state and local child care struggles.[50] According to the CALWV, the program should provide "adequate care of children whose normal home guidance and supervision is curtailed by the mother's employment or because the responsibility for the child reposes in one person."[51] League members spoke at state hearings, attended monthly meetings with other women's organizations, and actively encouraged chapters to study the child care problem in their own communities. In the areas most affected by the war, CALWV members served on local defense councils, joined welfare committees, and assisted with surveys of day care needs.

Initially the CALWV echoed mainstream views about mothers' employment. The best type of child care, the group argued, was provided "within the security of family life." As California mobilized its womanpower, it should appeal first to women without young children, and a public child care program should only be created under "special circumstances." Nevertheless, as women's participation in war-related industry increased, local leagues observed and documented the child care needs in their communities. What they witnessed gradually transformed their understanding of the nature and scope of the problem.

The CALWV differed with the national League of Women Voters office over priority accorded to child care, extension of federal funds, and control over centers. In July 1943 Mrs. George Rourke, legislative chair of the CALWV, informed the national League that "many groups and League members have raised the question as to our position, and recommendation on the two Congressional measures." The California League, preparing for its annual interviews with members of Congress, wanted to question candidates about their positions on the Thomas bill and Lanham Act. Three days later the national League responded that it would remain neutral. "Under League procedure," Mrs. Harris Baldwin, the first vice president explained, "it is not within the scope of any state League to ask its members to interview their congressional representatives on these bills."[52] The California group must follow the national position. Rather than worry about child care, headquarters wrote, the California League should concentrate on the national agenda, inflation and foreign policy. The CALWV and its local chapters prioritized different issues, however, because members had attended local defense council meetings on child care, helped conduct neighborhood surveys, and heard working mothers articulate their pressing child care needs.

Even before wartime emergency the California League may have adopted a different view toward child care and its educational benefits because of the presence of early childhood educators in its leadership. Harriet Judd Eliel, former state president and president of the San Francisco League from 1942 to 1944, for example, held BA and MA degrees in early childhood education from the University of California at Berkeley and had studied for a short while at Columbia Teacher's College. She served on the Bay Area Child Care Committee.[53]

The Los Angeles League of Women Voters (LALWV) also questioned the National League's position on the Thomas bill. From the early stages of planning for child care services in Los Angeles, some LWV members had dedicated their time to studying "family and child care: changing social objectives with emphasis on the relationship between federal, state, and local governments." These women pressed to change city zoning laws so that child care centers could operate in previously restricted neighborhoods.[54] Based on conversations with other child care advocates, the LALWV endorsed an extension of the child care centers program and implored the national League to "take the leadership" on preserving the federal child care program. The national office replied that "a sufficient number of other organizations [were] actively working on it," so League involvement was unnecessary. Given that the LALWV could not take a formal position on federal legislation, when Lanham Act funds were up for renewal in February 1944, the group asked members to compose letters to Congress to call "attention to the critical situation here on the Coast faced with the possibility of having our child-care centers closed for lack of funds" and urge legislators in Washington to reapportion Lanham Act funds.[55] League members in Los Angeles maintained that their support of child care was critical to larger statewide and national struggles.

The State Responds

Despite this extensive grassroots activity, California, like the federal government, proceeded with caution in its response to wartime child care demands. In May 1942, five months after Pearl Harbor, Earl Warren, then California's attorney general, issued a legal opinion that prevented the establishment of day nurseries in the state's school system. Despite rising pressure to implement child care, Warren announced that California "couldn't have anything like nursery schools or preschool child care in this state because the word preschool wasn't mentioned in the State constitution" and argued that the level of emergency did not warrant allowing local school districts to apply for Lanham Act funds.[56] Warren succeeded in delaying action on child care, but the legislature faced fierce political pressure to study and respond to the growing crisis. In January 1942, the state senate established the Interim Committee on Economic Planning and charged it with "gathering and analyzing all facts related to the transfer from peace-time industry to war production." The committee did not intend to look into the state's child care needs, but when it came to Los Angeles to hold the first series of hearings on housing, the Los Angeles Committee for Children in Wartime demanded a hearing on the subject. As Robert Kenny and John Phillips, the senate committee's chairs, put it, once they had spoken with the Los Angeles committee, child care's "relationship to our wartime economy was obvious."[57]

The committee hearings on child care in Los Angeles, Oakland, and San Diego caught the attention of citizens and policymakers. Groups that had been planning and assessing the needs of California's working families presented their views publicly to members of the state legislature and to the press. These arenas of public discussion were part of what feminist theorist Nancy Fraser has termed "the social," a "space in which conflicts among rival interpretations of people's needs are played out."[58] Throughout California's child care struggles, public hearings provided a place where working mothers and child care activists could confront elected officials who had blocked a state child care program. Organized labor, women's groups, nursery school administrators, educators, and mothers debated community needs and public policies with government bureaucrats and legislators. Susan Berry, a columnist for the women's section of the *Daily People's World,* a newspaper founded by the Communist Party and read by a wide range of progressives, told readers that the hearings in Oakland would allow citizens to "view at close range the stuff that history is made of . . . see progress in action."[59] The hearings were open to "all interested people," and hundreds attended. State officials might not have seen day care as a wartime priority, but local activists clearly did.

The jam-packed committee hearings highlighted the troubles facing industry, pointed to the anxiety of parents, and emphasized the need for a comprehensive child care plan. Statewide organizations, industry spokespeople, and government officials justified day care by acknowledging that women were needed for war work. Making day care "patriotic" and a "win-the-war" service tempered its potential threat to prevailing gender assumptions. "Every month, the number of women in industry is increasing," said Margarete Clark, chief of the state's Division of Industrial Welfare. "Authorities tell us that by 1943, 50 percent of all the shop employees in all industries will be women." Dorothy Baruch, education professor and aide to the Los Angeles regional director of the War Manpower Commission, testified about the number of children who would need nursery care as more women entered industry. Like those pushing for child care on the national level, they argued that production would decline or slow to a halt if there were no child care. Mrs. W. L. Leroy, president of a local PTA in San Diego, told the senators that California "must use women in war work whether we like it or not, and we must make greater use of our schools to meet the resulting problem in the care of our children."[60]

For the child care councils and committees that had been established in cities throughout California, the hearings of the Interim Committee on Economic Planning (also known as the Kenny Committee) served as a public forum to present their findings. The Bay Area Council on Child Care and the San Diego Committee for the Care of Children in Wartime reported on the overwhelming evidence of need developed from both a lack of adequate child care facilities and a rapidly increasing population of employed mothers. As of September 1942, of the twenty-five nursery schools operating in the Bay Area, only nine kept their doors open during most mothers' work hours.[61] Requests for care kept pouring in. In San Francisco alone, in the ten days before the hearing some five hundred requests were made to the public schools for child care. Thirty-one women placed classifieds seeking care for their children.[62] Representatives of local school boards backed up these statistics. One representative of the Vallejo city schools reported that "facilities for children have not kept pace with [our] increase in population."[63] Ellen Sweeny, director of Catholic Charities in San Diego, told the Kenny Committee that "Bayside Center, our nursery school, is taxed beyond capacity"; every day she turned away a parent who worked in war industry. The San Diego Committee reported that 92 percent surveyed wanted nursery school care for their children.[64]

Held in front of capacity crowds, the hearings gave working mothers a chance to speak for themselves, and they described the hardships that forced them to quit their jobs or place their children in an "unsafe situation." They were not being bad parents, these mothers told the committee; inadequate child care had left them no other option. Mrs. Joseph Marr, for example, quit her job at the General Cable Corporation because "the plant requires the children be taken care of and I have two that I couldn't find care for." She had pursued every possible avenue. "I inquired about day nurseries but couldn't get my children placed. Then I went to the cooperative nurseries but they wouldn't take the children. Then I had a woman come in but she did not work out well, so I had to quit the job." Dozens of working mothers in Los Angeles and San Diego told the committee similar tales. Others spoke of having to leave their children to fend for themselves. "I am the sole support of my three children," Mrs. Ellen Lamaster stated. "I know they should have guidance," she told the Kenny Committee, but she had to leave them unsupervised.[65] When a mother worked without arranging for proper care, said Mrs. Bessie Durfield, "I worry about [what the children] are doing, whether they are secure from bad influences. It's a constant burden for me."[66] These hearings placed working mothers on equal footing with more powerful witnesses such as the heads of state agencies and representatives of industry.[67]

At the end of the Oakland hearings the Bay Area Council on Child Care defined the basic needs of children while their mothers worked: "a place for play, for rest, for eating which is planned to give them adequate development from the standpoint of health, social relations, and understanding."[68] Advocates envisioned five types of government-sponsored facilities to meet these needs: all-day nursery schools with an organized educational, health, and nutrition program; day-long kindergartens; extended care before and after school; more licensed foster homes; and a service to guide mothers trying to find child care. In endorsing these recommendations the San Diego Committee for the Care of Children in Wartime warned state politicians not to do "too little, too late for children."[69]

When the hearings concluded, California's communities had convinced state leaders that immediate action was necessary to put a child care program in place. Kenny, the chair of the Economic Planning Committee, expressed full support: "The child welfare problem becomes more acute daily. Immediate establishment of nurseries as vital to expediting the war effort is imperative. The drafting of women for war work has increased beyond all previous expectations."[70] Until the middle of 1942 employers tended to hire white men first, but as more and more men joined the war effort and the labor shortage became more acute the employers focused on hiring women and African Americans. Kenny, a moderate Democrat from Los Angeles, articulated views held by many: To win the war, California industry needed womanpower, which was impossible without child care.

Governor Culbert Olson took the first steps toward implementing many of the suggestions made in Oakland and echoed in San Diego. Olson had been under great pressure from early childhood educators as well as local child care committees to establish centers. As Lois Meek Stolz, a nationally prominent early childhood educator, recalled, "Every place [Olson] moved around the state, some group of women would come with a protest signed by people urging him to provide child care."[71] After weeks of being pestered, Olson appointed a committee to create a state program and chose Stolz as its head. One of a small group of female social scientists trained in child development, Stolz was at the top of her field.[72] She earned a Ph.D. from the Teacher's College at Columbia University in 1924, having been encouraged by Patty Smith Hill, a leader in the nursery school movement, to specialize in child psychology, which was more open than other fields to female scholars. After developing an AAUW campaign to encourage college women to study young children, Stolz returned to Teacher's College in 1929 and served as director of the Institute of

Child Development there until 1939. Many credit Stolz with convincing Harry Hopkins, administrator of the Federal Emergency Relief Agency, to initiate government-sponsored nursery schools in 1933. Apparently, Hopkins and other Washington officials were so impressed by the prospect of hiring unemployed teachers and nutritionists that they set up the nursery school program that thrived under the WPA.[73]

Even though she had spent most of her career as an academic, by 1942 the fifty-one year-old Stolz also had experience in organizing and implementing day care programs. Fortunately for Californians, Lois Meek resigned from Columbia in 1939 after marrying Herbert Stolz, a physician and director of the Institute of Child Welfare at the University of California at Berkeley. Stolz's coupling of activism and child study dated back to her courses with John Dewey at the Teacher's College, which she claimed had instilled in her the belief that education was an important method for achieving social justice.[74] Her commitment to quality led her to mobilize students and faculty at Columbia to spread out across the United States to teach in and supervise the WPA nursery schools. Stolz was well qualified to inspire California communities to request Lanham Act funds. As coordinator of the state's child care program she could be certain that the Bay Area Child Care Council agenda, which she had presented to the Economic Planning Commission, would be carried out. When Olson's committee was formed Stolz told Californians that "local communities in the state have been attempting to meet the problem of caring for children of working mothers but have realized that it is too great for them to handle without assistance." For the next six months she worked tirelessly to establish public child care across the state.[75]

Despite Stolz's efforts and the buzz of local political activity, it often took months for the federal government to approve child care funds, so community organizations pitched in whenever they could. In Los Angeles, for example, Local 47 of the Musicians Union stated that until the government set up child care, "It is the duty of union organizations to establish nurseries now in order to prevent the confusion that will result immediately when women are drafted into war industries."[76] Speaking before the California Senate Committee to Investigate the Establishment of Nursery Schools and Child Care Centers, Lois Stolz asked for immediate emergency funds so that if Lanham Act money did not come through, communities could use state funds to open the centers. Appealing to the committee members' win-the-war attitude, Stolz pleaded, "It is just for the duration, just for the emergency so we could go [on] in California regardless of what goes on in Washington. These children have needed care since last March," and communities had tired of waiting. The slow federal response and the ambivalence of the state government frustrated Stolz so much that she jumped at Edward Kaiser's offer to direct and implement the child care centers at his shipyards in Portland, Oregon. Twenty-five years later she lamented the "government's stop-gap programs for young children," hoping they would someday rise to the occasion and sponsor comprehensive child care services.[77]

The state turned to other early childhood education experts for assistance in 1942 as it surveyed the child care needs of its rapidly expanding population. In 1941, the State Defense Council enlisted Elizabeth Lindley Woods to collect a list of volunteers who had training or experience working with young children. Woods, also an expert in early childhood education, received a Ph.D. in 1913 from Clark University, which under its president, renowned psychologist and child study advocate G. Stanley Hall, had become a national center for educational psychology at the turn of the century.[78] Woods taught at Vassar College and then worked as a psychologist and director of special education for the state of Wisconsin before becoming director of the Department of Educational Research and Guidance for the Los Angeles City Schools. This "teacher of teachers" supervised the Los Angeles WPA nursery schools during the depression, incorporating her standards into the federal program. A colleague described Woods as an educator who, throughout her career "sought new and better ways of providing early childhood education and making it available to as many children as possible and especially those in need."[79]

Woods's impressive credentials and commitment to quality child care prompted the state to appoint her as an advisor to the State Defense Council on the care of young children in defense areas. Understanding the need to recruit teachers and develop a systematic plan, Woods formed the California Committee for the Care and Training of Pre-school Groups in January 1942, made up of educators and women leaders in the field of early childhood education both inside and outside state government.[80] This group spent the year setting up a network for preschool care in California, outlining its main objectives in early 1942. Woods and her committee recruited personnel, established a training course for inexperienced teachers, surveyed defense industries to determine needs, and set up a procedure for mothers to apply for child care. Writing to Martha Chickering, director of the State Department of Social Welfare and head of the Committee of Health, Welfare, and Consumer Interests for the State Council of Defense, Woods declared, "We think we can secure a very complete picture of California's endeavor to insure the health and welfare of groups of pre-school children needing our care."[81] Woods drew on the established networks of nursery school and preschool educators that existed long before the war.

As a leader, Woods moved seamlessly between advocating for child care locally and on the state level. In addition to heading the state's preschool advisory committee, she spoke at hearings and small community forums and wrote a pamphlet, published in 1942, on preschool services in California. She made the case for group care with an educational emphasis, citing recent studies of child growth and development, and challenged the traditional notion that children under six should be at home with their mothers rather than in classrooms, learning. "When, how, and by what authority did we in democratic America decide that education should begin at six years of age?" she asked. Public awareness of "the preciousness of its on-coming citizens will make nursery school education possible for all families who desire it."[82]

Further action by the state depended, in part, on whom Californians elected as their next governor. The incumbent, Culbert Olson, a New Deal Democrat who enjoyed the support of organized labor, assured a group of Bay Area women of "his deep interest in the establishment of agencies for the care of children whose mothers are working in war industries." Women leaders connected to labor viewed Olson as more sympathetic to their needs that his Republican opponent, Earl Warren, who had "not made a single statement on this issue."[83] Unfortunately for these activists, Warren easily defeated Olson in November.

With the "old-guard Republican" as governor, the legislature at first felt little pressure from the executive office to establish state-sponsored child care. Warren continued to be criticized for his decision as attorney general that prohibited state operation of child care centers. The National Lawyers' Guild, for example, accused him of "holding back a flood of federal funds available to California for the establishment of vitally needed nursery schools for the children of war workers."[84] Stolz remembered the difficulties in setting up child care programs in California as "pure politics." Warren soon flip-flopped on the issue. Realizing that child care had become a critical war issue, he pressed the legislature to pass a law allowing California to establish child care centers under the Department of Education early in 1943.[85]

At the same time, knowing the federal government had agreed to fund child care, lawmakers took action to reduce the chance of publicly sponsored child care becoming permanent. The Child Care Center Act of 1943, which authorized communities to operate federally funded day care centers, prohibited "use for child care center of funds from district taxes or moneys apportioned to the district for school support."[86] Later that spring, the legislature passed an emergency bill to provide $500,000 for "supplementing the support of centers received from Federal Government, parents of children, and industries." California became one of only five states to appropriate funds for child care. Its policy was not as progressive as it seemed, however. It placed these funds under the control of the War Council rather than the agencies that supervised the child care program, the State Department of Education and local school districts, making it clear that child care was a temporary solution to the wartime crisis.[87]

The state proved to be quite stingy with supplementary funds.[88] Worried about the precedent that would be set by allocating state money, policymakers explicitly designated them to aid existing programs rather than establish new ones. In response to a Los Angeles woman's request for funds to help open an additional facility in her neighborhood, the state director of Civilian War Services stated that because the emergency child care program "is essentially a part of the war effort. . . . the obligation of supporting the child care centers is considered primarily a Federal responsibility."[89] California's coffers would not be used to expand or even extend this program.

The state legislature assured Californians that day care would be "effective only for the duration of the need for woman-power in war plants." In a May 1943 meeting of the State War Council, members concurred on the urgent need for child care but insisted the Council emphasize its temporary nature.[90] Earl Warren opened the meeting by highlighting that the child care problem in some "communities is very, very acute now," but he then acknowledged legislators fears' that child care was "an attempt of the part of someone to socialize the home and to relieve the mothers—relieve the parents of children in their care as a permanent thing."[91] For many social conservatives, child care posed a direct threat to the American family and American democracy. As Lieutenant Governor Frederick F. Houser cautioned colleagues in the state capital, "I am very much afraid that if this program is once established as part of the school system . . . that when the war is over, the 'camel having got under the tent,' you are going to find the program is permanently frozen on the school district, and I am very much opposed to having any permanent program of this kind."[92] Houser's fears were well-founded.

Centers Open: At Least for the Duration

In the spring of 1943, after numerous delays, federal Lanham Act child care centers started to open throughout California. In March, Elizabeth Woods wrote her dear friend Miriam Van Waters to express her frustrations. Van Waters, then serving as superintendent of the Massachusetts Reformatory for Women in Framingham, had been close friends with Woods since they grew up together in Oregon. Both studied with G. Stanley Hall at Clark University, and in Los Angeles during the 1920s they were part of a community of women professionals and reformers concerned with children. "No Lanham funds yet," Wood reported. "Our request went in in December. It took weeks to get it past the local offices (first WPA and then FWA), and on to the Regional FWA office in Salt Lake." A month later she wrote to Van Waters again, "Still no Lanham funds! Government bureaus are impossible when they attempt to manage community needs."[93] The city kept the twenty-three WPA centers in operation and opened nineteen new ones until the Lanham funds arrived, which finally happened that summer and fall. By November, approximately ten thousand California children attended Lanham Act centers, and by the following November twenty-four thousand were enrolled.[94]

Establishing the centers required overcoming many obstacles. They desperately needed trained personnel. The experienced teachers who had worked under the WPA were the prime candidates, but they could not satisfy all the staffing needs of the Lanham Act centers, and those with graduate degrees quickly qualified to become supervisors. Three metropolitan areas on the West Coast created training programs for preparing wartime child care workers. Housed at major universities in Los Angeles, San Francisco, and Seattle, they were training grounds for additional teachers and volunteers. The best-known of these programs was the Pre-professional, Directed Child Care, Teacher-Training Nursery School at San Francisco State College run by Lynette Messer, another graduate of the Columbia University Teacher's College. After hiring all the trained personnel they could find, many centers of necessity turned to those with little or no formal training. The federal government recommended a ten-to-twelve-week training course for volunteers who could be responsible for "supervising daily activities of children, such as playing, sleeping, eating." Volunteers could easily find training in urban areas like San Francisco or Los Angeles, but programs were not available in the state's more remote areas. In 1941, for example, the U.S. military established Camp Roberts amid the oak-speckled hills of Paso Robles, now the heart of the Central Coast wine country. At its peak, the army base housed forty-five thousand personnel, most of them in a tent city. Because some soldiers brought their families to Camp Roberts with them, the government approved a Lanham Act center to serve the children of military personnel and workers supporting the base. Staff and volunteers had to be recruited to the child care center.

Alma Winona Sample came to this small community with her husband in response to the call for people to provide support services for Camp Roberts. Sample, born in 1917 to Susan Mary Head, a member of the Red Lake Band of the Chippewa, and the reservation's first Anglo doctor, Louis L. Eliott, had grown up both on the reservation and with her white relatives. In 1943, soon after the Paso Robles child care center opened, Sample volunteered:

> My mother-in-law was living in town and she's a cook, a special cook so she took a job there at the center. It's very small. And she said it was such fun and this and that. So she said, "why don't you volunteer?" . . . I said, "okay" and I went. It looked like fun for me so I did it. About two weeks later she said, "Do you want a job as an assistant?" And I said, "okay." So I took the assistant job for two weeks. And about a month later, I was a director. It's really fast job growth. There, there wasn't anybody there and I didn't know any more except I knew I liked it. And had I gone to college I was going to be a teacher.[95]

For Sample, this opening led to a fifty-year career in early childhood education and a twenty-five year stint as director of a California child care center.

As Winona Sample's hiring illustrates, the Lanham Act did not limit employment to white women. Black, Asian, and Native Americans took jobs in the centers during World War II. During the war, black women enjoyed new opportunities in these programs. Katherine Flippin, an African American who had a thirty-five-year career in public programs for young children, got her start during the war. In 1929 she tried to become a teacher but had been turned away by the registrar of San Francisco State College. "What," the woman haughtily asked, "do you want to enroll here for? You could never teach in San Francisco."[96] In 1944 Flippin graduated from the eighteen-week training course at San Francisco State and worked in the college's child care center while attending college. Across the bay, Virginia Rose became the second African American woman to teach in Oakland's centers. Rose, raised in a politically active middle-class family, graduated from Barnard College and received her master's degree from the Case Western Reserve School of Social Work. In 1939 she and her husband, Joshua Rose, moved west with their two small children when he became executive director of the West Oakland YMCA. After settling in and giving birth to their third child, Virginia began to search for work. She doubted she could find a job in Oakland's Lanham Act centers because in 1943, as far as she knew, no African American women were employed there. When Rose applied for a job as a teacher, "the first thing the woman said was, 'I don't know if we have any openings for cooks.'" She replied, "'I'm not a cook,' and then I told her my educational background and experience. The woman rustled her papers. The next day, she called me about a substitute teaching job."[97] Rose became the director of two Oakland centers in 1949 and did not retire until 1982. Flippin, Rose, and other black women were pioneers in a profession previously closed to African Americans. Both women turned wartime employment into long careers as local leaders in the fight for adequate child care services.

Bolstered by a team of teachers and the backing of the state government, California's centers were in full swing by 1944. At its peak, the Lanham Act operated 3,102 centers serving 129,357 children across the United States. Because the boom in war production was heavily concentrated in rapidly growing localities in California, 25,566 children had enrolled in 536 centers—three times as many as in any other state—by May 1945.[98] Even then, the program did not reach as many eligible children as policymakers had envisioned. Countless war workers had to rely on other methods of child care, most commonly leaving their young children with an older sibling or a neighbor.

The Lanham Act centers that provided services to working families transformed child care practice and policy in California. Hundreds of women educators and trained volunteers were employed to care for the children of mothers working in war industries. For those with degrees in early childhood education, the centers provided a venue in which to carry forward their belief that all children should have access to early childhood education of good quality. The war enabled many women, like Winona Sample, to translate an interest in children into a career path. Black women who had encountered barriers to their aspirations found that the restrictions tumbled amid the wartime labor shortage. Mothers, even those who had at first been reluctant to place their children in a government-sponsored center, were pleased "not only that release for employment is possible, but also with respect to the influence on the lives of their children."[99] Educators and mothers considered this new public service not only as a way of assisting working families but also as expanding the educational opportunities and enhancing the development of young children. It appeared to be a promising first step in establishing a permanent federal child care system. When Harry S. Truman announced within weeks of the Japanese surrender that child care funding would end by October 1945, educators and parents who had cut their teeth in the Lanham Act struggles, along with the labor activists, welfare organizations, nursery schools, and the League of Women Voters, protested vigorously. They used newfound political skills and collective energy to ensure that wartime child care gains would not be snatched away in the postwar scamper back to "normalcy."

2

Postwar Hopes

The Fight for Permanent Child Care, 1945–47

On August 20, 1945, just six days after Japan surrendered, the Federal Works Agency (FWA) notified the public that it would end many of its wartime services, including the Lanham Act child care centers. Big-city newspapers devoted headlines to Japan's surrender, to soldiers returning home from the war, and to negotiating the peace. Buried in the metro and women's sections were brief articles on the end of federally funded child care. By contrast, the *Daily People's World,* the newspaper founded by California's Communist Party (CP) and read by a wide range of progressives, featured a front-page story highlighting women's dilemmas. Mrs. Novares, a San Francisco post office clerk, widow, and mother of three young children, told the reporter, "'Honestly, I haven't been able to sleep nights—wondering what I'm going to do . . . I will be forced to apply for relief or see my children run loose on the streets.'" Approximately twenty-one thousand other California mothers faced a similar predicament.[1] The FWA plan called for the end of federal child care funds within two months of V-J Day. Working mothers, particularly those whose employment would not end with the war, faced losing the best child care program available, which had given them peace of mind while they worked.

In California, the announcement that the Lanham Act centers would close touched off scores of protests by working mothers and child care workers. Elsewhere, similar protests had moderate success. Californians did more than mobilize to preserve federally funded child care, however. Fearing that the federal government would ultimately abandon them, the state's child care coalition turned its attention to Sacramento, waging a fierce political battle to convince the legislature to fund the centers. California was the only state to convert wartime centers into a statewide child care system. Washington, Massachusetts, and New York approved state funds for child care centers following V-J Day but appropriated so little money that the majority of their centers were forced to close. New York City, Chicago, Philadelphia, Baltimore, Detroit, Denver, and the District of Columbia provided funds to keep their defense-related centers open.[2] In the District of Columbia, mothers persuaded members of Congress that child care was essential to keeping families among the working poor and off public assistance programs like Aid to Dependent Children until 1950.

Several factors contributed to California developing this unique public service. First, the large numbers of migrants to the state during the war had it bulging at the seams, straining local services, continuing the housing crisis in some communities, and extending the need for state-sponsored social services. Between 1940 and 1945 the state's population increased from approximately 6.9 million to 9.5 million, and recent migrants gave no indication that they intended to return to their home states.[3] Second, Governor Earl Warren proposed spending some of the massive surpluses that resulted from wartime boom on social services. Although the CIO and others on the Left criticized Warren as a "fake liberal," the governor took pride in his nonpartisanship and shunned the demands of special interests. Historian Jackson Putnam has described Warren as "sincerely concerned with social issues, eager to work with anyone regardless of party label to realize his objectives and more than willing to compromise in attaining them."[4] Third, by the end of the war close to 20 percent of the children cared for in Lanham Act centers resided in California; the state had the nation's largest cohort of families that had experienced firsthand the benefits of publicly funded child care. Finally, early childhood education experts, intimately involved in the establishment of nursery schools and Lanham Act centers during the war, were especially active in California. Experienced educators believed that the time was ripe to mold a permanent child care system.

California's child care advocates, composed of labor unions, early childhood educators, African Americans, women's groups, Communist Party members, and left feminists, included one critical new group—parents, the overwhelming majority of whom were mothers.[5] These women enjoyed the benefits of the centers during the war, and some had already become involved in organizing on the centers' behalf. Now they faced a crisis. For many, the possibility of having no child care caused physical stress and mental anguish. One mother described being "headed for a very nervous condition" if funding were not continued. Another believed that lack of child care would affect the "future security of my family."[6] These mothers lay awake at night asking themselves what would working parents do with their children, and how could they make their communities, the state, and the nation aware that their day care needs would not change with the war's end.

The child care coalition participated in a national debate about reconversion. Citizens questioned the contours of the postwar welfare state and economic policies. What kinds of public services would the government provide, what types of protection would it give individual citizens, and in what ways would it regulate the economy? Many sought to ensure that postwar America lived up to its democratic promise. Initially, most progressives were optimistic about their chances of promoting a wide-ranging social agenda. This optimism, which infused the working class, was founded on what Marilynn Johnson has called the "rhetoric and ritual" of wartime unity. In order to address wartime crises, local political leaders had invited representatives of these groups to sit on citywide committees devoted to such pressing issues as housing, child care, and defense employment.[7] Progressive organizations hoped that this practice would continue as communities made the transition from war to peace. Furthermore, the programs and protections provided by the government between 1941 and 1945—public housing, rent control, fair employment, and child care—were seen not as temporary expedients but rather as model policies for a just society. When the federal government announced the end of Lanham Act centers, many in the child care coalition hoped that they could convince the state to support their continuation and perhaps expand them into a statewide nursery school program. During a year of study by the state legislature in 1946, educators and activists demonstrated the importance of child care and recommended the best method to meet the state's needs. Ellen Reese maintains that by securing state funding in 1946, advocates set the stage for California's unique state-sponsored child care program.[8]

This social-democratic moment was part of the national process of demobilization. Laura McEnaney has described the transition from war to peace as a time when "citizen-soldiers were now citizen survivors who came to define the reconversion not just as the ebb of their sacrifice, but as a nascent political culture of reciprocity and expectation between state and citizen."[9] Working-class Americans were not ready to say goodbye to economic remedies created during the New Deal and the war. Citizens who had endured wartime hardships—family separations, cramped living conditions, and wage freezes—did not want government assistance programs to evaporate with the end of the hostilities. Some advocated preserving government policies forged during the Depression and the wartime crisis, and others expanded this progressive vision.[10]

Day care activists had to contend with a society increasingly focused on a family ideal in which the breadwinner was male and the homemaker female. Although that ideal was only a reality for white, middle-class families, it shaped the dominant cultural ideas and policies of the postwar United States. The question of married women's participation in the labor force was among the most deeply fraught social issues after the war. Despite the myriad pressures that encouraged women to give up their jobs, many knew that doing so was an economic impossibility. Those who had always worked for pay, and most who had reentered the labor force during the war, had no intention of leaving the workforce; their income was essential to the survival of their families. Of Californians using Lanham Act centers in August 1945, 51 percent did not have husbands who were or had been in the service, implying theirs was not a war-related need.[11]

The employment of women after the emergency labor mobilization had been intensely debated since early 1945. Many feared that peace would lead to massive unemployment and a recession and argued that whatever jobs remained should be reserved for returning veterans. Some were concerned that women provided with child care services would continue working, not out of necessity but by choice. In a public opinion survey conducted in October 1945, 62 percent of respondents disapproved of a married woman earning money if her husband were capable of supporting the family.[12] The national necessity for women workers had ended with the war, but as those advocating for child care would point out, the familial necessity persisted. For some families, it even increased with the postwar purchase of a car or home.

When women working in war-related industries were surveyed about their own preferences, by contrast, the vast majority (70 percent) said they wished to continue working during peacetime.[13] Of these women, roughly 84 percent claimed that they had "no other alternative." In California, even after a round of postwar layoffs, many women continued to be employed, and their numbers remained far above prewar levels. In the San Francisco–Oakland area, for example, the number of women workers increased by 84 percent between 1940 and 1947.[14] Some scholars maintain that many women did not abandon high-paying war work for suburban domesticity but had been forced back into lower-paying, traditionally female occupations.[15] White women returned to "pink collar" jobs as secretaries and clerks while black women were pushed back into domestic service.

It was in this climate that California's working mothers struggled to preserve child care. They had to remind city council representatives, board of education members, and state legislators that many women still needed and wanted to work. As a teacher in the Santa Monica child care center put it, "It was a terrible shock to some legislators that at the end of the war the mothers didn't want to stop working. And that was a real blow. They thought the mothers were going to be delighted to go back." Wage-earning, however, was an economic imperative. After all, the teacher concluded, "They didn't want to be on welfare."[16] For a brief moment after the war, there was reason to hope for expanded child care services, if not across the nation then in the state of California. Progressive social issues were still on the state's political agenda. Cold war anticommunism had not yet tightened the noose around progressives' necks, forcing some to mute their voices and others into silence.

The child care coalition, alongside fledgling parents' organizations that helped establish California's Lanham Act centers, took concerted action to save the state's

530 child care facilities. Their initial goal was to secure an extension of federal funding in order to buy time to develop a state-level strategy. Advocates began by organizing meetings with parents who had benefited from the Lanham Act. Word of the closings had spread like wildfire through child care centers, aircraft plants, union halls, and PTAs. Parents met and formed groups in their neighborhood centers and appointed representatives to attend citywide meetings.[17]

The FWA's "bombshell" had working mothers in a panic, particularly those whose husbands were still overseas and those who were single parents. Without publicly sponsored child care they would have to return to the haphazard arrangements they had used before the war. Whether they believed in child care services as a right for every mother, as a service for those who needed it, or as a temporary measure until reconversion was complete, they agreed that it was time to take action. Mrs. W. R. Estes, a mother who was employed in an aircraft plant and belonged to Industrial Lodge 727 of the International Association of Machinists, summoned unionists to exercise their political voice: "We cannot sit back and relax—we must be ever alert—become more conscious of how large a part politics play in our lives. We must inform ourselves and take an active part" in keeping the centers open.[18]

Across the nation, working parents openly criticized the planned closings. Most who spoke out were working mothers with husbands still overseas.[19] In Cleveland, where nine hundred mothers enjoyed publicly funded child care during the war, a day care committee was established, and its members made personal visits to county commissioners, the Ohio congressional delegation, and the governor to acquaint them with their grievances. In Philadelphia, mothers carried petitions to the mayor, packed the gallery at city council meetings, and demonstrated in front of city hall carrying signs reading "Child Care Centers vs. Orphanages." They demanded that day care become a permanent part of the school system. Parents in Washington, D.C., took similar action as they struggled to make the city aware of working mothers' needs, and special committees on child care sprung up in other cities and towns across the country.[20]

Mobilizing at the Grassroots

Mothers and community activists in Los Angeles and the San Francisco Bay Area galvanized supporters immediately after hearing that Lanham Act centers were slated to close. Activists printed and distributed thousands of emergency bulletins publicizing community meetings. They appealed to city councils and boards of education to support their pleas to the federal and state governments. Working mothers flocked to the meetings, which sparked months of demonstrations, letter-writing campaigns, and public forums. As they began speaking to one another about their shared child care struggles, working mothers formed political organizations, led and directed by mothers themselves, dedicated to saving California's child care services. On September 16, 1945, the Los Angeles Parents' Council wrote to Earl Warren to announce the creation of a county-wide parents' group "for the purpose of marshalling all community forces to work for the continuation of the child care center program."[21] These working mothers would be the guardian angels of the state child care system for more than twenty-five years.

Members of the child care coalition, state and local lawmakers, and other supporters congregated to discuss political strategy. On August 28, 1945, about four hundred people attended a forum in Los Angeles at the Van Ness Avenue School, "which resulted in an overflow crowd, with persons standing in the hallways and outdoors."[22] The meeting was originally intended for Van Ness center parents only, but once the word got out, parents and teachers from centers throughout the city and even from outside Los Angeles showed up. The "standing room only" crowd prompted Los Angeles's Emergency Child Care Committee to sponsor a countywide meeting the following week. Beach Vasey, Warren's assistant who attended the meeting, recommended to the governor that "it would relieve a great deal of emotional steam if, in the event you plan to include this subject in your call [for the emergency legislative session], to so announce at or before the mass meeting. This would transfer the emotional pressure from you to the Federal administration and the Legislature."[23] Vasey had witnessed the stress that the centers' uncertain future caused among Los Angeles parents.

During the war, mothers spoke out less on their own initiative and more often because labor organizations and community day care committees mobilized members and brought working women to hearings and public forums. After two years of government-sponsored, safe, affordable child care and political encouragement from left feminists, labor unionists, and other progressives, however, working mothers with a personal stake in this pubic policy issue stepped into the political arena and began to speak and organize themselves. The new activists included wives of servicemen, single parents, factory workers, and office clerks, but all repeated the same theme: They must work to support their families, and they refused to leave their children to "roam the streets."[24] White mothers as well as black spoke out at meetings held in child care centers, housing projects, neighborhoods, and communities.

In Aliso Village, an integrated Los Angeles public housing project built in 1943, close to one hundred residents responded to the call of its Emergency Mothers Committee and planned a Save Child Care and Housing rally that took place in the school auditorium on August 31, 1945. Bertha Marshall, the committee's head, boldly told the *Daily People's World* that closing the wartime centers was "designed to get women out of industry and back into the home.

It smacks too much of Hitler's 'kirche, kueche, and kinder.'"[25] More than once these "fighting mothers" found themselves in face-to-face confrontations with unsympathetic witnesses. At a hearing held by the state assembly's education committee in Los Angeles on September 26, 1945, for example, a male witness who suggested that the state end its child care program "was met with feminine boos, hisses, and other exclamations of disapproval."[26]

Support for the actions of working mothers came from a variety of sources that publicized mass meetings and committee hearings and urged readers to take action. Among the most important was the *Daily People's World*. An editorial on "how to fight for continued child care" encouraged readers to write letters and send resolutions to Earl Warren and the chair of the Federal Works Agency, Major General Philip Fleming. Calling the end of these services "one of the worst casualties of the reconversion period," the *People's World* proclaimed that it was "up to the labor and progressive movements as a whole to take up the fight for continuance of child care centers in California." Just five days later the front page featured a six-point program on "How to Keep Child Care." Readers were to keep writing, to "speak on this matter at your union lodge, club or church organization," and to convince their friends and neighbors to register their support for state-sponsored services.[27]

As fears about the imminent closing of the centers spread, more and more Angelenos took a keen interest in the issue. Just two weeks after the Van Ness Avenue meeting, an interracial crowd of approximately 1,400 parents, labor activists, business leaders, and legislators crammed into Polytechnic High School to discuss the child care crisis.[28] Members of the assembly and a representative from the governor's office joined the parents and community welfare and education leaders at both meetings. Democratic Assemblymen Ernest Debs and Augustus Hawkins had previously sponsored child care bills. In "an emotional" speech, Hawkins criticized Warren for not "supporting the liberal legislators in their fight for child care center extension."[29] Working mothers and educators waged a letter-writing campaign to the governor and legislators requesting that the topic of child care be included in the special postwar legislative agenda. Two days later, twenty-two mothers at the Union Avenue child care center in Los Angeles met and composed individual telegrams to Governor Warren.[30]

Across the state, African Americans pursued a dual strategy of promoting state child care services alongside community-based centers. The *California Eagle*, Los Angeles's oldest African American newspaper, vociferously supported the statewide campaign. At the same time, however, black residents of East Los Angeles raised money for a community-sponsored child care center. Scholars have observed that black families did not use state-sponsored child care, relying instead on family members and neighbors, but my research reveals that African Americans played a vital role in the struggle for public care.[31] Given their past frustrations with liberal programs, black activists did not want to rely exclusively on the government for social services. The Avalon Child Care Guild, established in August 1945, carried out a wide-ranging campaign that won endorsements from the city's political leaders, including Mayor Fletcher Bowron and the Social Services Department as well as financial contributions from wealthy white liberals. Carlotta Bass, editor of the *California Eagle*, urged working mothers to organize and support this community program as well as government-sponsored care. "Where the need is greatest, the fight is fiercest," she admonished readers.[32] In September, John Anson Ford, a member of the L.A. County Board of Supervisors, sponsored a successful resolution urging the continuation of federal aid for child care. "The sudden enforced abandonment of child care centers will cause irreparable damage and hardship" to southern Californians, he warned. The guild's fundraising campaign culminated in a benefit concert at the Shrine Auditorium by the Southernaires, a well-known African American singing group.[33]

Mothers and community activists in San Francisco and the East Bay, like those in Los Angeles, organized to appeal for the continuation of child care centers. Advocates formed a special committee to address mothers' needs, including groups that had "originally fought through red tape and opposition" two years before. The Bay Area Child Care Committee, representing labor, parents' groups, the Community Chest, and the San Francisco League of Women Voters, coordinated appeals to Truman and Warren. Twenty-five of the city's thirty-three child care centers organized parents and teachers to protest the FWA's decision. At a "lively session," working mothers pleaded with the board of education to continue this essential program. Some even spoke about a "permanent child-care program for working mothers—war or no war," which they described as "an educational philosophy California educators have been trying to avoid for years." This group of mothers explained that, as heads of their families or wives of servicemen, their child care needs would not diminish in the coming months.[34] In Berkeley and Oakland, where two thousand children attended Lanham Act centers, mothers applied pressure on their boards of education as well.

The Berkeley school board needed convincing. Although federal housing projects still teemed with workers and their families and eliminating centers in these projects would place undue strain on the community, board members were hesitant to support public child care. School administrators sought to avoid having child care under their jurisdiction because they feared the centers would compete with schools for scarce funds.[35] Tensions over the role of women bubbled to the surface in these debates. Some board members went so far as to claim that mothers who used child care received a publicly sponsored luxury. When a skeptical board member told a crowd of parents that the "mothers who have children in centers just put them in so they could go to bridge parties," a mother responded, "We're holding down jobs and hardly have time to go to bridge parties. The boss wouldn't like that." This portrayal of child care resembles Ronald Reagan's later depiction of mothers on public assistance as "welfare queens." Mothers persuaded board members to reconsider their position. One member told the *Daily People's World* that he had never thought seriously about the necessity of affordable care because "he'd never realized the community need" for it.[36]

The high concentration of war industries and organized labor in Oakland inspired the city's board of education to take a more proactive approach. In a letter sent to every parent with a child in the centers, the board suggested that they write to the FWA and Earl Warren, visit their state representative, and talk to their union locals in order to alert those in Washington and Sacramento to the needs of Oakland's families.[37] The Antioch school system called Earl Warren's attention to the fact that employment had not declined; indeed, some companies continued to expand. Child care centers would "meet a real need," the school district argued.[38] Cities that experienced the strain of California's population boom expressed the greatest urgency.

Nonprofit day nurseries and nursery schools shared working mothers' and sympathetic school boards' alarm at the announced closing of the federal centers. Many educators favored government-funded care for preschoolers. The Golden Gate Kindergarten Association (GGKA), which operated several nursery schools, lobbied for the continuation of federal funds and became one of the leading voices for state-supported child care. At its executive board meeting on August 6, 1945, the GGKA braced for "an increased attendance when that time comes, for there will still be mothers who are working as well as war widows who will out of necessity be working and whose children will need day care."[39] The association sent letters to the Federal Works Agency and the Regional Housing Authority expressing its desire for child care centers with an educational emphasis, which would continue in the buildings constructed for the Lanham Act program. In the event that state funds were not forthcoming, the GGKA prepared to expand its services for young children. At a minimum, the association sought state permission to operate nursery schools in the Lanham Act facilities. The GGKA and other nursery school operators knew that the need for care was "tremendous" and would be ongoing. The association reported that at their schools alone, "two to five people are turned away a day."[40]

The success of studies and questionnaires in illuminating working mothers' day care needs during the war convinced local organizations to distribute them again. As he debated what action the federal government should take on child care, Harry Truman requested evidence from local areas regarding their continued needs. San Francisco and Los Angeles conducted surveys just before the war's end that demonstrated a pressing and persistent need for day care. In June

1945, the San Francisco Board of Education sent surveys to 1,200 parents with children in Lanham Act centers. Out of the 898 who returned the questionnaires, 884 said they needed to continue working, 797 could not find other arrangements for the care of their children, 819 claimed that their jobs would still be available to them, and 327 had husbands overseas.[41] Approximately 88 percent of respondents had no doubt that publicly funded child care was irreplaceable. In Los Angeles, a Welfare Council study found that 99 percent of Angelenos believed that the program was still necessary. Rosalie Blau, who conducted the Association of Nursery Education of Southern California survey, stated that a "majority of the child care center nursery schools will continue to be necessary in postwar planning."[42] Many migrants intended to remain in the state. The next step was to translate this empirical evidence into a persuasive lobby to extend child care funds.

Advocating for Federal Funds

Like many Americans, child care advocates held out hope that New Deal–era social programs would be preserved and even expanded after the war. They appealed to three levels of government: members of Congress and President Truman in Washington; the governor and members of the legislature in Sacramento; and local boards of education and city councils. In the fall of 1945 the federal government was their first priority. Activists appealed to policymakers to preserve such programs as rent control, price controls, and public housing. In a series of "frantic" appeals, working mothers pleaded for the continuation of Lanham Act centers because the "need was as great now" as it had been during the war. The closing of nursery schools would "strand servicemen's wives" and widows. Spokespeople for cities transformed by the war cited statistics to prove that the "emergency" had not ended. The Oakland school board underscored the fact that "two-thirds of the 1,200 children from approximately 650 families" using the centers "are offspring of war veterans' wives now holding down jobs." Throughout the state, community representatives claimed that between 40 and 75 percent of mothers with young children in the centers were widowed or still had a husband overseas.[43] How could the federal government abandon the families of its servicemen they asked? The state's working mothers tried to capitalize on veterans' social status, because the GI Bill had proved the government's willingness to finance soldiers' transition to peacetime life.[44]

Advocates turned to Governor Earl Warren for assistance, and he appeared to understand the crisis that would ensue in California if the centers shut their doors. By the end of September, Warren had received more than a thousand letters, petitions, telephone calls, postcards, and telegrams. In a telegram sent to the Emergency Child Care Committee of Los Angeles, he let community groups know that he had heard their pleas: "I understand the federal government has indicated its intention to cut off the Lanham Act funds for child care centers and am urging the President not to do this, but if the decision is adhered to, I realize a serious problem will be created in some parts of our state and will give the matter serious consideration."[45] A few days later, Helen MacGregor, the governor's private secretary, whom Warren's biographer described "as one of two chiefs of staff," reminded Warren of his promise to encourage the federal authorities to continue Lanham Act funds. She emphasized the urgency of the situation, reporting that "the Los Angeles County centers will have to begin preparations for closing on September 13th if funds are to be withdrawn on the 30th and the City centers will have to do likewise on October 13th." MacGregor added that extending the centers' funding would allow state education and welfare committees time to evaluate the need for child care.[46]

Warren heard from a number of state legislators who believed the crisis was not over. Senator T. H. Delap from the East Bay questioned the termination of Lanham Act funds: "Personally, I cannot understand why this sudden action was taken." He then described the situation in his district: "Richmond is still an over-populated community and the excess population is here because of war work and a large part of such excess will no doubt be here for at least another year." Assemblyman Everett Burkhalter, who represented North Hollywood and many of the workers employed in the aircraft industry, wrote on behalf of the two thousand children and their mothers who "have come to depend on these facilities being unable to pay high-priced help to care for their children." Kathryn Niehouse (R-San Diego), the only female member of the legislature, wrote, "I am having scores of letters and telephone calls each day from both business men and mothers of children using child care centers. They are appealing for funds to keep them open." Other legislators from areas dominated by war industry echoed these sentiments.[47] Warren did not receive a single letter from a legislator urging him to close the centers. If there were opponents in the legislature, they remained silent.

The governor warned President Truman that the closing of California's 530 centers "would cause a great wrench in our community life" and emphasized the extraordinary impact that doing so would have on the state, "where we have had such an influx of people during the war."[48] He informed Truman that he would ask the legislature to outline the state's position on child care in its special session, but until then federal funds must be extended. The wartime emergency was not yet over.

Members of the child care coalition appealed to liberal members of Congress to make their case in Washington. In particular, mothers and organizations in California and across the nation turned to Helen Gahagan Douglas. The glamorous former actress had quickly become the voice of blacks, labor, and women after her election to represent an inner-city Los Angeles district in 1944. Because of her later defense of civil liberties as the cold war suppressed vocal dissent, Douglas would be best known as the "Pink Lady," an appellation used by her 1950 senatorial election opponent Richard Nixon. On September 19 Douglas highlighted the importance of extending child care funds, telling colleagues, "I am receiving protests from women's groups not only from my own state but from many states in the Union. Mass meetings are being held in city after city to protest the closing of day care centers throughout the country. The closing of day care centers is developing into a very desperate situation." She emphasized that "the program was set up because there was a need. That need still exists. It is part of the demobilization program. It is the human side of reconversion."[49] Clyde Doyle, a moderate member of Congress from Long Beach, which had been dramatically affected by the growth of war industries, also supported keeping the Lanham Act centers open. Appealing to Truman on behalf of "thousands upon thousands of parents and citizens of California," Doyle insisted that the federal government provide money for child care during this critical period.

Together with nationwide protests, the recommendations of prominent political figures such as Earl Warren persuaded Harry Truman on October 4, 1945, to request that Lanham Act funds be extended until March 1, 1946. The federal government must continue supplying child care during reconversion, Truman declared, to "give working mothers more time to make other arrangements for the care of their children, and State and local governments additional time to provide the necessary . . . funds."[50] Doyle answered Truman's request by introducing the bill that provided $5 million to keep the Lanham Act centers open as the state and the nation debated the future of public child care.[51] Truman's decision to extend child care fit with his limited support for wartime government programs and regulations. Although he agreed to end price controls on items such as meat, gasoline, and clothing, as a means of dealing with the massive postwar housing shortage he continued rent control and funding for housing construction.

While this bill granted the extension for which advocates had been working, it all but signaled the official end of federal funding. With temporary funds from Washington the battlefield soon moved to the state capitol and city hall. Warren tried to convince the federal government that its "responsibility is not over" because half the mothers were "either wives or widows of servicemen." In response, FWA administrator Philip Fleming reminded Warren that centers had been established "with the understanding that such assistance would be terminated when women workers were no longer needed for war production."[52] The federal government would not fund child care beyond the wartime emergency. Claiming war-related needs proved to be a very effective argument in securing a temporary extension of funding. The "emergency" rationale, however, had an unintended consequence: It limited the arguments that advocates could make in the future. What seemed to be a smart rhetorical strategy in 1945 hurt activists' later efforts to secure permanent child care services on both a state and national level.

Mobilizing for State-funded Centers

When it became clear that Truman would only approve short-term child care funding, California progressives pressured the state legislature to provide child care services for working families. Dorothy Clancy, coordinator for Los Angeles's Central District Parents Council for Child Care Centers, told Earl Warren that the council would now attempt "to secure state participation."[53] With the help of union locals and educators, parents formalized center-based, citywide councils. These loosely knit groups spent the remainder of 1945 and 1946 holding meeting after meeting on political strategies, attending committee hearings, and bombarding politicians with their views on why and how the state should offer public child care for working families. Each organization had its own methods of accomplishing this goal, but advocates coordinated their efforts in cities and across the state.

The California League of Women Voters (CALWV), an active supporter of the Lanham Act centers, studied the issue of permanent state funding, and its enthusiastic wartime support made the statewide League seem like a natural ally. Following its customary pattern of "intensive study" before taking a stand, however, the CALWV declared that it would recommend only a temporary extension of the centers until it had conducted a study of the present and future needs of California's working mothers. In September 1945 it instructed local leagues to make the "Care of Children of Working Mothers" their number-one priority. The statewide League *urged that all Leagues, whether or not your communities have the wartime Child Care Program, or have expressed concern about future needs in this field, will respond to this call for information and direction.*"[54] If a local chapter concluded that its "community would benefit by a permanent public program for working mothers," then it was asked to determine how the government should carry out a child care program.

In the fall of 1945, the San Francisco League surveyed the city's needs, interviewing experts and touring the federal child care centers with their director, Marion Turner. In its report, the group reminded the membership that more than half the women who had children in San Francisco's centers worked in "essential civilian activities" and would remain in the workforce after reconversion was complete. When the interviewers asked Turner's opinion of a means-based system, which would provide child care only to mothers unable to afford private programs, she vehemently objected to granting the government power to determine which women needed child care. "It is not legitimate to submit the problems of a home to an outsider," she told them, and "it's not possible to judge fairly family values." To her, a means test required government invasion into the personal lives of individual families, making the service more like a welfare program. For the next twenty-five years advocates would echo Turner's desire to keep child care from becoming like Aid to Dependent Children (ADC), which subjected beneficiaries to demeaning investigations by caseworkers. With ADC already viewed as invasive and mothers on welfare looked upon with disapproval, the last thing advocates wanted was a similar model for state-funded child care. One league member reported that she "was impressed with the simplicity and common sense used throughout" the centers; much to her surprise, "there was good care, good nourishment and no sign of waste. The policy was to have the atmosphere as homelike as possible with the only definite routine being mealtime and rest."[55] Turner had allayed fears that day care was an inadequate substitute for a mother's care.

In November the California League issued its second report on "Child Care Center Policy." Armed with the results of local study groups and informed by roundtable discussions at the state conference, the League struggled with its official position. Despite evidence from the San Francisco Center the CALWV concluded that it would support the continuation of child care only as "an emergency program for the postwar transition," not as a permanent service. The compromise represented a consensus position for the group, which needed more time to determine the "best permanent position of the League." Members had voiced "widely varying views" about state services.[56] One wrote to the San Francisco Center that public child care should be provided only for the neediest mothers. She also cautioned that "the opportunity for increased freedom is too tempting to human nature and to mothers of young children no matter how intelligent—and it would cause abuses of the original intention of the program."[57] The CALWV's slow process and its equivocal outcome frustrated nursery school educators, labor organizations, and working mothers who wanted to take decisive action right away.

Organized labor, represented most prominently by the Congress of Industrial Organizations (CIO), positioned itself to play a vital role in California's child care battles. Hoping to build on the success and power it achieved during the war, the labor movement promoted a broad, ambitious social agenda.[58] The CIO and its women's auxiliaries had been leaders in the grassroots push for child care services during the war. Moreover, labor organizations represented many of California's working women. The war had expanded union membership and given the CIO's Political Action Committee (PAC) a well-respected place in the democratic process.[59] The CIO was confident that it was now "universally accepted as a skillful, active proponent of the most well-prepared, well-organized all around program for the people of the State."[60]

Organized labor, its female membership increasing, had begun taking strong stands on women's issues, and in supporting child care it defended a woman's right to earn. Early on, scholars maintained that labor was "relatively inactive" in the campaign for child care and that what action there was "emanated from individual parents in unions who were concerned with the program."[61] Yet in 1945–46, persuaded by female members and an active women's auxiliary, the California CIO Council placed the weight of its 150,000 members behind the centers. Speaking before the Assembly Interim Committee on Education in late September, Harry Brown, the CIO legislative director, caused the greatest stir in the audience when he suggested that child care should be extended beyond the transition period. He spoke of the centers as "permanent institutions open to working mothers" and asserted that there should be "no qualifications to attend. Women should not lose the right to earn a living because they become mothers."[62] Labor leaders contributed to the barrage of letters sent to Earl Warren before the 1946 special session.[63] When the Los Angeles CIO planned a rally to fight for "jobs at decent wages" and full employment, it included child care on the list of demands. Organizers extended a public invitation to the newly formed Parents' Council for Child Care Centers to join the mass meeting on the steps of city hall. At the two-hour rally that blocked traffic during rush hour, a working mother of two whose husband was overseas addressed the crowd.[64] With an increasing number of female labor activists, both in unions and auxiliaries, male labor leaders began taking stands on issues critical to female members.[65] For the California CIO, child care ranked as a top priority in 1946.

The CIO Women's Auxiliaries fought hard for child care during the war and continued to work on the issue afterward, even as women were driven from their wartime jobs and the focus of auxiliaries shifted to maintaining their membership and solidifying their place within the CIO. Despite these difficulties, the auxiliaries continued to work on women's issues. In September 1945 the CIO Women's Auxiliary War News urged members to help working mothers and war widows by persuading Truman and the state legislature to make child care permanent in California. The CIO Women's Auxiliary Council in Los Angeles worked alongside other citywide women's groups to press for the centers' continuation.[66] Waitresses' Local 48 in San Francisco joined the state CIO Council and the CIO Women's Auxiliary in the campaign. Labor feminists and their allies were among the most assertive advocates for publicly funded care.

With so many voices speaking for child care services, the state's progressive coalition put a unified set of recommendations before the 1946 legislative session. A year earlier, the CIO Political Action Committee brought progressive organizations together to form the interracial California Legislative Conference.

The conference gathered again on January 5 and 6, 1946, the day before the emergency legislative session called by Earl Warren began. Planners sought to attract as many organizations as possible. The Emergency Legislative Conference pulled together what a reporter for the *Labor Herald* described as the "biggest, strangest lobby ever seen": a vast, diverse collection of organizations ranging from the Communist Party and the CIO to the New Council of American Business, the League of Women Voters, and the Southern California Association for Nursery School Education. This gathering of "rank-and-file" Californians believed that Governor Warren's proposals did not do "enough to meet the problems of full employment, adequate housing, real social security, ample unemployment insurance, industrial development, veterans' welfare and all the other issues facing us." The conference laid out a progressive agenda of government action uniting the interests of "the farmer, the worker, the housewife, the mother and child, the businessman, and the veteran" in a "single pattern of progress and security." Sympathetic radio announcers broadcast information across the state on "how the people's program [was] drafted and what it contained."[67]

In addition to a permanent state program of adequate child care, the six hundred delegates supported a diverse social democratic platform that included full employment, fair housing, affordable public utilities, and health care.[68] The child care panel at the conference attracted many of the groups in local and state-level child care coalitions and featured their newest addition—local parents' councils. They put together an ambitious ten-point proposal, stating, "The position that child care centers should be made available to the children of all working mothers, and all mothers who are incapacitated by illness, as well as for children in motherless homes."[69] Taking advantage of this moment when anything seemed possible, the panel asked for universal child care, calling upon the state to establish centers in any community that demonstrated need. They insisted that child care become part of the state education system, including certification for teachers and a coordinated parent participation program; that the ban on using local funds for centers be lifted; that a means test be rejected; and that these services be made permanent.

A few groups dissented. In a minority report the California League of Women Voters supported education-based nursery schools and child care only for the duration of the postwar transition. Viewing child care as merely custodial, the CALWV favored a nursery school program that would serve as a "part-day educational program, participated to a significant degree by the parent."[70] In the end, though, 431 of the approximately five hundred organizations represented at the conference approved the child care panel's report. For the remainder of the decade the CIO-led Legislative Conference pushed for permanent child care centers, sponsoring the most liberal legislation and denouncing any means test.

The Battle in Sacramento

As the legislature opened its extraordinary session on January 7, 1946, Governor Warren spoke about the enormous changes the state had witnessed during World War II and the new set of problems that needed to be addressed. "Our tremendous population increase—our industries that blossomed so quickly during the war and threaten to fade even more rapidly after it—make it impossible for us to remain static," he warned.[71] Warren laid out an ambitious plan for reconversion, including housing, urban redevelopment, race relations, mental health, and child care. He acknowledged the emergency rationale for the centers and encouraged the legislature to ascertain "what the permanent policy of the State towards these institutions is to be."[72] Although not advocating a state-sponsored child care system, Warren left the door open for doing so. As a self-described pragmatist and independent progressive, he sponsored many postwar social programs but was cautious not to promote an activist state lest he alienate members of his own party.[73]

The legislature plunged into the debate on whether child care centers should be continued permanently or temporarily. The question of permanent funding would take eleven years to resolve as the state made one temporary appropriation after another. Legislators introduced many child care measures, ranging from eliminating government-sponsored centers to establishing a permanent program. Heated arguments about the role of the state in child care involved the larger question of whether mothers with young children should be employed outside the home.

As part of an anti-statist political agenda spearheaded by the Republican Party that enjoyed some Democratic support, Assemblyman Gardiner Johnson (R-Berkeley) and Senator Jack Tenney (D-Los Angeles) introduced legislation that would continue child care only on a temporary basis. Tenney, described by many as the "California version of Martin Dies" and the zealous head of California's Un-American Activities Committee, introduced the bill. Tenney had voted in favor of child care as a wartime necessity but always tempered his support by warning against the "socialist origin of the plan." In September 1945 he told the newly formed Parents' Council for Child Care that he would support child care as long as it was needs-based and at least three thousand mothers qualified.[74]

Tenney's motive for introducing moderate legislation was clear: "to forestall efforts of the left-wing group in the Assembly from passing permanent legislation of the subject."[75] Johnson, like Tenney, maintained that by making the emergency argument "the Assembly has beaten off attempts to rivet into the school system child care centers operated day and night without much regard to actual need." Johnson claimed that "the pressure for the permanent establishment" of child care centers was "fanned by a left wing philosophy of government" and "aided by the tension of post war disturbances around us."[76] Most senators and assemblymen agreed with Johnson and Tenney that the state should pass a short-term extension but evaluate its day care program before making a long-term decision.

Augustus Hawkins, an assemblyman representing south-central Los Angeles and the only African American in the state legislature, introduced a bill to make the centers permanent. Referred to as "our little Giant" by the African American community, the five-foot-five politician, who had been inspired to become a public servant by Upton Sinclair's campaign to End Poverty in California (EPIC) in 1934 and had served as legislative director of the CIO's PAC, would champion child care for the next two decades.[77] During the war, Hawkins's district had become predominantly African American as blacks migrated from the rural South to work in defense plants. When an increasing number of black women became welders and riveters, child care "became very, very popular" among Hawkins's constituents.[78] The ambitious legislation he introduced drew support from labor unions, parents' groups, and the Emergency Legislative Conference. His bills called for a $5 million appropriation for operating the child care centers through mid-1947, made the centers a permanent service for California's working families, and required the centers to be available to any working mother with young children. Hawkins, a staunch advocate for working families and civil rights, was an active participant in the postwar progressive coalition and developed this legislation in collaboration with labor leaders, educators, members of local child care councils, and black activists from his district.[79]

Once Republicans had introduced a temporary child care measure, however, it was almost guaranteed passage. Speaker of the Assembly Charles Lyons (R-Beverly Hills) represented the views of many Californians when he said that child care should not receive continued support on educational grounds or become a responsibility of the state. "During this period when industry is unsettled," he had told the Woman's City Club of Los Angeles in September 1945, "when many mothers must support the family until the return of the husband or until he finds a job—perhaps for a period of a year or eighteen months, I deem such provision necessary."[80] Most legislators concurred that child care should be continued only during the period of reconversion.

Those who completely opposed state-run child care services represented a small but vocal constituency. Opponents inside and outside the legislature had an anti-statist vision that included a return to the way things were before the war and fewer government-sponsored social programs. The strongest attack on the child care program came from Senator Harold Levering of Santa Monica and Earl Desmond of Sacramento. Desmond, a Catholic, accused Tenney and the other sponsors of "making the child a subject of the state" and leaving an "'opening wedge'" for communism. "The place to rear a child is in the home and not under the care of state teachers," Desmond contended.[81]

The temporary provision of state funding for child care centers prevented a battle over elimination of the child care program and persuaded some lawmakers against a permanent program to support this more moderate proposal. It allowed the legislature to approve child care without having to acknowledge that mothers' participation in the labor force was not temporary but irreversible. After the defeat of Hawkins's proposals, the child care coalition was "forced to retreat" and support the Tenney-Johnson measures. In February 1946 the legislature appropriated $3.5 million for the program and extended state funding for child care centers from March 1, 1946, to March 30, 1947.

Before the final vote, legislators resistant to the idea of permanent child care pushed through the most consequential change that took place during the session, instituting a "means test." This provision required that no child be admitted to the state's centers without evidence that "the parent or person having custody of the child proved they are financially unable to provide otherwise for the care of the child."[82] Publicly sponsored care would resemble other public assistance programs aimed at mothers—most notably, those receiving ADC—and only be offered based on need. Since passage of the Social Security Act of 1935, the U.S. had developed a two-tier welfare system, a stratified system of provisions that made Social Security and unemployment insurance seem like entitlements based on employment whereas public assistance programs, particularly ADC, were regarded as a form of "dependency" and granted inferior levels of funding. Adding to the stigma, the state subjected ADC recipients to supervision, moral judgments, and invasion of privacy. The state's child care program would now admit children based on financial need, but because it was under the jurisdiction of the Department of Education it would not subject working mothers to moral judgments or scrutiny by a caseworker. Child care centers became an income-based rather than universal social provision but were not stigmatized as a form of public assistance. The measure moved the state-sponsored program away from providing child care as a social right and offered it only for the state's needy citizens.[83]

Despite the newly imposed means test and temporary financial support, the $3.5 million appropriation for California's centers represented the most ambitious public child care program in the nation. Although keeping the centers open can be seen as a "worthwhile victory," this battle forced advocates to make the first of many compromises. In order to provide service for some of California's working families, the state child care program became based on financial need and not an entitlement.[84]

The Tenney-Johnson bill included funding for a comprehensive study of preschool services in California.[85] The joint committee held hearings, reviewed nursery school, kindergarten, and child care programs, and gathered information and statistics on the need for these services.[86] The state explored whether the centers should continue as an educational measure, rather than a purely custodial one. Proponents would spend the next year trying to remove the means test and make the program permanent, and opponents had a year to abolish it entirely.

The Year of Study

Advocates had reason to be optimistic about gaining a permanent program during the year of "exhaustive study" by the legislature. The anti-statist impulse had not completely dismantled publicly funded social services. Nationally and locally, social provisions remained despite a vocal minority who believed that government should shrink at war's end. The means test only passed by the narrowest of margins. The Joint Committee on Preschool and Primary Training held "open and impartial hearings to secure information and opinion from experts and from laymen affiliated with all the major groups of citizens," including experts in early childhood education.[87] In a meeting of the Northern and Southern California Associations for Nursery Education, the director of research for the joint committee informed the predominantly female crowd of nursery school educators that "some kind of permanent policy should be established. This is the first time in the history of the State that such a problem has ever been proposed through the people of the State, and if we grant that it is most important in the field of education, this is indeed a remarkable opportunity. The laws are not written, money is not provided, and the people can have whatever they wish. . . . This is a truly historic period for early childhood education."[88] That same month the Southern California Association for Nursery Education (SCANE) wrote in a fundraising letter, "California stands ready to listen to all the needs and values of nursery education for young children and their parents. . . . This is a vital year."[89]

Representing almost two hundred teachers in private nursery schools and child care centers as well as others concerned with early childhood education, SCANE made an education-based argument to convince the legislature and Californians in general of the value of "all-day nursery education."[90] Because the bill for state-sponsored nursery schools had failed in 1945, educators promoted a child care program that incorporated the educational principles they had hoped to instill in a public nursery school system. They believed in the importance of educating young children outside the home, providing not just a custodial service but a school "where valuable learning and necessary experiences take place."[91] These women, trained in early childhood education, had the expertise to steer the state in the right direction.

Led by Rhoda Kellogg, graduate of Columbia Teacher's College, a bastion of progressive education in the 1920s and 1930s, the Golden Gate Kindergarten Association (GGKA) had a longstanding commitment to preschool education. Founded in 1892, Columbia Teacher's College emerged as a leader in the academic study of preschool education, relocating the center of the progressive education movement from Chicago to New York. By attracting prominent researchers, the college exposed students to such progressive movement leaders as John Dewey and pioneers in preschool education such as Patty Smith Hill. The college played an influential role in establishing the federal nursery school program during the New Deal.

Kellogg had been politically active from a young age as a suffragist in Minnesota. In 1919 she was arrested alongside Alice Paul and others in the "watchfire" demonstrations in front of the White House and spent her twenty-first birthday in jail.[92] During the war Kellogg had supervised the Vallejo School District's eleven Lanham Act centers. With a strong belief that educating children at a young age would lead them to become good and productive citizens, Kellogg helped the GGKA become one of the most vocal advocates for state-sponsored child care and nursery schools in the 1940s. Hired in March 1945, she served as the GGKA's supervisor for forty years. When it came to the state-supported centers, the GGKA pushed for a combined nursery school-child care program that employed educational principles similar to those used at the GGKA's schools, which encouraged children to develop their individuality at an early age. At the same time, the children "not only learn to do things with their hands and minds—but, most importantly, they learn how to get along with others."[93]

Kellogg and the GGKA board saw the uncertain direction of the child care at war's end as an opportunity and sought to make their educational philosophy central to the state program. With Kellogg at the helm, the GGKA played a prominent role in the process to secure funding from the legislature in 1946. Frustrated with the "unwillingness" of the LWV, PTA, and Community Chest to take decisive action, Kellogg abandoned the idea of a unified recommendation. She focused instead on making certain that the GGKA's views reached the desk of every legislator. Her speech before the Assembly Education Committee in January received such a "warm reception" that she rushed back to San Francisco, mimeographed the material, and hand-delivered it to committee chair Gardiner Johnson in Sacramento so it would be on the desk of every assemblyman before the vote.[94]

Kellogg's statement emphasized the strong educational program that had existed in many of the Lanham Act centers and the potential educational benefits of child care. Countering the argument that Lanham Act schools had poor standards, Kellogg told the committee that as the supervisor for the Vallejo nursery schools for two years she had observed a rapid improvement. When they first opened, Vallejo's wartime centers were sparsely equipped and overcrowded. Over time, with improved facilities and the influence of well-trained teachers, the centers adopted established nursery school practices. In fact, she told them, "the curriculum of the four and five year old groups in the good Lanham centers was such as to put the average kindergarten program to shame."[95] In Kellogg's view, child care should continue to be supervised by the Department of Education to protect it from becoming solely custodial. In the four-page statement filed with the legislative study committee, the GGKA pressed even harder for a well-rounded program in early childhood education. "To set up a program of nursery education and a program of before and after school care," the GGKA advised, "is to ask the school to extend the scope of its work just as it did when it took over kindergartens and when it put in supervised recreation and hot lunches." State child care was not a radical move the educators assured policymakers; rather, it was another important step in a comprehensive program of early childhood education.[96]

Many others in this cohort of early childhood educators appeared as expert witnesses at the four hearings held in 1946 by the Preschool and Primary Education Committee and continued to advance an education-based argument for care. They joined the stream of parents, labor organizations, community child care committees, local school administrators, child care supervisors, and others who addressed the state's "long term and long range needs with respect to preschool training." Elizabeth Woods, director of guidance for the Los Angeles City Schools and one of the administrators of the Lanham Act child care centers, came before the committee to praise state-supported centers. Most, Woods stated, "were staffed with sufficiently trained teachers and operating with high enough standards of health, care and educational programs to warrant being classified as nursery schools." Helen Christianson, a professor at UCLA who had trained child care workers during the war, described age three as the most important stage in a child's development and a nursery school as an ideal place to "stimulate learning and development of children too young to go to kindergarten." Christianson concluded by reminding the committee that "we have to realize that our society, our housing, our way of living have changed tremendously and have put new demands on all of us" and that publicly sponsored nursery schools would help working families and young children adapt to these changes. Finally, when the committee headed north to the Bay Area in late April, Lois Meek Stolz, who had returned to California from the Kaiser Shipyard's child care center in Portland, Oregon, touted the advantages of nursery school education. In her testimony she emphasized that no quality preschool program would separate the child from its family and that a range of services should be available to meet the needs of different families, some of whom required full-day nursery schooling and others only a morning or an afternoon.[97] Stolz and other advocates realized that many working mothers simply needed supervision for their children, but they hoped for much more: that California's program would provide care for preschool children and take into account all the educational philosophies and ideologies that nursery school educators had been promoting since the 1930s. Much like the female professionals of the Progressive Era, the state's early childhood educators created a postwar "female dominion" that directed child care policymaking for the next twenty years. Lanham Act centers had given these women new professional authority.[98]

Alongside professional educators, California's left feminists employed a number of arguments to preserve the gains made during the war and asserted the need for child care as a woman's right. These women, active in the overlapping labor, consumer, peace, and civil rights movements, believed that achieving women's equality entailed addressing structural inequalities based on race and class. Few referred to themselves as feminists, but they promoted causes and policies now considered feminist. Historians refer to these women as left feminists in order to distinguish them from the feminists of the National Women's Party (NWP), who since the early 1920s had devoted themselves to passage of the Equal Rights Amendment and allied themselves more closely with political efforts on the Right. Left feminists had varying degrees of connection to, or distance from the Communist Party; some were members, whereas others were progressives, social democrats, or socialists. They all faced crippling political attacks, however, in the increasingly anticommunist climate after the war.[99]

Tillie Olsen, a former member of the San Francisco Board of Education's Child Care Committee and past president of the California CIO Women's Auxiliary, used her column in the *Daily People's World* to push for a woman's agenda. Olsen grew up in Omaha, Nebraska, the daughter of Russian Jewish immigrants. As a teenager she joined the Young Communist League (YCL) and in the 1930s immersed herself in radical politics. In these years she gained attention for both her political and literary accomplishments. In her postwar column she criticized the federal government and organized labor for being inattentive to child care. Olsen used the column, which ran for three months in the spring and summer of 1946, to highlight the progressive movement's irksome tendency to ignore women. She recognized that the immediate aftermath of the war provided a window of opportunity in which to change women's position as workers. Those who had lost their jobs when the war ended or remained active members of their unions, she insisted, must pressure labor leaders to improve women's status. Without women's activism, Olsen wondered, "will there be support worked out for putting child care centers and nurseries to care for the children of working mothers on a permanent basis in California, under the public school system?"[100]

Women in the Communist Party advocated for child care as part of their quest for women's rights. The CP, which had gained a foothold within CIO unions during the war, remained indistinguishable from the CIO mainstream immediately afterward. Communists had gained political influence in the CIO because of its efforts to unify all progressive forces.[101] Dorothy Healey, a leader in the California Communist Party, described this period as the party's "most productive years in southern California." The Democratic Party, labor leaders, and communists, even if they disagreed about some political issues, "would remain allies on the most pressing domestic issues."[102] Communists organized alongside and together with other labor councils and organizations to press for permanent, state-sponsored child care. Although women were never a dominant force in the leadership, the CP educated them on their oppression and allowed them to gain experience as organizers. In order to recruit women members during the war, party leaders promised to protect women's jobs and take the lead in promoting child care.[103] In 1946 the Thirteenth District of the CP issued a pamphlet, *Child Care Centers: A Political Football,* which stated boldly, "Child care centers are a public service; a right of the people, just like fire, police, and health services. The Continued Fight for Child Care as a right is a continued fight for the rights of women and for the extension of American democracy!"[104] Communists were among the few to argue forthrightly after the war that child care facilities with federal and state support were a necessary step toward women's equality.

Communists organized women on the grassroots level in communities as well as at work. Dorothy Healey, then organizational secretary of the Los Angeles County Committee of the Communist Party, called a meeting of all "mothers of children present in child care centers" as well as working mothers who wanted access to this service. She believed that working mothers' political activism was essential to working-class support for child care and reminded all local communist clubs that "if we are to mobilize enough working class support to save child care, that those mothers with children in centers consider that this one meeting at least take precedence over other tasks." In Healey's opinion, the child care program secured during the war marked a major gain in the struggle for women's equality. To preserve that gain, working mothers would have to galvanize the working-class community.[105]

The short-lived Congress of American Women (CAW), a left feminist organization formed in 1946 by a cross-class, multiethnic group of women to back progressive causes after the war, promoted child care in the most explicitly feminist terms. The organization, founded on International Women's Day, March 8, 1946, attracted women who believed that gender equality was intimately linked to issues of race and class. CAW drew its strength from labor activists, African American women, the CP, and others under the progressive umbrella. Its nationwide Commission on Child Care and Education pushed for the continuation of wartime centers in 1946.[106] One of CAW's two largest chapters was in Los Angeles (the other was in New York City). Gerda Lerner, a local and national leader in CAW and later a distinguished historian of women, remembers its interracial membership mobilizing for child care. Despite the end of federal funds, "the need for childcare was as great as ever. We wrote letters to the newspapers, petitioned our representatives and, in 1947, organized a cooperative play group to take care of our most urgent needs."[107] The CAW mobilized individuals to preserve California's centers, not on a temporary basis but as a right for mothers who worked. Mabel Grey, an African American, represented the organization on the state legislative conference's child care committee in 1946. In a flyer two years later CAW implored the citizens of Los Angeles to *Save Our Child Care Centers.* Although they acknowledged the centers' wartime roots, the women clearly understood their contribution to women's equality: "Child Care Centers give mothers the *right* to work!"[108] Tragically for the women's movement and public child care in California and the nation, CAW disbanded in 1950 after accusations of communist connections by the House Un-American Activities Committee (HUAC). According to Amy Swerdlow, in 1948 CAW's outspoken position on child care and price controls and its opposition to the Truman Doctrine made it an "obvious target" for HUAC.[109] In 1946 and 1947, however, before being labeled subversive, CAW successfully mobilized women at the grassroots to preserve the state's program.

Child care advocates remained hopeful because little opposition had been voiced at the hearings held by the joint committee. Monsignor Thomas J. O'Dwyer, director of hospitals and charities for the Archdiocese of Los Angeles, told the committee that "with the return of normal conditions, the reintegration of the home should be one of our primary concerns." According to O'Dwyer, child care centers responded to a social welfare problem not faced by "normal" mothers. The Catholic Church repeated its "traditional opposition in respect to state aid in educational matters of this sort."[110] The mayor of San Diego, Harley E. Knox, expressed a similar view. No institution could "substitute" for the care a child received in his or her own home, and social policy should discourage families from sending both parents into the labor force.[111] Governor Warren, too, received very few letters from citizens who objected to child care. Those who opposed it drew on familiar themes: belief that married women should not work outside their homes or that public child care was socialist and un-American. These citizens advocated shrinking government social programs and questioned the morality of mothers using child care. But such views remained in the minority.[112]

After nine months of compiling data and listening to Californians' opinions, the technical staff presented a four hundred–page report to the Preschool Committee on January 17, 1947, and the committee, in turn, spent the next two months deliberating over the future of the child care program. Presenting its recommendations in March, it acknowledged that California parents needed child care but argued that the extent of this need had changed. Stressing that "child care centers as provided under and designed to fill a wartime need should be discontinued," the committee recommended that "child care services should be continued under peacetime needs with state aid to meet the requirements of needy parents and their children."[113] As the 1946 "urgency" measure had suggested, no child could be admitted to a state-supported center without proof that his or her parents were unable to afford private care. The means test had become central to the program's survival.

Facing a Republican majority in both houses of the legislature, Assemblyman Ernest Debs, the Los Angeles representative who had attended many community child care meetings in late 1945, was the lone voice of dissent in the joint committee. "The majority recommended that the centers be continued only on the basis of serving needy parents and their children by limiting the amount of income," he said. "This will exclude from the program more than 50 percent of the children now using the centers." Centers, he continued, not only helped parents who must work but also provided many young children with high-quality care that they otherwise might not have received.[114] Like other progressives, Debs believed that child care should be available to children of all working mothers, regardless of income level, and that the service should extend beyond demobilization. Unfortunately for the state's working mothers and their supporters, Debs stood alone on this issue.

Progressives were disappointed with the committee's recommendations but knew that saving state child care made California exceptional. In 1946 many other states closed down child care programs; by July of that year California housed more than one-third of the remaining Lanham Act centers, all sponsored by state or local governments.[115] A year after federal funding ended, California's public child care provisions far exceeded those of other states. These struggles only renewed activists' convictions that they should fight for state-sponsored care. Out of the battles emerged a new group of activist mothers, energized and ready to demand adequate care for their children. They joined early childhood education experts and teachers who believed that a public nursery school system was important to the future of children in a democracy. Rather than promote a separate public nursery school program, these women viewed the state's child care program as the place to carry forward their educational mission, and they would play a significant role in California politics for the next two decades.

PART 2

Mobilizing during the Cold War

3

Child Care
"Is a State Problem"

Working Mothers and
Educators Take Action, 1947–51

On a spring evening in 1947, thirty-four mothers assembled after work at the Van Nuys Child Care Center in Los Angeles County to draw up and sign a petition imploring Governor Earl Warren to "support an adequate Child Care program," a permanent, state-supported program offering child care to all. They regarded the recent recommendations of a state legislative committee on child care as woefully inadequate. After holding hearings, collecting data, and listening to expert testimony, the committee had ignored the opinion of many Californians by endorsing a temporary program restricted to low-income parents. "We, the undersigned, favor continuous legislation for Child Care for all working mothers at reasonable fees, and the elimination of any means test," wrote the incensed mothers.[1] Such meetings were held in child care centers across the state after the federal government announced that it would close Lanham Act centers in 1945. As battles over publicly funded child care extended through the late 1940s and into the 1950s, the working-class women like those who gathered at the Van Nuys center were joined by a group of predominantly middle-class early childhood education experts as well as teachers and directors in the state's centers. Over the years that coalition of parents and educators generated a core group of activists who could be organized on a moment's notice to fight for child care legislation in Sacramento.

The activism of California's working mothers demonstrates that citizens far removed from the levers of power could participate effectively in state politics. In the discursive space created by the child care centers, where working mothers congregated to pick up children and discuss legislative strategies, a significant transformation in consciousness took place. Women struggling to meet the competing demands of work and child rearing came to realize that the survival of their families depended on making time to write letters, attend hearings, and organize petition drives. Many had never thought of themselves as political activists or felt a need to speak out, but now they learned to translate their individual needs into collective action. In participating in an institution that "fostered identification with democratic values" they gained a sense of themselves as rights-bearing citizens.[2] Examining the lobbying conducted by these newly politicized mothers and educators widens our definition of politics to recognize informal venues such as child care centers as sites of political mobilization.[3] This more capacious definition of political action, in turn, reveals the direct influence that these grassroots efforts had on California's elected officials.

These women entered politics at a moment that seemed distinctly unwelcoming to progressive political forces. By 1947 the political tide in California and the nation had turned as the cold war escalated and a fearful contest for world domination began to define U.S. foreign and domestic policy. In March 1947 President Harry Truman declared it America's responsibility to support "free peoples" abroad by halting the spread of communism. In the November 1946 congressional elections, political newcomer Richard Nixon defeated the incumbent, Jerry Voorhis, by labeling him a communist. Republicans gained fifty-five seats in the House and took control of Congress for the first time since 1928.[4] A year later the House Un-American Activities Committee (HUAC) investigated the California film industry. The "Hollywood Ten" received national media attention when they refused to answer HUAC's questions and were jailed for contempt, and many more "suspected communists" and their associates were blacklisted.[5] On the state level, Senator Jack Tenney dedicated his own Un-American Activities Committee to rooting out "reds" in California. Focusing on communist infiltration of the University of California at Los Angeles and the atomic research projects at the University of California at Berkeley, the committee's hearings received "sensational press coverage" for "exposing Communist front organizations."[6] This repressive political atmosphere narrowed the parameters of acceptable debate.

Those who had been child care's strongest allies during and immediately after the war found it increasingly difficult to devote time and energy to the issue. California's most radical child care advocates—the Communist Party, the Congress of American Women (CAW), and the Congress of Industrial Organizations (CIO)—faced accusations and suspicions of disloyalty that muted their political voices.[7] These groups contributed statements of support but could muster little else. Moderate groups such as the California League of Women Voters (CALWV) were so afraid of being associated with anything that could be labeled communist that they were very cautious in their advocacy after 1947.[8] In most of the country this conservative climate was strong enough to sink child care centers and erase any memory that they had existed. In California, a persistent, dedicated cadre of activist mothers and educators prevented the centers from being abolished. The repressive political atmosphere makes their successful effort to save the centers even more remarkable.

Every year between 1946 and 1951 state legislative debates forced California's working mothers to face the prospect that the centers would close their doors. For the first six months of each calendar year, they lived with uncertainty and had to endure the stress of wondering how they would care for their children without the centers. In response, mothers flocked to meetings after work. At first parents and educators relied on haphazard organizing strategies and ad hoc committees to keep centers open. They continued to receive support from women's, labor, and veterans' organizations, but working mothers, teachers, and early childhood education experts quickly realized that they must assume a leadership role. For these neophyte activists to command the kind of respect that organizations like the League of Women Voters enjoyed, they had to establish their own statewide organizations, forge new tactics for gaining allies in the legislature, and find novel venues for spreading their message about child care.[9] Advocates faced little organized opposition, but state legislators offered only a temporary annual extension of services. Yet California's piecemeal provisions for working mothers far exceeded those of any other state. The passionate pleas and political dedication of mothers and educators achieved victory after victory.

By articulating a dual needs argument, contending that services for their children would benefit society, working mothers and educators gradually made their vision of child care central to legislators' views of the public services.[10] Their words and ideas filtered into state-level policy debates. In the process the women gained new friends both inside and outside the legislature who advocated for child care. Many male policymakers recognized the necessity for child care services for mothers who had to work outside their homes, although eventually it became clear that the model policymakers favored fell far short of the one politicized mothers envisioned.

Educators Get Organized

Leaders in nursery school education and teachers in child care centers joined parents in their fight to institute a permanent state-supported child care system. The group included Elizabeth Woods, who held a Ph.D. in child psychology and had chaired the California Committee for the Care and Training of Preschool Groups; Lynette Messer, a graduate of Columbia Teacher's College who directed the Child Care Teacher-Training Nursery School at San Francisco State College during the war; and Rosalie Blau, who served as a head teacher in Los Angeles's first Lanham Act center.[11] All had been involved in early childhood education since the WPA nursery schools in the 1930s and had worked to secure wartime funding. Now they coordinated the efforts of parents and educators throughout the state. Their training led most to advocate progressive methods of education, and they functioned as part of a much larger statewide network of teachers and activists.

Child care teachers such as Docia Zavitkovsky in Santa Monica and Virginia Rose in Oakland valued the high quality of the care provided in California's centers. Zavitkovsky, like Rose, got her start in the state's centers during the war. Born in Panama in 1913, Docia Humphrey Cusbee, the daughter of an engineer who worked on the construction of the Panama Canal, received her B.S. in education and M.S. in education administration from USC in the 1930s and intended to work at the community college level. Then, in 1935, she attended the California Pacific International Exposition. "They had a nursery school," she recalled, "and it had a one-way vision glass. . . . That's when I looked through this glass and there were these, they weren't two-year-olds, at that time, they were three and fours, and they were fascinating. And I thought, that's what I want to do!"[12] In the following years she gained experience by working in two preschools, and in 1939 she married Charles Zavitkovsky. Their daughter, Ann, was born in 1942. Charles enlisted in the army in 1944 and was sent overseas. With her nursery school experience, Zavitkovsky was asked to volunteer at the McKinley Center in Santa Monica and then was hired permanently and soon after made director of the center. She would work in Santa Monica centers for thirty-nine years until retiring in 1983.[13]

From the beginning, teachers like Zavitkovsky and Rose helped local parents' councils disseminate information about political activities, watching the children while mothers held letter-writing parties and strategy sessions. Early childhood education experts and teachers had a personal interest in the centers becoming permanent, not only because they offered professionally rewarding employment but also because they showcased educational theories they had been promoting since the 1930s. In their view, child care centers should serve as nursery schools, educating preschool children as well as their parents.[14]

Through the late 1940s and into the early 1950s constant legislative battles forced educators to become savvy political activists. Two well-established organizations, the Northern California Association for Nursery Education (NCANE) and the Southern California Association for Nursery Education (SCANE), led the way. Their officers and members had been involved in developing the state's nursery schools and child care programs since the 1930s, but they lacked political expertise. In 1945 neither group had a legislative officer. During the war, these organizations advocated for the state program.[15] Rosalie Blau and Elizabeth Woods traveled frequently from Los Angeles to northern California to participate in statewide child care committees and testify at hearings. As Zavitkovsky recalls, "We had a northern and southern group and we met [together] every year. . . . We were a close-knit group and also were very supportive" of each other.[16]

At war's end these organizations committed themselves to turning the state's "emergency" centers into a statewide, publicly funded nursery school system. When the legislature granted a temporary extension of the centers in 1946, both southern and northern associations increased their memberships and expanded their legislative activities.[17] By 1948 NCANE and SCANE each had a legislative committee that met once a month to discuss political strategies and organize with parents and other child care advocates. These educators and teachers viewed centers "not merely [as] custodial facilities but as settings where valuable learning experiences take place." Teachers played an active part "in interpreting the role of the centers and of good child care programs to the community through membership in community organizations."[18]

John Weber, a young veteran who the Department of Education hired in 1946 to supervise the child care centers and held that position until 1970, was a very important ally for child care advocates. In 1947 he launched monthly meetings with administrators and directors of centers throughout the state. Weber not only championed the centers to the state's Department of Education, local school boards, and the legislature, but he also devoted enormous time and effort to nurturing those outside the political structure and helping them communicate with politicians in Sacramento.[19]

Early childhood education experts turned to teachers and center administrators to extend the reach of their political activities. For example, Lovisa Wagoner, who headed the laboratory nursery school at Mills College, wrote to Ruth Howarth, director of child care centers in Redwood City, encouraging Howarth to mobilize teachers there. Wagoner suggested that it might be "a good idea to send to each director of a Child Care Program, application blanks inviting all the teachers to join. Could a letter from you, saying the Nursery School Association of Northern California needs the support of everyone interested in the education of young children" go out in the next few months? "The support of all people professionally interested in children is imperative, as you know. If all teachers in child care programs join forces with the Association to support such legislation, bills that are desirable would stand a much better chance of being passed."[20]

Teachers were eager to join the campaign. World War II had instilled in them the conviction that child care centers had a patriotic mission and provided valuable services to the children and the community. Docia Zavitkovsky remembered that "enrollment cut across all economic lines and made for a very good program because one wasn't concerned whether he was at the poverty level or whether one was on Aid to Dependent Children (ADC). . . . You were involved because you were freeing a person to work for the war effort and there was a great deal of feeling about doing something supportive to the national effort." During those years teachers formed close relationships with mothers. "I met with them all the time," Zavitkovsky recalled. "I was just available to them and I would meet with a parent" and "get the phone calls, what they were unhappy about or happy with."[21] Teachers had regular contact with mothers when they picked up or dropped off their children at school or encountered them at parents' council meetings. At the McKinley Center in Santa Monica as well as in other centers throughout the state, teachers and mothers shared a space that became central to their political campaign.

Parents, like educators, had much to learn about the political process. In Santa Monica, Zavitkovsky observed, "Neither the parents [n]or the staff were informed in terms of the legislative process, [so] we had a great many meetings."[22] During the yearly battle for child care, parents, teachers, and directors "learned how to organize and fight for what they wanted."[23] Winona Sample, a Red Lake Chippewa who became head teacher of the Paso Robles Child Care Center during World War II, described herself as a political neophyte. "Oh, I didn't know really anything about [politics] because I was twenty-four, five, six, very young. I knew Indian politics. . . . But I learned very fast and I learned well about the bills and everything."[24] Sample had no idea that accepting a job in the state's centers meant committing herself to political action. Even the teachers, who played critical roles in the movement, were ultimately upstaged by a group of mothers who captured the attention of the press, the governor, and the legislature.

Mothers Organize

At the end of the war parents in government-sponsored centers mobilized to convince the state not to close these critical institutions.[25] As it became evident that child care would not be permanently secured through a single decisive political battle, they built institutions to marshal an increasing number of mothers to campaign for state-supported centers. City and local parents' councils were formed "to develop activities toward the continuation of a permanent child care program in California." They elected officers, created letterheads, and met on a regular basis. To hold mothers' interest year-round the councils also provided parent education, bringing together head teachers with parents to discuss children's needs.[26]

The councils nurtured politicized women and catapulted some into state and citywide leadership roles. Women who led parents' councils traveled to state conventions, spoke to assembly committees, and forged alliances and friendships with other women in similar positions. They took these conversations back to their child care centers as well as into their neighborhoods and public housing projects. Like women who shared a common workplace, they experienced similar daily struggles, juggling employment and child care through the use of state-sponsored centers.[27] Attending monthly parents' meetings, letter-writing potlucks, and child care rallies had a consciousness-raising effect on many who realized for the first time that they were not alone.[28]

From 1946 on, at least once a month and even more frequently when child care legislation was before the state legislature, centers were transformed into sites of political education and mobilization. Rooms that during the day echoed with the laughter of energetic toddlers were filled by mothers discussing their newest political strategies and swapping stories about the trials of being a full-time parent and full-time worker. These meetings were attended almost solely by women, although dedicated fathers joined them occasionally. As they sat in the centers where their children played and learned during the day, many realized that they had a shared stake in decisions made in Sacramento. The state's child care centers served as what Nancy Fraser has termed alternative "publics," sites "where members of subordinated social groups invent and circulate counter discourse to formulate oppositional interpretations of their identities, interests, and needs."[29] Parent education groups became "free spaces" where some working mothers gained a group identity, became more assertive, and blossomed into political activists.[30]

In addition to educating parents about child care policy and coaching them in how to persuade legislators, parents' councils encouraged members to exercise the right to vote. Virginia Rose of the Oakland parents' council recalls that "one year we were deputy registrars. And we sat at little card tables to get people to register to vote . . . as many of us as could, that had the time. Because we wanted our parents to be able to vote." Like other teachers and parents, Rose believed that the parents' groups should not only teach mothers to advocate for child care, but also educate them to become active and engaged citizens.[31]

Parents' councils also promoted racial tolerance and understanding. Having multiracial clienteles made the centers venues for forging interracial understanding and navigating racial and ethnic differences. As one founding member recalled, "Nobody ever thought anything about it—we just were [integrated], from the start."[32] The parents' groups and the physical space of the centers helped bridge the divides between black, white, Asian American, and Mexican American parents and teachers. African American teachers, said Rose, "had to learn to be sensitive to their [white parents'] feelings. Not just be opposed to their feelings but to be sensitive to them." Racial understanding did not always come easily, and racist views did emerge occasionally in parents' meetings. But when it came to working for child care, parents and teachers put aside their differences.[33]

With the assistance of teachers and directors, parents' councils spearheaded letter-writing campaigns every year the legislature debated child care. In Los Angeles, women gathered at potluck dinners at centers to write to their legislators and Governor Warren. "Some evenings," Rosalie Blau remembered, "we'd all stay and have dinner. Then, a few teachers would care for the children while the mothers wrote letters." Docia Zavitkovsky observed that potlucks ensured good turnouts by making it "easy for them" to participate. As Winona Sample described the potlucks at the Redwood City Center, "Parents would come in and their hot, big hot dish would be there—their salad, dessert. And they'd be eating and they'd have a business meeting—have a speaker, have views with something about legislation or [have] a legislator in. . . . And they came fifty, sixty people at a time, you know."[34] Political action was nurtured in the publicly sponsored child care centers of California's rapidly growing cities. A constant stream of new mothers who had a stake in their future made the centers places at which to discuss political strategy and tactics. Despite the frequent turnover in clientele, the shared experiences of these mothers and space created by the centers made social learning possible. The centers also preserved the collective memory of a movement that relied on a new cadre of activists every few years.[35]

In September 1948 the San Francisco Child Care Council spearheaded the formation of a statewide organization at a parents' convention in Long Beach. The California Parents' Association for Child Care (CPACC) aimed to establish permanent child care program in California by coordinating the political activity of the local parents' councils and the approximately twelve thousand parents they represented, so that they might have a more effective voice in Sacramento.[36] Because mothers who had children in the centers changed from year to year, advocates considered a permanent organization critical to success.

Mothers and Wage Letter-writing Campaigns

The letter-writing campaigns carried out by the parents' councils provide a powerful example of how child care centers mobilized mothers to influence public policy. Although only fragmentary records of parents' groups have survived in the archives, the letters reveal a great deal about the women who wrote them, their political views, and how they slowly gained a sense of solidarity and community with other mothers in similar circumstances. From the end of the war on, parents' councils in conjunction with teachers and child care administrators, organized mothers and some fathers to flood Governor Warren's office with letters. Every year between 1945 and 1950, when the child care centers faced elimination, thousands of working mothers wrote to the governor and to their legislators.

In 1947, for example, Earl Warren received close to thirteen hundred letters from parents, teachers, and statewide organizations.[37] More than half came from parents of children in the centers. Of these, 35 percent indicated they were working mothers, and 29 percent identified themselves as single mothers who were the sole supporters of their children. Approximately 30 percent of the single mothers were widows, and 16 percent were divorced. Most of the letter-writers lived in the three urban areas with the largest number of child care centers; more than half of the letters came from Los Angeles and a quarter were from the San Francisco Bay area. In 1946, and throughout the rest of the annual campaigns, women made up at least 90 percent of the correspondents; in 1950 only 3 percent were male.[38] Most had only one child; fewer than 10 percent had three or more. Although it is not possible to identify most letter-writers by race, the racial breakdown of children in the state's centers in 1947 is known: 83.5 percent were white, 8.5 percent African American, 4.2 percent Mexican, 1 percent Japanese, fewer than 1 percent Chinese, and 2.1 percent identified as other.

Women of color were among the parents who participated in the letter-writing campaign.[39] Indeed, black women played a critical role in these early organizing efforts. The California Council of Negro Women rallied its membership and the *California Eagle,* the state's black newspaper, kept readers informed of important legislative activities. "Procrastination must not be the thief of time in this case," the editors pleaded with mothers after federal funds were cut off. "Write . . . urging [elected officials] to work and fight to preserve all child care centers."[40] In January 1947 *Eagle* columnist W. J. Wheaton reported after visiting a state center, "The institution as a whole should be fostered and financed as a regular educational program of the state. . . . Aside from the strain and worry eased from the shoulders of parents who are compelled to work and have no other means whereby their offspring may be cared for, children in the day nurseries are being taught principles of democracy, which will prove an asset [to] the nation in the inculcation of democracy."[41]

Before the Great Depression, political letter-writing had been carried out mostly by urban, upper-class males. During the administration of Franklin D. Roosevelt, however, a more diverse set of Americans began to view it as a right and duty of citizenship; working-class, rural, and female citizens wrote to politicians in larger numbers in the 1930s. Part of this change can also be attributed to Eleanor Roosevelt, who encouraged citizens, women in particular, to contact her about their concerns and struggles. By 1950 women accounted for half of all political letter writers nationwide. Leila Sussman attributes the shift both to FDR's and his successors' encouragement of the practice and to the far-reaching impact of New Deal policies on the lives of average citizens. In California, the state's wartime child care centers prompted working mothers to express their concerns to Earl Warren.[42]

Letters to the governor and legislature played a central role in the movement to preserve California's day care services. The sheer bulk of the correspondence was impressive, but it also mattered that the majority of the letters centered on women's individual stories and experiences. Writing to the governor, one scholar maintains, exemplified "citizenship in practice."[43] Some working mothers had taken part in union organizing during the war, but for many, sitting down to write the governor or a legislator marked the first time they had played an active part in politics. Taking up their pens, the women made their personal struggles part of the public record. By sharing their problems with the governor and others in political power they identified themselves as part of a constituency that politicians had to take into account. They provided a mass of firsthand testimony on the need for child care services and clear, well-constructed arguments for state-sponsored centers. Organized letter-writing drives were also consciousness-raising experiences. The act of writing forced working mothers to hone their arguments and think about how best to communicate their child care needs. Posting a letter indicated that they believed that their views mattered.[44] Mothers realized that their struggles with day care were not unique or individual; rather, they were collective, and solving them required political action.

Some wrote brief messages outlining the necessity of a permanent child care program, but many others went far beyond the call for a "short note" and sent three- or four-page letters.[45] Mothers furnished Warren with the intimate details of their lives. Some revealed how much money they earned, how hard they worked, how hard their husbands worked, or how they became divorced and the sole supporters of their families. They gave the children's names and ages. Some even enclosed pictures, asking Warren how he could leave their adorable son or daughter without care. Mrs. Thomas A. Emmons wrote explicit descriptions of the hardships her family faced. "Undoubtedly," she told the governor, "you have the statistics regarding the number of working mothers and the undesirable living quarters here in Los Angeles." To drive home her point, Emmons included a photograph of the converted bus in which her family lived while saving to buy a home, part of a *Collier's* magazine article on the postwar housing crisis in the West.[46] This is the "bus in which our boy must spend his days if I am forced to quit working," she explained.

As the parents and teachers of the Manhattan Beach child care center aptly put it, they wrote "to give [Warren] a little more intimate picture of the need the Centers fill in our children's and our lives."[47] Clearly, the mothers believed that if the governor spent a day walking in their shoes, he would support the program. No doubt some selected the details of their lives that would elicit sympathy and garner support from the state's political leaders. They used storytelling as a means of contending for influence in a democracy.

Many letters expressed acute awareness of the disparity in power between the governor and the women. It is difficult to gauge whether the degree to which they were being deferential, however, given that they were instructed to be respectful and "not demanding" in the letters. One mother closed asking Warren to "take heed" of her opinions and those of other mothers "in order to have the Child Care Centers carry on, as you were voted into office to carry out the

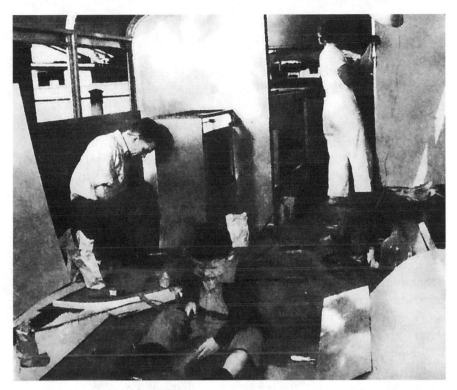

Figure 1. Mr. and Mrs. Thomas Emmons in their converted bus, Culver City, Calif. *Collier's*, Dec. 14, 1947. (Photograph by Ike Vern Pix. Reprint by permission of Jane Vern Anderson)

desire of the 'little people.'" Adding her "voice to those of the thousands," Irma Keal reminded the governor of how much power he had. By supporting child care legislation, she urged, "you—one man—can do so much." Another woman wrote, "This must be a time when all working mothers regret that they have not taken a more active interest in politics. Something which vitally concerns us and our children has come up—the continuing of extended day care—and most of us feel powerless to do anything about it."[48] Others suggested that although they were not politicians, their views on child care were valuable. As a mother from San Francisco put it, "We haven't the time, money, or ability of reaching those who should plead for us," but "I hope you will not hesitate in granting the financial help needed."[49] Mothers pragmatically acknowledged their ultimate dependence upon men like Warren to decide the fate of child care, but their letters showed increasing awareness of a place for them in the political process. A widow with a two-year-old daughter announced as she closed her message, "This is the first time I've ever written a legislator, a Governor, or a Congressman. I suppose this is the first time a bit of proposed legislation hit so close to home."[50] Marjorie Richardson, after telling Warren that was her very first letter to a political leader, explained that "When I read the notice that the schools will very possibly be closed if the bill wasn't passed, I realized I had remained still too long."[51] For many of the women, writing to Warren was their first step into political activity.

Many letters revealed women's strong identification with other working mothers and consciousness of their class, linking their individual situations with those of other families.[52] Some indicated that they had gained this sense of solidarity from interactions with other parents at the child care centers. Rather than appealing to the governor only on behalf of their individual needs, they pleaded to preserve child care services for *all* working mothers. Kathleen Kay of Playa Del Ray informed the governor that "fifty of us mothers who must work to support our children have been meeting weekly to discuss ways and means" of convincing legislators to adopt a permanent child care system.[53] Others extended their connections to working mothers throughout the state and identified with others across the country. "These schools fill a long felt need in a working nation," observed a mother from San Francisco. "Working women: widows, divorcees, wives of disabled veterans, and widowers, and many others have . . . been beset by the same problem. . . . 'How shall I take care of my children while I am at work carning a living?'"[54] Mary Jones Dmitrieff aligned herself with working-class women when she wrote, "You see I am not talking of the career woman. . . . I am speaking for the benefit of the factory worker, salesgirl, waitress, hairdresser, and the office girl who have two or more children."[55]

This collective consciousness became part of these women's notions of what it meant to be a "good" mother. Like African American women, single mothers, and poor women on welfare, California's working mothers had to redefine good mothering outside the dominant model of the full-time homemaker with a husband who could support her and their children.[56] Gloria Rouzar, a widow from Hollywood, wrote that "one of the important things provided by the nursery schools is the blessed peace of mind a loving mother feels knowing that though she must be parted by economic necessity for many hours a day, from her beloved children, that they are getting, in most instances, safer, better care than she alone could provide." She reminded Warren that "we mothers who have to work, want to work to provide the best possible things for our future Americans" and avoid taking government charity. Publicly supported child care centers alleviated the anxiety and distraction that came from not knowing whether their children were safe while they were at work. "To you," one woman said, "this may seem to be a small problem, but to us mothers it seems to be our only solution to bringing up our children to be good citizens for the future

America." Bringing up their children to be good citizens meant working rather than taking "handouts" from the state, and the mothers sought to counter criticisms commonly aimed at single parents. One protested that working mothers should not be seen as "'trash' that 'dump' their children on someone else while they flit over the country-side." Women like her, she maintained, were "conscientious mothers who are trying to give their children good care and yet make a home for them, give them an education, better them despite the fact they have a broken home."[57]

The working mothers challenged postwar gender conventions. They did not dismiss the reigning domestic ideal, but they pointed out the gap between ideal and reality. A woman from Los Angeles explained, "As parents we would like to be at home, if we had one, if we could keep one up, but in so many cases we are in no position to do anything but keep 'in the swim of things.'"[58] Mrs. W. B. Robinson opened her letter to the governor by directly stating the problem: "Woman's place may be in the home, but there are certain extenuating circumstances which can make that desirable status difficult to attain."[59] Another mother reacted to a senator who had introduced legislation to eliminate child care centers in 1947: "One of the senators made the statement that the woman's place was in the home! This is just as silly and unthinking a remark in this case as that of Mary Antoinette when she said, 'let them eat cake!' I'm sure we'd all like to stay home with our babies—they're little so short a time. But unfortunately they—and even we—must eat!"[60] Most of the women would not have called themselves feminists, but their arguments centered on identities they had constructed as both mothers and workers. By expressing a desire to be at home with their children they echoed idealized views of motherhood, but at the same time they challenged conventional notions of motherhood by working outside their homes and proclaiming their right to child care services.[61]

Many spoke directly from the heart, but they also made deliberate appeals to Warren as patriotic citizens. They grounded child care demands in their traditional role as nurturers, responsible for raising the nation's children. At the same time they made these claims on behalf of what historically have been considered masculine attributes of citizenship—independence and wage-earning.[62] Child care would allow women who must work outside the home to fulfill their material responsibilities. Jean Ramsey spoke especially for those who were divorced or widowed when she asked, "How else can we possibly take care of our children and know they are as well taken care of?"[63] Alluding to the dominant discourse that deplored dependency on public welfare programs, some stated that child care services would enable them to avoid becoming dependent on the state for their livelihoods.[64] Eunice Shreve told Warren that "most of us would much rather care for our own children" but rejected any thoughts of going on Aid to

Dependent Children (ADC) because "earning our way is preferable to relief."[65] Shreve's comments suggest that she, like many other working mothers, had become aware of the "pervasive attacks" that had already begun on ADC after the war.[66] With child care that enabled them to support their children through employment rather than depending on the state, the mothers could be considered full citizens with benefits of American citizenship previously reserved for men.

The governor's office took notice of the letter-writing campaigns, and they made a difference when it came time for the governor to sign the child care bill in late June 1947. Beach Vasey, the governor's special assistant, reminded Warren that "we have a legal file drawer full of letters urging approval of child care center legislation." Parents' voices had made their way into the state's child care debates. In fact, Vasey's recommendations reflected the influence of both parents and educators. The final bill, sponsored by two moderate legislators and eventually signed by Warren, represented a "compromise between the school of thought that we should have no child care centers and those who believe that we should have free child care centers regardless of the ability of the parents to pay."[67]

Mothers wanted a child care program "without restrictions" but lobbied for the middle way when they had no other choice.[68] The following year, Vasey informed the governor that "for a period of months we have been flooded with correspondence from individuals and organizations of all sorts favoring . . . child care centers. No attempt has been made even to count this correspondence, which has been most numerous and prolonged." A state senator declared that he "had received more mail on child care than on all other legislative issues combined during the 1948-49 session."[69] The yearly barrage made voting against child care impossible and persuaded some policymakers to support the sort of program that parents and educators advocated. At the same time, their arguments and claims constrained options in the future.

Advocates Descend on Sacramento

At council meetings, parents and teachers organized groups of mothers to speak with state legislators in the capital. For educators whose organizations paid their expenses the trip to Sacramento was not a hardship; for working mothers, by contrast, it required careful planning and entailed some expense. To attend hearings and lobby for child care services, they had to take time off work and depend on friends and neighbors to watch their children. Speeches by impassioned mothers became an annual ritual in Sacramento between 1947 and 1957, forcing legislators, the press, and the public to take notice. According to one member of the senate, parents' testimony "presented the most effective means of applying pressure for child care."[70] On April 22, 1947, for example, thirty-five parents and teachers found care for their children and substitutes for their classes and made the 380-mile journey to Sacramento on behalf of the 3,500 parents who benefited from Los Angeles's 115 child care centers. Forty others from the southern part of the state spent all night traveling by car, bus, and train. Despite their exhaustion, parents and educators enthusiastically went door to door in the legislature, seeking to gain new allies for a permanent child care program and, most immediately, aiming to defeat a bill proposed by Senator W. P. Rich that called for an end to state-sponsored child care.[71] A few of the women had experience dealing with politicians, but lobbying was an entirely new experience for most. Docia Zavitkovsky recalled one now-famous story about two parents who represented the centers in Santa Monica. "We were asked to send delegates to Sacramento to speak on behalf of the program and they were to go as advocates. . . . They went up to the desk and, instead of registering as advocates, they registered as 'agitators,' because they didn't know what it meant to be an advocate or what advocacy was all about."[72]

White and black middle-class women's groups and veterans' organizations joined the parents and educators in Sacramento that April. A coalition including the Council of Churchwomen, the Congress of Parents and Teachers, the California Federation of Women's Clubs, the California League of Women Voters, and the California Council of Negro Women assisted in the push for permanent, state-sponsored child care centers. Tarea Hall Pittman, a community activist and civil rights advocate who was then president of the California Council of Negro Women, remembered busloads of women pouring into the state capitol.[73] Governor Warren addressed the crowd, promising to sign any child care measure that came across his desk. Pittman viewed the governor as being genuinely concerned about the issue. At the hearing that afternoon and evening, a number of women reminded the legislature that "without the facilities for daytime care of their children, they would be unable to hold their jobs and support themselves."[74]

That spring day mothers and their supporters testified for hours, forcing an education committee hearing to remain in session until 11 P.M. "The assembly chamber still echoed today with the voices of earnest young mothers who pleaded with members of the education committee," Eva Lapin, a reporter for the *Daily People's World*, wrote in her column the next morning. "Don't play politics with child care," one mother told the committee. "You must give us a chance to work to support our families with the confidence our children will be well cared for.[75] In February, after an earlier set of hearings, the headline of the *San Francisco Daily News* read: "Politicians Read Riot Act by Angry Parents.[76] Mothers and their supporters knew that legislators held the power, but they were determined to make their voices heard in the state capital.

Figure 2. San Francisco mothers and fathers leave by chartered bus for Sacramento to advocate for child care legislation, May 25, 1947. (*San Francisco News-Call Bulletin* newspaper photograph archive, BANC PIC 1959.010—NEG, the Bancroft Library, University of California, Berkeley)

Spelling Out Ideology and Strategy

In early 1948 California's child care advocates outlined a permanent program. With the leadership and funding of the southern and northern California Association for Nursery Education, the coalition produced a twenty-six-page report on the "needs of young children in our democratic society," describing a state child care program as a "democratically acceptable means of reducing the pressure on city people and preserving and strengthening the city family and its constituent members."[77] The mark of early childhood educators is evident in *A Brief Inquiry into the Need for a Child Care Program in California*. The pamphlet emerged from collaboration among Messer, Theresa Mahler, Rosalie Blau, and Elizabeth Woods as well as leaders of the state parents' organization and public school administrators from the cities with the largest numbers of child care centers—Los Angeles, San Francisco, and Oakland. As these educators and parents met to compile and edit what they saw as an essential new tool in their lobbying arsenal, they drew on facts and figures from a parent-initiated study as well as principles of progressive education. The pamphlet outlined the arguments parents and educators made in the face of rising conservatism during the late 1940s and 1950s, paying special attention to mounting criticism of ADC and its clientele as well as the increasing power of the Red Scare.

The publication laid out a sophisticated and historically grounded argument for government-sponsored child care beyond wartime emergency. Centers were necessary because economic changes forced mothers to work outside the home. Like those who wrote letters to Warren, the authors argued that child care would prevent juvenile delinquency and nurture "socially healthy, well-adjusted adults." Rather than destroying families, the report claimed, child care "helped and strengthened" children and families. Finally, it maintained that child care was not charity but rather "a functioning educational as well as custodial unit" based on modern ideas of early childhood education that provided a suitable substitute for a mother's care.[78]

A Brief Inquiry excluded the opinions of the more radical mothers, especially those who believed that publicly supported child care should be available to any family regardless of income, an option that was not politically feasible. With the shift from the war against fascism to the cold war and the turn away from New Deal welfare policies toward a politics of domestic containment, child care proponents surveyed a new political landscape.[79] Mothers and educators had to take a deliberately moderate approach, upholding mothers' domestic role while pushing for a service that enabled them to earn wages. "Of first importance in American life today," they concluded, "is the preservation of the family as a self-reliant, independent, responsible social unit."[80] Emphasizing families' heroic efforts to survive despite challenging social conditions, they filled the pamphlet with testimonials from parents who explained the ways in which child care had helped them raise their children with dignity. In families where economic necessity sent the mother out to work, child care and a good job were critical to remaining "self-reliant and independent." In a state with what one scholar described as an "anti-welfare state legislature," arguments linking child care with economic self-sufficiency would prove particularly effective.[81]

The pamphlet was clear on how centers would "encourage improvement in the quality of all nursery schools on the Pacific Coast."[82] Advocates defended the program against opponents' claims that child care centers attempted to replace the love and time of a parent by arguing that they promoted children's physical and intellectual development. Children learned how to function in a group setting, were taught proper eating and sleeping habits, and were exposed to art, music, and literature. A child would benefit from a high-quality early education that "provides him with a richer, wider world, where he makes gains in experience, knowledge, and understandings that will serve as a foundation for later school success."[83] Training California's children according to recent child development principles assisted working families in raising good citizens, advocates maintained.

The pamphlet countered accusations that child care was communist-inspired. Advocates emphasized that democracy began at home, but a democratic family did not require a stay-at-home mother. It required "warm affectionate child rearing" and self-reliance, which families facing inadequate housing and the rising cost of living with a single income, especially those dependent on a woman's wage, could achieve only with the help of child care services.[84] Advocates redefined the democratic family to fit the realities of working mothers' lives while representing stable families as a bulwark against communism. Like the mothers in the annual letter-writing campaigns, the authors of *A Brief Inquiry* contended that child care was good for the country as well as for working parents. These arguments were harbingers of late twentieth-century discourse about helping poor families stay off welfare. The authors claimed that with child care services, "Parents develop the independence and self-reliance desirable in an American citizen." They concluded, "Every family that is preserved or strengthened is a gain for democracy. Without child care many of these parents might, in the face of insurmountable circumstances, and in a state of despondency, become prey of crack-pot agitators or the victims of subversive political agents."[85] By maintaining that independent, wage-earning by mothers and fathers were a stronghold against communism, advocates used one cold war ideology to undermine another: the notion that all mothers belong at home with their children.

Parents and educators distributed the pamphlet to members of the state legislature and other organizations in hopes of gaining new allies and changing the minds of old foes. In February 1949, the California Parents' Association for Child Care included the pamphlet in each letter they wrote to members of the Assembly Education Committee. The state association praised it "as probably the most valuable service made on behalf of continued legislation" in 1949.[86] Theresa Mahler, legislative chair of the NCANE, sent *A Brief Inquiry* along with a letter to all new state legislators. "Each year since 1942, and again this year," she told them, "the problem of the care of children of working mothers and of children from other homes which are unable to provide adequate supervision of their children has been subjected to debate in the California Legislature." The bulletin, Mahler promised, would assist them in learning "the background, the present problem, and the prospects for the future" of child care.[87]

As mothers, teachers, and childhood educators gained political experience, they employed a wide range of methods to convince legislators of child care needs. Keeping with their theme of bringing legislators face to face with the experiences of children in the centers, the coalition produced a film that told the story of child care in five Los Angeles centers.[88] Citing national statistics about women employed in industry and the "considerable percentage" who were mothers, the film let the audience know that "California recognizes this as a continuing civic problem, and has made provision to help and supplement the home by establishing child care centers, operated through the State Department of Education, with high standards of health and educational guidance."[89] The film reassured the audience that centers did not undermine American families or take mothers' roles. Rather, centers helped women remain good mothers by providing safe and affordable care while they worked outside their homes. It also described the experiences of children who spent their days in the state's centers. The camera took the viewer through crowded city neighborhoods to a mother's workplace, showing her relaxed in the knowledge that her daughter was safe at the child care center, and then into the center itself, following young children as they played and learned.[90] The coalition reinforced women's role as mothers while refashioning the image of good motherhood: a woman who spends her day in an office or a factory and places her daughter in the safe environment of the state's child care centers.[91]

Figure 3. Child care centers pamphlet, California Parents' Association for Child Care Centers [n.d]. (Courtesy of Center for Oral and Public History, California State University, Fullerton)

In addition to offering statistics, visual evidence, and personal testimony, child care advocates tried to sway legislators by inviting them to visit child care centers. In 1946 mothers from the Baldwin Park Child Care Center informed Ernest Geddes, a small businessman in Pomona and a Republican assemblyman, that the federal government was going to stop funding and asked him to "come over tonight or tomorrow night" to attend "a meeting to see what we can do about child care centers."[92] As he recalled to a reporter years later, initially "I told them that as an economy-minded Republican I couldn't do anything about it" and that "they had a New Deal congressman and he could get what was coming to them." The next morning Geddes observed the center. Sitting silently, unnoticed in the back, he "watched the children play, heard them say Grace before their meals. Something happened inside me and I haven't been the same since."[93] From that moment until his retirement in 1960, Geddes joined left-leaning legislators Augustus Hawkins and Ernest E. Debs to build a consensus in support of child care within the assembly. Face-to-face contact with children in the state's centers transformed his views about child care, a tactic so effective that it was adopted across the state. In March 1949, Birdice Phillips, principal of the Shurtleff School in Napa, wrote to NCANE's legislative chair that "I have personally written an invitation to Mr. Nathan Coombs, State Senator, and Mr. Ernest Crowley, Assemblyman, to come have lunch at the center" to learn more about the high-quality early childhood education program.[94] Mothers also believed that if Earl Warren visited the centers he would see for himself the need for their continued presence. "My dear Governor," Mary Jones Dmitrieff inquired, "have you ever visited one of these Child Care Centers? I know you have been in Los Angeles on numerous occasions so perhaps you have visited these centers and know why I am appealing to you. You can go into any one of the centers, that remain, at any time during the hours of six A.M. to six P.M. and you will always find the children doing something worthwhile to benefit themselves."[95] In Santa Barbara, Republican assemblyman Thomlinson "gave several hours of his time in which he visited the Centers, studied the program in them, and discussed the situation with us quite thoroughly." A few months later, he voted in favor of the child care bill.[96]

The coalition appealed to each legislator's particular interests, adapting their tactics to the individual. In 1949 Theresa Mahler set out to convince San Francisco's Senator Gerald O'Gara, a devout Catholic highly critical of the child care program, that he should help parents and teachers preserve the centers. O'Gara, like the Catholic Church in general, resisted the idea of the state rather than local governments providing aid to education. He objected to the centers for three reasons. Ineligible parents took advantage of them; they did not provide caseworkers; and by 1949, he believed, the need had diminished significantly. O'Gara was finally persuaded when the Association for Nursery Education demonstrated to him that Catholic families relied on the child care program.

Mahler told him that at least 51 percent of the Oakland families with children in the centers were Catholic and explained that "the one Catholic agency in West Oakland has a long waiting list. So we do know that child care is helping those Catholic parents in the strengthening of home and family."[97] In December O'Gara wrote to Governor Warren, declaring that state funding for child care was "of the greatest importance to the people of San Francisco, and that it is not possible at this time to transfer the burden of supporting these child care centers from the State to local property owners."[98] Activists had secured another key ally.

By 1950, legislators had incorporated the mothers' definitions into their correspondence and official statements. Sam Yorty, a Los Angeles assemblyman who later became the city's popular and controversial mayor, drafted a letter to Warren in which he argued that the senate "must end the vacillation and indecision which results in an annual period of anxiety on the part of citizens in need of the assistance rendered by Child Care Centers." California families should not have to worry that the legislature would not keep centers open. Frank Kraft, a Republican senator from San Diego who had introduced child care legislation every year since 1948, reminded Warren that the centers were of "extreme importance to the mothers in my district who use these centers, and to me." Later that year Kraft explained that his views had been influenced by his contact with mothers and teachers as well as by watching his two widowed sisters struggle to raise their children alone. "I have become well acquainted with the splendid work done by the Centers, with personnel, and with the mothers to whom the centers are a Godsend," he recounted.[99]

In the early years after the war, the Catholic Church was the most vocal opponent of state-supported centers, which were believed to pose "serious dangers to sound family life and our social structure."[100] Church leaders praised the valuable service the centers had provided during the wartime emergency but were adamant in upholding the common view that now mothers should return to their primary roles at home. The church spoke most vehemently against nursery educators' desire to make the state's centers a first step toward a comprehensive public nursery school program. For the church, nursery schools threatened to tear apart American families and encourage mothers to take jobs outside the home and "shirk their family and social responsibilities." Working mothers, that is, were acceptable on the sole condition that they did not "seek employment by choice but only by necessity." Throughout the late 1940s, Catholics sent telegrams and memorandums to legislators in hopes of counteracting the well-coordinated campaign conducted by mothers and educators. Eventually, however, after repeated defeats, the Catholic Church abandoned its organized opposition.[101]

A small number of individuals wrote to Warren and their legislators to oppose the state-supported centers. In contrast to the thousands of letters Warren received from child care supporters each year, the governor's mailroom counted only a handful of letters from those not in favor of the centers.[102] Some who objected to spending public funds on child care argued that state support for child care services ran counter to fundamental American values. Drawing on conservative rhetoric and rejecting social programs, Mr. M. F. Taylor wrote in bold letters, "I am sick of this New Deal, Communistic, CIO, Socialism, this Un-American stuff." Others claimed that centers followed the practices of communist countries by shifting the responsibility for raising children from its rightful place in the home to the state. Finally, many accused parents who put their children in the centers of "falling down in their duty—in leaving the care and rearing of their children to some outsider."[103] Some contended that mothers were taking advantage of this public service and spending the day at the beach or in bars while California taxpayers paid for their child care. Like the Catholic Church, these letter-writers defended dominant models of gender. But the opponents of child care remained relatively ineffective because their numbers were so small. Parents' and educators' appeals were more subtle and persuasive, targeting traditional values while simultaneously undermining them and disarming opponents' accusations that child care centers threatened democracy or American families.

Debating a Means Test

After the state took over child care centers from the federal government, the types of families using the centers changed significantly. When the Interim Committee on Preschool and Primary Training conducted its year-long study in 1946, more than 60 percent of children in the centers lived in families where both parents worked outside their homes. By the time the Interim Committee on Social Welfare conducted its investigation four years later, one-parent families made up 56 percent of the centers' clientele. Much of this change came as a result of the means test that took effect on July 1, 1947, which gradually eliminated many of California's two-parent families whose income was above—sometimes just barely—the income ceiling.[104] With the means test firmly in place, the state's centers became part of the needs-based welfare system alongside such other postwar programs as school lunches, federal housing assistance, and, in the 1960s, Medicaid. Access to the centers could no longer be claimed as a right by all working parents in California although the coalition fought to expand the state's definition of need throughout the postwar period.[105]

In early 1946, when the state first took over administration and funding of the centers from the federal government, it did not specify financial limits for eligibility. By September, just five months later, enrollment in the centers had reached nearly sixteen thousand, an increase of almost three thousand children. Administrators soon realized that the legislature had been wrong in assuming that the numbers of children in the centers would drop as servicemen returned from overseas; they had erroneously anticipated that men's return to the labor force would mitigate the need for women to work. The March 1946 legislation stipulated that the state child care program would "'provide for children of those parents who were financially unable to provide otherwise.'"[106] The state had left it up to local governing boards of the centers to obtain proof of parents' eligibility, and, consequently, some localities continued to embrace a loose definition of "needy," waiting for state policymakers to impose restrictions.

Resistance to a means test appeared long before an official decision was made. The San Francisco Child Care Council wrote to Walter E. Dexter, state superintendent of public instruction, that it viewed implementation of family income standards as "unworkable, undesirable, and unnecessary." Council members objected to any sort of means test for two reasons. First, in many communities the state-supported centers represented the only affordable child care option or even the *only* option. Second, a means test placed the determination of a family's need for child care services firmly under the state's authority. Income standards for eligibility were unnecessary, they believed, because parents "are the persons best informed and best qualified" to determine the financial necessity for placing their children in the centers.[107]

In November 1946, the State Department of Education imposed an across-the-board fee increase to avoid running out of operating funds before the March 1947 renewal date. Raising the fee for each child by one-third placed centers out of reach of many families. More than two thousand children were withdrawn because their parents could not afford the higher fees. With the legislation extending child care passed on June 30, 1947, the state imposed a monthly income ceiling of $225 for one-parent families and $275 for families with both parents working. Parents whose earnings exceeded the new income limits were forced to withdraw their children.[108] Many others who were required to pay the new fees found it financially impossible to do so. For the next decade the coalition tried to eliminate the means test or raise the income ceilings to a more "reasonable" level. Local school districts, parents, and educators compiled statistics and collected stories that illustrated the test's dramatic effects on their communities, families, and child care enrollment.[109]

Residents of Bellflower, an unincorporated community north of Long Beach whose population had tripled since 1940, sent Governor Warren a copy of the child care study they conducted at the end of 1946 to explain why so many families had withdrawn from the centers.[110] Of the mothers who filled out the questionnaire, 67 percent blamed higher fees for their decision to remove their children from the center. One mother gave a detailed description of her dire situation: "My two sons have been enrolled in the nursery school and child care program since it was first started in Bellflower four years ago and have been in almost constant attendance. Because of the increasing fees and my meager salary, I have now been forced to remove them."[111] This woman also cared for her mother and two elderly relatives. Her situation illustrated what the San Francisco Child Care Council had contended was wrong with imposing unreasonable fees and an unrealistic means test: The policy did not account for individual needs or for the myriad of factors that might make it financially necessary for a family to place a child in a publicly supported center.

The close relationships between educators and the parents who relied on the centers became apparent as John Weber held meetings with directors of child care centers in both northern and southern California. At the Southern Section meeting held just three days before Governor Warren signed the 1947 means test provision into law, for example, directors posed numerous questions about test administration. Mary Alice Mallum, director of the Santa Monica child care centers, asked the group's opinion on a particular case. She described a mother of two whose earnings were well below the income ceiling but "after several years struggle" had obtained alimony from her ex-husband, which pushed her over the ceiling. Mallum argued that "she has just started receiving alimony and may not continue to, over a year" and, consequently "should be allowed in the Center, I believe." Women on welfare often faced a similar situation when they had court-mandated child support payments deducted from their paychecks even if they did not receive the payment. Ruth Koshuk, director of the Bellflower Centers, asked Weber, "Is it still possible for committees of local districts to make exceptions and allowances for special cases of high expenses?" Weber emphasized that exceptions could be made "only within the law. We must stick to the law."[112] The state-mandated means test stripped local directors of the ability to evaluate, case by case, whether a family was "financially unable to provide" for its children's care. Another director spoke on behalf of World War II veterans struggling to support their families. They "came back and bought homes to re-establish themselves," she said, but that meant they had high expenses, and with incomes just above $275 they were denied this state-supported service. Weber shared administrators' disappointment with aspects of the state's means test, admitting, "It is too bad, and serious. Many people, P.T.A., welfare workers, etc. were concerned about this group during the legislative hearings. But they could not get it into the law." Koshuk proposed that directors collect testimony from those eliminated or turned away from the centers: "We will need them to fight [for] legislation next year."[113]

Many women who had suffered from the income restrictions criticized the means test in their letters to Warren and other state officials. Presenting stories of personal hardship, providing statistics on the numbers of women forced to leave their local centers, and appealing to the governor's sense of what was fair and just, they ardently advocated a more inclusive child care program. The Los Angeles-based Parents' Council for Child Care Centers reported that "Ever since the higher fees there have been a steady stream of withdrawals from the child care centers, literally by the hundreds. It has not been because other care was found. . . . In most cases our children are now 'on the streets.'"[114] They expressed outrage at the state's decision to raise fees without consulting citizens and working families, which had left many mothers in a desperate situation. Responding to the possibility of a means test in 1947, Patricia Lomax, corresponding secretary of the Richmond Child Care Council, wrote to Warren on behalf of the five hundred parents with children in the city's centers and rejected the idea of restricting publicly funded child care services to the poor. "This emphasis upon poverty as a pre-requisite to adequate child care," Lomax said, "seems to us to ignore what ought to be the fundamental approach to the problem—that is, the needs of children in terms of their effective maturation."[115] The educational benefits of the centers, they argued, should determine policy. In individual letters, mothers shared with Warren their difficulties after the means test took effect. In many cases the earnings that placed families over the income ceiling allowed them to move from temporary housing to their own homes, leaving trailers, converted buses, and boardinghouses behind. Mrs. Wanda Huish, wife of a veteran and employee of the Veterans Administration, asked the state superintendent of schools to "make an exception and let our little girl receive this care and training." Wanda and her husband earned slightly more than the income ceiling allowed, but, she explained, "In order to pay for our home, buy groceries and meet our living expenses, it is necessary that we both work."[116] For this family and many others, affordable child care meant the difference between living in unsuitable conditions and owning a home. Postwar policies, like the G.I. Bill and increasing tax breaks for home ownership, favored the purchase of homes, but many families could only pay for mortgages with wages earned by working mothers. Thus families that used the state's centers were like most working-class families immediately after the war.

The legislature did grant some exemptions to the means test. Military families gained access to publicly funded child care as a reward for patriotic duty. The provision first applied to veterans attending college under the G.I. Bill, and in 1951 it was extended to families in which the father had recently been drafted or returned to the armed forces because of the Korean War.[117] Women employed in traditionally female occupations—nursing or teaching—also received an exemption because the population boom in California had caused a severe shortage of qualified professionals. Because these were viewed as critical public service occupations, advocates pushed the state to continue offering them child care. Finally, the state gave an exemption to parents harvesting crops during agricultural emergencies; in practice, however, that did little for children in rural areas or migrant workers' families. Since the legislature had stopped the construction of new centers by 1947, the number in agricultural regions remained woefully inadequate even though the low wages of agricultural workers meant that most already qualified under the means test. By 1950 the state had strictly defined who had access to the state's centers: veterans, workers in essential industries, and low-income working families.[118]

These exemptions did little to soften the effects of the means test although, occasionally, mothers and educators opposed to the test found a sympathetic hearing. Throughout their careers John Weber and Frank Wright both spoke out frequently on behalf of mothers' needs. Wright declared that a woman "who has minor children to support should not be penalized by the fact she appeared to earn more than the maximum amount."[119] Many legislators and citizens shared Wright's view, but during the yearly child care battles the opinions of those who supported income restrictions prevailed. Each year between 1947 and 1951 the legislature approved child care and gave its stamp of approval to the means test. When the assembly's Interim Committee on Social Welfare made its recommendations in January 1951, after six months of studying the program, the only change it advocated was adjusting the income ceiling to reflect the increase in the cost of living since 1947. The rise was hardly noticeable: a measly $20 increase for one-parent families.

Success Is Preservation

By 1948 mothers and educators in California had to relinquish arguments for child care as a social right for all the state's working women. They did, however, succeed in preventing the elimination of publicly funded child care, defying the trend that swept across the rest of the country. By 1950, only Washington and Massachusetts also continued to provide child care, and each state had fewer than ten centers. While California's program had been cut back significantly since its wartime peak when it served twenty-five thousand children, the state's centers amounted to almost 80 percent of the nation's public child care services.[120] In the conservative political climate of the cold war, saving state-sponsored child care signaled a major victory.[121] Mothers worked for child care so they could simultaneously be good mothers and breadwinners. In the process, they gained a new sense of themselves as citizens who had a stake in the political process. Educators' arguments that centers produced good citizens and protected American families added strength to the mothers' cause. The coalition demonstrates that the political activism of women on the state level preserved some of the social democratic promise implicit in this wartime program. Within the constraints that fiscal and familial conservatism imposed on welfare policy, reformers built a strong case for state-supported child care. They continued to believe, however, that working families deserved much more.

4

"We Need to Stand Together"

*Theresa Mahler, Mary Young, and the
Coalition's Victory in the 1950s*

When asked about Theresa Mahler in 1998, Mary Young recalled, "She depended upon me for a lot." In fact, Mahler and Young relied not only on each other but also on a wider network of mothers and educators to sustain their lobbying efforts for child care in the 1950s. During legislative sessions they spent hours on the telephone, strategizing and allocating tasks.[1] Young's responsibilities ranged from helping to write and edit speeches to contacting parent representatives across the state and organizing letter-writing campaigns. As legislative chair for the Northern California Association for Nursery Education (NCANE), Mahler served as the key spokeswoman for nursery school educators and child care supervisors throughout the postwar struggles to secure permanent, publicly funded child care. A soft-spoken, unassuming woman who became president and later legislative chairman of the California Parents' Association for Child Care (CPACC), Young spoke on behalf of California's low-income working families, particularly single mothers. Without the leadership of women such as Theresa Mahler and Mary Young, California's centers might have disappeared in the 1950s.

When Governor Warren signed child care legislation on June 30, 1951, it appeared that advocates had much to celebrate. For the first time since the state took control of the centers in 1946, the legislature had granted them a two-year rather than only a one-year extension. It also authorized the first rise in the income ceiling for eligibility since 1947. In December 1950 Warren finally announced that he would lend his "full support'" to proposals to fund the centers on a permanent basis.[2] He had previously been sympathetic to working families' child care needs but had resisted putting the full weight of his office behind the program. Earlier that year, the assembly had unanimously endorsed the child care bill. Permanent child care legislation finally seemed attainable.

The coalition that had been battling to save the centers since 1946 knew all too well that they could not rest on their laurels. Advocates would have to work for a permanent program when the extension ended in 1953. California's low-income working families would spend another two years wondering whether they might lose safe and affordable care. The coalition still faced a number of substantial road blocks. Powerful opponents who believed the state should not pay to care for the children of working mothers remained in the legislature, mostly in the senate. In particular, senators from so-called cow counties in rural areas did not want their tax dollars supporting a program that mainly benefited urban areas.

By 1950 the cold war had pushed American politics and culture far to the right as reactionaries waged a concerted campaign against communism at home as well as abroad. In an atmosphere of suspicion and innuendo that painted all progressives as "Reds," many activists were convinced that it was too risky to push to expand services. Although none of the women leaders was ever investigated for suspected communist affiliations or sympathies, they downplayed past associations with left-leaning groups and moderated their arguments. The coalition increasingly relied on a nonconfrontational, cautious brand of activism.

The political activities of Mahler, Young, and their supporters suggest that although women's reform activism survived well into the 1950s it took a new form. The child care coalition influenced policy by drawing strength from women's networks while collaborating and strategizing with some of California's most powerful men. The success of nursery school educators and mothers in preserving state-sponsored child care illustrates what Estelle Freedman has termed "pockets of quiet persistence" among women's organizations in the years after World War II.[3] Despite the challenges it faced, however, the coalition that Mahler and Young led did not disintegrate but continued to influence public policy.

Theresa Mahler advocated child care from an ideological perspective she had learned from the nursery school educators who had shaped her views of child development. Mary Young represented the new mother-activist, part of the constituency of Californians who had experienced government-sponsored, education-based child care services during and soon after the war. The quality and convenience of the care, and the peace of mind they felt about their children's well-being while they were at work, prompted Young and other working-class mothers to take action to preserve permanent child care. When welfare programs were increasingly stigmatized and under attack, women like Young understood how critical the state's centers were to family independence.[4]

Although the organizations Mahler and Young represented were not limited to women, they remained female-dominated. By 1954 single mothers made up more than 65 percent of parents of children in the state's centers. Mothers had always composed a majority of the active members of the parents' councils.

NCANE and SCANE had a few male members, but no man had been in the state leadership since their founding in 1929.[5] CPACC had a few men in its leadership but most rank-and-file members were mothers. The success of the women's campaign, however, depended on the assistance of key male politicians and allies.[6] Mahler and Young collaborated with powerful men in the legislature and the State Department of Education, as well as with male lobbyists, and their male allies taught them how to navigate the male-dominated political domain. At the same time, they relied on women activists to convey the needs of working mothers and the educational benefits of child care centers. Soon they began looking to women's groups to help them achieve their objectives in Sacramento. Ultimately, it was clear to both sides that although Mahler, Young, and the child care coalition could speak out on their own behalf, present persuasive statistics showing that California's families needed the centers, and organize statewide campaigns, decision-making power rested with California's eighty assemblymen and forty senators, all but one of whom were men.

To persuade male legislators Mahler and Young drew the well-established networks of educators and mothers into the political process. Mahler relied on longtime nursery school educators and close friends in the profession such as Elizabeth Woods and Rosalie Blau to sustain and inspire her. Young looked to other mothers to help her at the grassroots, stuffing envelopes, writing speeches, and attending meetings of local boards of education and civic groups. Most parents with children in the centers were single mothers like Young, some formed close, enduring friendships.[7] Strong emotional bonds proved vital to women's ability to carry on protracted, grueling political battles.

Mahler and Young, who differed in manner, experience, and leadership style, became central players in the coalition of early childhood educators and mothers that spearheaded the campaign for permanent child care centers throughout the 1950s and 1960s. Although the women were extraordinary leaders, their paths to activism resembled those of other participants in the coalition. Trained by progressive educators and leaders of the nursery school movement, Mahler got her start as a nursery school teacher during the depression in Los Angeles and taught in one of the city's first Lanham Act schools. Like many others trained in early childhood education she found that the publicly sponsored centers offered an opportunity to put her skills to work. When the war ended Mahler committed herself to transforming the state's child care centers into high-quality preschools. Young, by contrast, had no previous experience with politics or child care but, like many mothers of her time, had struggled to find a safe place to leave her daughter while she worked. Advocating for child care on behalf of their voluntary associations allowed both women, who lacked formal education past high school, to achieve professional status at a time when fewer than 14 percent of California women held professional positions.[8] Mahler and Young grounded their activism in a female network of educators and mothers. The two often worked as a team, but differences between their constituencies led to occasional conflicts or divergences of opinion. The eleven-year campaign for state-supported child care culminated when advocates finally wore down policymakers "with sincerity and persistence" and persuaded legislators to approve child care services on a permanent basis in 1957.[9] Through their leadership and perseverance, Theresa Mahler and Mary Young can take their share of credit for the victory.

The "Shy Young Lady"

Mary Young grew up in an Irish Catholic family on the Great Plains. Born on a farm outside Franklin, Minnesota, on May 10, 1915, to Irish immigrants Andrew James Lynch and Alice Alworth Lynch, Mary Elizabeth was the eldest of eleven children. When she was ten the family moved to Watertown, South Dakota, a town of about ten thousand in the northeastern corner of the state, where her mother had grown up. The sandy hills surrounding Watertown made it an ideal location for growing potatoes, and Mary's father leased a farm and moved his family four miles southeast of town. When she was not in school or helping with chores, Young could be found with her nose in a book. Her mother, an "avid reader," had passed a love of reading on to her eldest daughter, who frequently checked out an armful of books from the Watertown library. Alice Lynch told her daughter that she hoped to send all of her children to college.[10] But when Mary graduated from high school in 1932 that dream seemed out of reach. During the Great Depression farm prices dropped catastrophically, and most farmers hoped to sell their crops for enough to cover the cost of production. "Times were rough in South Dakota," she recalled, and there was simply "no money" to pay for college. "Next year," Alice Lynch announced determinedly, "Mary and I are going to raise chickens so she can go to college."[11] The next year never arrived, however; she died in the winter of 1933, leaving a six-week-old baby boy and nine other children for Mary and her father to care for.

Still committed to Mary's education, her father initially asked the neighbors to look after his children so Mary could attend nursing school in town. After she had been in school for a few months it became clear "that her family was not managing very well without her."[12] That winter she returned to the farm and took over the household, cooking, cleaning, caring for the baby, and becoming a surrogate mother for her siblings. Mary's caretaking continued until her sister finished high school, agreed to take over, and encouraged Mary to apply for one of the new federal government jobs. After spending a year assigning Social Security numbers to residents of northeastern South Dakota, Mary took a job as a secretary with the Prairie States Shelterbelt Project, a land conservation program, in 1938. In the winter of 1940 she came down with strep throat.

In those days, before antibiotics, strep was a serious disease that might lead to rheumatic fever and cause heart valve damage. After Mary spent months in and out of bed, her doctor suggested she move to a warmer climate to improve her health, so in October 1940 she went to the Southwest, eventually landing in Pasadena, California, where her uncle lived. There she joined the 3.5 million other Americans who migrated to California between 1940 and 1950 to seek jobs in the state's expanding war-related industries. After recuperating at her uncle's house Mary quickly found a job as a billing clerk at the Star Truck and Warehouse Company in East Los Angeles. In 1943, bored by her job and eager to become involved in the war effort, Mary tried to join the Marine Corps Women's Reserve, which offered new challenges and excellent benefits to twenty-three thousand females.[13] Unfortunately, however, a Marine Corps doctor disqualified her for medical reasons. Mary spent the remainder of the war working at Star Truck and Warehouse.

Like many other women of her generation, Mary met a soldier, engaged in premarital sex, and unintentionally became pregnant. Unlike most of her peers, however, she did not marry the father of her child. Her story began like those of many others. After work one evening, on her way to meet a girlfriend to go dancing at the Palladium in North Hollywood, Mary saw a handsome Marine, Harvey Young, board her bus. "He caught [her] looking at him," so he sat down beside her and struck up a conversation. They dated a few times before he was sent into combat in the South Pacific. They stayed in touch by writing letters, and when he returned in 1946 Young asked her to meet him for an evening in San Diego. They spent the night together despite Mary's concerns about pregnancy. "But sure enough I did get pregnant," Mary recalled ruefully. "He went east and I never heard from him again . . . and I didn't know what to do." Without her mother or close female friends to consult, Mary faced an enormous decision. Abortion was illegal and only available with a high cost and risk, so Mary felt she had only two choices: give up her baby, Debbie, for adoption or raise her by herself. She decided that she could not give up her daughter and confronted the reality of raising her in a society that viewed "out-of-wedlock" births as "abnormal" and mothers of children born out of wedlock as neurotic.[14] She joined the approximately a hundred thousand unmarried women who gave birth in 1946. A war-related increase in such births had begun in 1944.[15] Because of the booming economy and the availability of jobs, increasing numbers of women like Mary chose to keep their children because they were confident they could support them. Hoping to protect her daughter from the stigma associated with illegitimacy Mary chose to take Harvey Young's name even though he was never part of her life again.

After Mary gave birth to Debbie, she moved to San Francisco, where she knew a couple who also had a young child. She hoped that she had found a solution to her struggles when she moved in with her friends and their little boy. They agreed to share child care duties; Mary would give the babies dinner at night and her friend would care for them during the day. One night, when the friend spoke about going to the grocery store, Mary asked who had watched the babies while she shopped. "Oh, they're sleeping," was the reply. Mary was dumbstruck. The woman had left her infant unsupervised. At that moment she realized she could not jeopardize her daughter's health and safety and would need to move. Mary "had a difficult time" finding child care for Debbie. "I think she was in three or four different places," Mary recalls, "until she was nearing two years old." She was overjoyed when she heard about the state's child care centers in 1948. "Well," she confessed to her pediatrician, "I've applied at the child care center, but I've lied about her age"—a common practice for mothers desperate to find quality care for their children.[16] California's centers required children be at least two years of age, and Debbie was two months shy of her second birthday. The doctor, who had been very uncomfortable with the previous child care arrangement, assured Young, "I'll go along with that!" Mary then enrolled her daughter in the Frank McCoppin Child Care Center. "I thought it was so great because I had no worries," she says. "I could just leave Debbie at the nursery school" and go to work.[17] She shared the sense of relief that other mothers experienced once their children attended state centers.

Mary Young's political activism began in 1951, when Florence Winning, the head teacher at the McCoppin Center, asked, "How would you like a free trip to Los Angeles?" Young said she would love to go but asked, "What's the catch?" "You have to go to a meeting," Winning responded, "an all-day meeting, and report back." Young agreed because she would be able to see her father, who had just moved from North Dakota to Los Angeles. She "didn't know anything" about politics or the state legislature before she boarded the bus for the annual conference of the California Parents' Association for Child Care (CPACC). "I got an education," she recalled.[18]

On October 13, 1951, when she stepped into the crowded ballroom of the Alexandria Hotel, which was decorated with an exquisite Tiffany stained-glass ceiling, Mary found herself surrounded by hundreds of other mothers, both black and white, whose children were enrolled in the state's child care centers.[19] The convention was designed to give parents information to take back to their centers and communities. Mary listened intently to speeches by state leaders of the parents' organization as well as a keynote address by Frank Wright, then the associate superintendent of public instruction and one of the most vigorous advocates of child care in the state's Department of Education. Mary was excited about being part of a larger movement as speaker after speaker marked the organization's success and looked to a promising future.[20] Several hundred other mothers and a few fathers learned how to educate their communities about child care, the inadequacy of the means test, and achievements made during the previous legislative session. The convention exposed Young and her peers to the history of the struggle for child care and inducted them into the campaign.

This convention was the third CPACC had held since its founding in 1948. The previous year John Weber, state supervisor of child care centers, had praised the "development within the organization itself from that of a sincere but sometimes groping group of parents, to a more soundly established association in which the same sincerity is accompanied by mature and well-considered thinking and planning."[21] Gradually, CPACC became a well-functioning institution and gained credibility among child care supporters. No longer described as angry or confrontational, the parents' groups won respect from state officials for "the orderly intelligent way in which they presented their problems to the various legislative committees. It certainly is a great improvement over what some of us experienced two or three years ago."[22] This shift in tactics required parents to postpone their demand for permanent child care for all California families, but it paid off politically. Well-established women's organizations such as the California League of Women Voters (CALWV) listened to parents' groups as they debated their position on child care centers.[23] CPACC became increasingly visibile in Sacramento and across the state. In order to teach the growing number of mothers with children in the centers how to navigate California's political system, CPACC sponsored regional meetings of parents in northern and southern California, testified at hearings throughout the state, and sent a representative to the governor's Mid-Century Conference on Children and Youth in 1950. Mary Young became part of this maturing organization.

Betty L. Bachman, legislative chair of CPACC since its inception three years earlier, addressed the 1951 convention. Bachman, whom many credit with the parents' association's early success, grew up in a political family. Her father, James T. Lapsley, had served on the city council of Burbank, California, for twenty-one years and had been a member of the Republican State Central Committee.[24] A married high school science teacher with one son, Bachman gained access to the state's child care centers through the teachers' exemption from the means test, although because of her income she paid the highest possible fee.[25] A bright young woman and a "competent lobbyist," Bachman exhorted conference participants to tell other Californians that "there is nothing of Socialism and regimentation in this necessary program for working mothers." Urging them to pay close attention to the candidates for office that November, Bachman argued that child care laws "will be no better than the men who make them."[26] Members of the Parents' Association for Child Care should become well-informed citizens by focusing on electoral politics as well as lobbying the legislature. Bachman also encouraged mothers to think beyond the child care issue and expand their political voices.[27]

Like other mothers attending the state convention for the first time, Mary heard new strategies for organizing, learned how to publicize child care centers in her community, and received an education on how the legislative process worked.[28] Young returned to San Francisco energized and armed with a wealth of information gleaned from conversations with mothers from other local parents' associations. She shared these strategies with mothers at her daughter's center. "I came back and I told them that the most successful thing that they were doing in Southern California was getting pot-luck suppers, getting parents to take part."[29] Soon the parents' group organized a committee and began holding supper meetings to plot its political activities.

With her growing enthusiasm for organizing, Young was elected president of the Child Care Parents' Association of San Francisco and became the key spokeswoman for the 1,300 parents with children in the city's centers. In her new position, this intelligent but reserved woman began recruiting other mothers to join her but recognized immediately the obstacles she faced in trying to organize women who, like her, were sole supporters of their families. She emphasized that taking political action required sacrifices. More than once Young persuaded a reluctant mother who would tell her, "Oh, I can't do it, I have to work." Young's response would be that she understood the difficulties of juggling motherhood and work but "we all have to work." When they realized that every mother who advocated for child care was a volunteer, they often "changed [their] tune."[30]

A Determined Woman

Theresa Mahler grew up in a privileged environment but felt confined by traditional gender roles. Born on September 15, 1902, to Louis Schlichter and Marie Vetter Schlichter in Baltimore, Maryland, Theresa was the oldest child. Louis Schlichter, a successful businessman, provided generously for his family, dressing his children in expensive clothing and paying for them to travel every year with their mother to visit her relatives in Vienna. Marie Schlichter came from a prominent Austrian family. For many years her father, who could read and write in nine languages, served as chief translator for Francis Joseph III, who ruled Austria from 1848 to 1916. Despite growing up in a rigid Catholic family, Theresa's mother had a strong business sense and was very independent-minded. Like most men of his era, Theresa's father viewed higher education as a male preserve. He believed that women were suited only for vocational training and refused to indulge Theresa's desire to attend college although she loved to write and composed poetry throughout her teenage years, hoping to become a writer. Nevertheless, her father forced Theresa to drop out of high school after one year and enrolled her in Eaton and Brunet Business College, where she earned a secretarial certificate in nine months. Meanwhile, he paid for her younger brother to attend an excellent private school in Maryland and then the University of Southern California. Such restrictions only fueled her determination to learn. Years later Theresa wrote, "Interruption of formal schooling did not lessen my interest in education, and my participation in classes (on the university level) has continued for the satisfaction involved and not 'for credit.'"[31] Her ambition and desire to prove herself served child care advocates well in later years.

At the age of seventeen Theresa fell in love with Harry Edward Mahler, who worked for her father. Although they were fond of each other, their relationship was marked from its start by their divergent interests and class status. Harry Mahler grew up in a poor family that had always scrambled to make ends meet. He was an expert in electrical systems but never understood the importance of formal education. They married in 1919, and a year later their first child, Jeanne, was born. Migrating to California along with two million others during the 1920s, Harry moved the family to Los Angeles in 1926, hoping to find work in the booming motion picture industry. Eventually, he found a job as a sound engineer at MGM Studios.[32] Theresa soon gave birth to their second child, Karl, and they settled into raising their children.

Through the lean years and more prosperous times, Theresa devoted herself to motherhood. She set high goals for the children and made sure they took advantage of all the opportunities she had missed; early on, they learned that "in order to please her, [they] had to do well in school." Jeanne Mahler studied anthropology at the University of California at Los Angeles and eventually completed medical school at the University of California at San Francisco. Karl Mahler received a master's degree in public administration and joined the U.S. Foreign Service, spending most of his adult life abroad. Theresa also took Jeanne and Karl on outings, made sure they interacted with other children, and exposed them to cultural activities such as theater and the opera.[33]

Mahler's commitment to education may have begun as a reaction to the restrictions she had faced, but it developed as she volunteered in her daughter's experimental elementary school, which was supervised by Elizabeth Woods. Woods, a psychology professor and preschool advocate, "interested [her] . . . in this whole idea of having children learn in different ways and giving them an opportunity to do."[34] The observation and participation classes for kindergarten and primary students had been instituted by Barbara Greenwood, a kindergarten training teacher who had started the first nursery school in California at UCLA in 1923. In 1934-35 Mahler signed up for evening classes with Gertrude Laws and Helen Christianson, Greenwood's colleagues, and they exposed her to their strong belief in the benefits of educating preschool children, particularly when "coupled with a program of child study for parents."[35] In 1935 Mahler qualified for a special secondary education credential to teach child growth and development as well as parent education. With this degree and Woods's recommendation, she accepted a position as an education leader in parent-observation groups at a Los Angeles nursery school that was combining preschool with parent education. Woods immediately noticed Mahler's intellect and became her mentor, a role she played for many early childhood educators from the 1930s through the 1950s.[36] Although Mahler's lack of official academic credentials was not a hindrance to her career, it troubled Mahler and fueled her professional ambitions. In a job application she confessed that "for the sake of requirements sometimes I wish that I could add letters after my name, or say that I needed but a credit or so. But I happen to be one of those persons whose education has been a broad, rather than a formal one."[37] In a field controlled and dominated by women and struggling to stake out its professional authority, Mahler's demonstrated flair for teaching proved more important than her lack of a college degree.

Mahler advanced quickly through the ranks in Los Angeles's nursery school program. In her early thirties, with two older children, Mahler taught parent education classes in local WPA nursery schools, which Woods supervised for the city. When the federal government began sponsoring wartime centers for the children of working mothers in 1943, Woods turned to Mahler to take on an important job: supervising the care and education of fifty children and teaching a parent education course at a newly opened child care center in North Hollywood, near several of the local aircraft plants that employed sixty-two thousand women by 1944.[38] Mahler even trained new teachers for the centers that proliferated around the city during the war. In 1944, when she applied for official nursery school credentials, Woods sent a letter of recommendation praising Mahler's "outstanding" work and declaring that Los Angeles could not find a "better trained person for her position."[39] By the war's end Mahler had taught the "in-service training course" to approximately six hundred teachers employed in federal centers. Woods recommended her appointment as supervisor of the child care centers for the Los Angeles School District.[40]

Mahler's stellar reputation caught the attention of Marion Turner, director of San Francisco's centers. Turner, who had studied under Patty Smith Hill at Columbia Teacher's College struggled with health problems, and she offered Mahler a temporary job as a supervisor in the San Francisco Child Care Centers in May 1946.[41]

Mahler and her husband had drifted apart over the years. She saw the San Francisco job not only as an opportunity to continue her career with the state's centers but also as a way to put some distance between herself and her husband. The divorce was extremely difficult for Mahler. "It just broke her completely," her daughter remembered, yet she seized the chance to begin a new life away from her husband when she assumed a supervisory role in California's second-largest child care district.

The move proved to be a boon for the San Francisco centers and the California Associations for Nursery Education. Mahler had spent many years working with southern leaders such as Rosalie Blau and Elizabeth Woods; by moving north, she provided a key link between SCANE and NCANE. Mahler, whom her daughter described as "a good organizer and a smart enough woman to recognize that big improvements could be made and that if anyone was going to do it, she would have to do it," became the legislative chair for NCANE, and from 1946 until she retired in 1971, she spent "countless hours and untold energies . . . devoted to fighting the battles for all children and the children's center program in California."[42]

Mahler worked with Turner supervising the San Francisco Child Care Centers between 1946 and 1949, and after ill health forced Turner to withdraw, Mahler took over the position. Turner, from whom she received a valuable political apprenticeship, recognized that for child care center legislation to succeed, educators and mothers had to recruit powerful allies. Turner began by enlisting the help of Lawrence Arnstein, her next-door neighbor and executive director of the San Francisco Social Hygiene and Health Association. Arnstein's commitment to improving public health and aiding the unfortunate was rooted in the Progressive Era, when he worked briefly at Lillian Wald's Henry Street Settlement House in New York City. Arnstein, who had served on the San Francisco Board of Health since 1913, came from a wealthy family that made its fortune in the woolen business. He retired from that work in 1942 in order to devote his time to public health and had access to some of the Bay Area's most powerful men and women.[43] "Mr. Public Health," as he was often called, turned his expertise as a lobbyist to advocate for the child care program. After Turner took Arnstein on a tour of a San Francisco center, she told him, "I have heard about your experience in Sacramento and with the legislature and with the Board of Supervisors. You know many people and how to organize community efforts"[44] She implored him to use his powerful connections and expertise to help the child care cause. It was the beginning of a twenty-five-year commitment. Arnstein's efforts on behalf of child care only slowed when he reached his eighties and nineties; even then he was still writing long letters in support of the cause.[45]

When Mahler accepted the job in San Francisco, Turner introduced her to Arnstein, who became a mentor and powerful ally. Mahler took to advocating and pressuring the legislature for child care services as if it had been her life's calling. Her daughter remembered that she "had this extraordinary ability to see how things should be organized and what needed to be done to make it better and in which ways you had to go to get it going. . . . She quickly realized that the only way to get anywhere with promoting the child care program in the way she wanted it to be developed, you had to play politics because unfortunately the money didn't come from trees."[46] Mahler spent most of her free time during the first six months of every year advocating for state-supported child care in Sacramento. In the late 1940s she became what a colleague later called "the best informed person I have met on state and federal legislation affecting young children."[47] Conversations with Arnstein and her experience during the war convinced Mahler of the importance of developing a coalition that drew many organizations into the child care constituency. Impeccably dressed and known for her serious demeanor, Mahler seemed ideally suited to inhabit the male world of politics and that of the female activists.[48]

She put her ideas to work developing legislative strategy. From the outset, she wanted NCANE to extend its coalition well beyond its natural constituency of parents and educators and sought to figure out which groups might support a permanent, publicly funded child care system. In 1947 Mahler suggested that NCANE lobby the state League of Women Voters to consider permanent child care as a priority issue. She directed nursery association members to call on friends and acquaintances in the LWV, send them informational material, and push them to make child care one of their "active projects." Throughout the 1950s Mahler asked NCANE and SCANE members to raise awareness and seek support from other women's organizations. She often turned to her colleagues and longtime friends from the nursery school association for support and advice. Elizabeth Woods and Rosalie Blau served as her two most important confidants and advisors; by 1950 the three had attended meetings, developed nursery school policy, and collaborated for more than fifteen years. Mahler knew that Woods's involvement in local reform activities and her longtime contacts in the Los Angeles area would be an invaluable resource. In 1953, for example, she implored Woods to persuade a southern California Republican women's organization to "soft-pedal their opposition" to a permanent child care program. Although she knew that Woods, a Democrat, lacked direct influence in the organization, she was confident that Woods's longtime connections in Los Angeles women's networks meant she "must know some people who do."[49] Mahler's cooperative work with Woods and Blau strengthened the ties between the northern and southern branches of CANE. The three women coordinated regional activities, kept one another abreast of legislative activities, and worked tirelessly to secure permanent child care.

Mothers and Educators Collaborate

At first glance the differences between Theresa Mahler and Mary Young appear to outweigh their commonalities. Their family and class backgrounds were strikingly different, and the women came to maturity in distinct historical periods. Mahler dedicated her professional life to promoting early childhood and parent education, whereas Young was introduced to child care when she placed her daughter in the state's centers in 1948. The two women had contrasting leadership styles as well. Mahler was described as an outspoken, extremely determined woman who liked to "take charge" and Young as someone who spoke in a soft voice and chose to lead from behind. Yet Young and Mahler shared some important qualities. Like many intellectually curious women of their time, both were denied a formal education. They both believed in the educational value and economic importance of child care and dedicated themselves to lobbying the legislature on behalf of working mothers and their children.

The women, Mahler representing educators and Young speaking for mothers, worked together to convince everyone involved in the centers to fight to preserve publicly funded child care services. The collaboration began in 1952 as Young became increasingly involved in the San Francisco Parents' Association for Child Care Centers. In one of the citywide meetings, the tall, outspoken, and somewhat distant Mahler noticed the mature, composed, and intelligent Young, who, unlike many others, was unintimidated by Mahler. As they formed an activist partnership they bridged the gap between mothers' and educators' organizing efforts.

As the 1953 legislative session began, Lawrence Arnstein wrote to Fred Luke, the past president of CPACC, to express concern about no "definite assignment of the legislative work in the Parents' Groups." Not only did he believe in the importance of the parents' voice in the legislature, but he also recommended continuity in parent leadership. With an experienced legislative advocate, the coalition would not continually "have to re-educate" political neophytes. With Mahler's stamp of approval, Arnstein pulled Young into the statewide organization and initiated her into the male bailiwick of the legislature.[50] She served as CPACC's legislative advocate for twelve years.

The quiet but enthusiastic Young had advanced rapidly in the leadership of the parents' group. She gained statewide attention when she was appointed second vice president of CPACC in April 1953 after a mother resigned suddenly.[51] Jeanne Miller, Mahler's daughter, remembers that her mother identified Young's strong work ethic and exceptional organizing skills and worked hard to "persuade her of the importance of what [advocates] were trying to do" in the legislature.[52] She was chosen to assist Betty Bachman in Sacramento and represent parents' organizations from the northern portion of the state. Her calm demeanor and moderate political beliefs exemplified the well-mannered and professional image the parents' association wanted to project. Armed with a title and the authority that came with it, Young dove headlong into the legislative process.

The first year was spent learning how to navigate the legislature from three veterans of the state's child care battles, Lawrence Arnstein, Betty Bachman, and Theresa Mahler. Young needed training and encouragement before becoming comfortable as a lobbyist. During the 1953 legislative session Arnstein rode the

Figure 4. Mary Young, speaking at California Parents' Association for Child Care Centers annual convention, El Segundo, Nov. 11, 1964. (Courtesy of the Center for Oral and Public History, California State University, Fullerton)

bus to Sacramento with Young to acquaint her with lobbying and the ins and outs of the state capitol. Years later he told her that he hardly recognized the "shy young lady that I went to Sacramento with the first time" in the sophisticated political activist she became.[53] Young vividly remembered their first meeting. Arnstein, she said, "gave me some sage advice, showed me around the Capitol Building and told me who to contact first. I can tell you I was not only pretty nervous, I was downright scared." Arnstein also helped smooth the way for Young's visits to legislators' offices that spring. "My nervousness was somewhat allayed," she revealed, "when I would mention my name and the group I was representing, and then heard them say: 'Oh, yes. Mr. Arnstein was just in here and he told me you would be stopping by!'"[54] As he had done with Mahler, Arnstein extended his expertise and political clout to the parents' association's newest advocate. Young did not become a savvy, self-confident lobbyist overnight, but she thrived in her new role.

Young gradually assembled a strong constituency of parents who were active in their local, city, and statewide parents' associations. With the assistance of Mahler, the executive board of the Child Care Parents' Association of San Francisco, and teachers in the city's centers, Young produced a pamphlet that was distributed to new parents. The brochure offered a brief history of child care legislation and highlighted the critical role played by the parents' association. It reminded mothers and fathers that "it is the privilege and duty of parents to attend these meetings and to join actively in the development of the child care program."[55] Indeed, the brochure emphasized that "the continuation of the centers is the personal problem of the parents who need the service." Young adopted the approach used by Mahler and Bachman, recognizing that parents must be informed on the issues and ready to take action. Grassroots participation was essential.[56] In the process, the parents developed what political scientists call "social capital," which translated into power and influence in Sacramento.[57]

Setting an Agenda

Young, Mahler, and Bachman linked two child care networks: one of dedicated professional educators and their male political allies and the other state and local parents' associations. In 1954 they met with their leading supporters in the state department of education, John Weber and Frank Wright, center directors, and Assemblyman Ernest Geddes to develop a legislative strategy. They had to decide whether to ask California's new governor, Goodwin Knight, to introduce a child care bill as part of his special legislative agenda and figure out how to persuade legislators that the means test was detrimental to many California families.[58] Knight had replaced Warren in October 1953 after Dwight Eisenhower appointed the former governor to the U.S. Supreme Court. Although more conservative than Warren, Knight had observed his success as a centrist and noted the support he had received from organized labor. Knight, however, had taken no position on state-supported child care; advocates had to start from scratch to secure the governor's endorsement. Because 1954 was a budget session, the coalition also had to convince legislators to extend the program's funding from the legislature. The new rules passed in 1951 had reduced the number of families that could use the state's child care centers because the income ceiling did not keep pace with the rising cost of living, and fees for families exempt from the means test rose substantially. Mahler, Young, and their male allies—Lawrence Arnstein, Frank Wright, Ernest Geddes, and John Weber—deferred the goal of expanding the program and making it permanent and concentrated on preventing any further backsliding in coverage.

The contraction of the state's centers was a bitter blow. When the new law took effect 746 families whose income exceeded the guidelines for eligibility had been forced to withdraw or were refused enrollment. The restriction's most devastating effect was on families that qualified for the exemption: veterans in college, teachers, nurses, agricultural workers, and "workers in essential industry." Previously, these parents had to pay the full cost only if their incomes were very high; fees were calculated on a sliding scale. Now every family in the exempt categories had to pay the full cost, regardless of whether they earned $1 or $50 over the monthly ceiling. For many, the fees were prohibitive. Exempt families fell from 21 percent to 8.9 percent of total enrollment between July 1951 and March 1952.[59]

The means test continued to wreak havoc on child care enrollment as well. Although the legislature raised the income ceiling in 1951 and 1953, it did not keep up with inflation. Between July 1952 and February 1953 approximately four thousand families had their applications denied because their income exceeded the ceiling—even though more than half of them made less than $50 more that the upper limit.[60] Many needy families were denied access to care.

The decline in the number of families using the centers weakened advocates' arguments about the program's vital importance to Californians. The Korean War enabled proponents to revive the rationale that the wartime emergency necessitated public support for child care, but the federal government did not extend social provisions for working women and failed to provide funds for child care.[61] With enrollments declining, how could advocates prove that these services were necessary on a permanent basis? Adversaries cited the decline as evidence of a postwar return to "normalcy," by which they meant mothers returning to their rightful places at home. The child care coalition had to demonstrate the need for state-supported child care services.

Advocates secured statistics from child care directors that illustrated the large number of families adversely affected by the new regulations. In 1952 Mahler asked NCANE members for "cooperation in obtaining significant letters from parents as to how the present income ceiling affects them, particularly the full cost families," and those who had withdrawn or been prevented from enrolling children.[62] As the state's supervisor for a large district, Mahler had access to center administrators and relied on them to provide information for her legislative work. In her monthly legislative bulletin she highlighted the injustice of the full-cost fee. Families whose income barely exceeded the ceiling had to pay much more in proportion to their incomes than families whose income fell just below it. Mahler understood that convincing fiscally conservative legislators to raise the income ceiling and/or lower fees would require massive effort and urged center directors to mobilize support among civic groups in their areas for such a task.

The CPACC organized a letter-writing campaign to put a human face on the statistics. Mahler, Young, and Bachman believed that letters from parents would be most effective but advised educators to "double check" them. In 1952 Mahler recommended that the letters "be screened by the director working with the parents (or parents groups)." Center directors should send only those "considered most effective" and make sure they were mailed in envelopes "*written by the parents.*"[63] By 1953 Mahler had produced a "Do's and Don'ts" list of instructions for writing to state legislators, guidelines that struck a careful balance between encouraging parents to "write sincere letters in your own words, on your own stationary, and in your own handwriting" and reminding them that "when you write do it right." A "righteous" tone was inappropriate, and letters must not be confrontational or discourteous.[64] While Mahler cast her political net widely in her calls to action, her correspondence indicates a certain reluctance to give mothers control over their own political activities, yet parents' groups and local organizations often sent letters to Sacramento before receiving instructions from teachers or administrators.[65] Tension between the organization's leaders and the grassroots had existed since the first campaign. When mothers took pen in hand they tasted the thrill of putting their experiences and ideas into their own words and sent them directly to representatives in the capital. Mahler and other educators understood that parents spoke with the greatest authority about the benefits of child care but feared allowing them autonomy. In 1954 Young was careful to disseminate accurate information and give clear instructions, hoping to prevent costly mistakes. In January, for example, Governor Knight had received letters from mothers asking him not to close the centers, but given that the centers were not in jeopardy in 1954 the letters had done nothing but irritate him. Leaders directed parents to focus on the means test and prohibitively high fees. Young and Bachman said that letters should not make it "appear that we have an organized campaign." Parents' letters should come from many different regions and arrive at a rate of approximately twenty each week. Advocates hoped to convince rural as well as urban senators to support child care.

Parents and educators waged a broader publicity campaign to make Californians aware of the need for the centers and persuade more who qualified under the current means test to enroll their children. The San Francisco parents' association, with Mahler's assistance, produced a handout for working parents to deliver to employers, arming them with statistics showing that child care centers "are good business" and asking the employers to write to their legislators in support of child care. Young and the parents' group hoped that the pamphlet would widen their base of support. Soliciting new applicants for the centers was equally important. In Oakland, parents who belonged to labor unions placed articles in local newspapers "telling the locations of the centers and the advantage to a working mother to having her child attend."[66] The *Legislative Bulletin* encouraged parents' groups to publicize the centers in order to fill them to capacity and demonstrate the continuing need for child care.

Public Debate

In October 1954 the Senate Interim Committee on Social Welfare set out to determine whether the centers still deserved state support by holding hearings on child care in San Francisco and Los Angeles. As before, the hearings provided a forum for voices ranging from mothers and educators to labor unions and women's groups. Women predominated; in San Francisco they made up seventeen of the twenty-two speakers.[67] Witnesses explained working mothers' child care needs directly to senators who held the ultimate power to support or kill the program.[68] Unfortunately, not a single one of the senators had a center in his district. Worse still, only one of the five committee members represented an urban area; the others hailed from predominantly rural areas and were known for their stinginess in allocating state funds to the cities, especially for social services.[69] The senators resisted authorizing state support of child care by interrogating and badgering witnesses throughout the three days of hearings. In addition to offering passionate, well-informed testimony, the CPACC invited the men to visit public and private nursery schools in Los Angeles and San Francisco.

The San Francisco hearing served as a baptism by fire for Mary Young. Public speaking did not come naturally to her. "Mary," her teachers always admonished, "you must speak louder." Indeed, Young tried to avoid public speaking altogether and often persuaded others to stand in her place. She was much more comfortable organizing within female networks than on male political turf. Leading from behind the scenes she was in her element, whether organizing letter-writing drives, motivating mothers to take action, or joining other speakers at parents' meetings. As newly appointed second vice president of CPACC, however, Young faced her fears and appeared before the Senate Interim Committee on Social Welfare. As she did throughout her career, she performed two roles, speaking both as the official representative of this professional organization and as a working mother benefiting from the center herself.

Young's testimony before the committee and her personal reflections on the experience provide a window into the arguments the parents' association wanted to deliver and the process of learning to lobby on behalf of the ten thousand families that depended on the centers. Young relied on Betty Bachman, her predecessor, for advice, encouragement, and validation. Proponents sought to convince the committee that Californian's need for child care extended far beyond wartime necessity. The last witness before the lunch recess, Young followed a host of distinguished speakers, including representatives from the State Department of Education, labor unions, child care directors, and a state senator. With a mixture of trepidation and conviction, she presented the centers from the perspective of those who knew them best—parents. Reminding the senators that most parents could not testify at the hearings because they had to work, Young spoke as their representative "to say what only they might say with authority—they are liv-ing the Child Care program as no one else is."[70] Leaving the issue of the means test to other witnesses, she spelled out the centers' importance to California's working families. The program allowed families to stay together and provided children with safe, trustworthy, and educational care. For the mother who must work, Young maintained, "the welcome that [she] receives in the evening from a happy, busy, thoughtful child . . . make[s] up in part for the necessity of spending the day away from them."[71] She described her daughter's positive experiences at the centers as well as similar stories she heard from other mothers. Parents, she emphasized, preferred state-supported child care to the federally funded welfare program, Aid to Needy Children. The mothers believed in working to support their children rather than being "a burden on the state."

Presenting this image of parents who used the centers as upstanding citi-zens was especially important to CPACC, because it countered their opponents' objections that state-supported group child care was un-American and that mothers who relied on it were immorally ceding maternal responsibilities to the government. In a letter to Bachman, Young described the restrained style in which witnesses presented themselves. The chair of the committee, John Murdy (R–Orange County), praised their "orderly" presentation; Young thought he "had expected histrionics."

She expressed considerable alarm when Colleen Norton, an African Ameri-can, self-employed bookkeeper and mother of three, ventured outside the realm of what was considered "respectable" behavior by employing a confrontational style. Her political views as well as her decorum seemed dubious; Young told Bachman, "we've all been suspicioning she is communistic as she puts out a lot of questionable chatter."[72] In an era when appearing combative or uncoopera-tive could elicit allegations of communist sympathies and damaging personal attacks, the parents' association did all it could to preserve its moderate image. Norton had identified herself as an officer in the Parents' Association, but she had not been cleared to speak by the group.[73] What troubled Young was the lack of deference and sense of entitlement Norton exhibited as she debated with senators and even challenged them directly. Young reassured Bachman that after Norton's potentially damaging testimony, she let the senators know that Norton was not speaking for the parents' organization. Hearing from a black woman who admitted to being a recipient of Aid to Needy Children may have troubled Young as well. Negative reports constantly circulated in the media linking public assistance with African Americans even though they formed a small minority of recipients. Although the parents' association had been integrated from the beginning it may have followed a strategy similar to that of welfare advocates who, while promoting the importance of ADC to poor families, "remain[ed] silent on the issue of race."[74] The success and continuation of the child care program depended on maintaining their profile as a group of well-behaved white women who conformed to the image of good mothers.

Coalition leaders sought to persuade Californians that child care centers were not charity. Working mothers explained why they did not believe that using state-supported centers meant taking a handout from the government. At the Los Angeles hearings, Bachman argued that the centers fostered self-reliance by allowing parents to continue working. In fact, families who used child care contributed approximately $30 million to the state's economy each year. "We are contributors to our society and proud that we are able to be," Bachman reminded the senators.[75] The mothers were loath to "associate [with] the word 'WELFARE.'"[76] To persuade "economy-minded" legislators, in 1953 Lawrence Arnstein commissioned a report that illustrated the economic benefits of having mothers remain in the labor force and use state child care centers, which cost much less than Aid to Needy Children, later called Aid to Dependent Children, or ADC, and then Aid to Families with Dependent Children, or AFDC. Single working mothers made up 65 percent of those using the centers, and without child care it would be necessary for them to turn to welfare, which would cost approximately $8 million annually, three times the cost of operating the centers.

Avoiding the stigma of welfare made sense in a political climate that was increasingly antagonistic toward the welfare system as its utilization grew after the war. Conservatives expressed particular hostility toward groups that had finally been able to obtain benefits and services in northern and western cities: divorced or unwed mothers and increased numbers of African American women.[77] Child care advocates might be faulted for repeating and reinforcing the demonized stereotype of welfare mothers, yet they sought to spare centers the "politically instigated attacks" that the ADC program faced. As welfare professionals in the state and across the nation promoted "self support through employment for poor single women as a way to break the cycle of dependency," California's child care program provided a model for keeping families off welfare.[78]

The coalition rallied supporters to appear at the hearings, and the majority of witnesses affirmed the centers' benefits. One reporter observed that "no one appeared to argue that the program should be abandoned or curtailed, and there were some suggestions that it be expanded."[79] Frank Wright and John Weber, who represented the State Department of Education, advocated that child care services be established on a permanent basis. Local labor councils and unions, which had long supported child care but suffered in the reactionary political climate, reminded the senators "that working mothers are a permanent and essential part of the economy of the State" and attested to the centers' importance to their female members.[80] The most vocal groups were those representing many women, including the Culinary Workers Union, the Waitresses Union, and the

Cannery and Packers Union. Rank-and-file women told male leaders that child care centers made them better workers because they were "free from worry as to the care of their children." During the postwar period labor feminists were pushing for child care both nationally and locally.[81]

The few voices of opposition came from private nursery school owners, a representative of the California Manufacturers Association, and committee members themselves. Private school owners claimed that they could provide services for working families. In their view, state-funded child care centers wasted taxpayers' money (not to mention cutting into their own profits). The Manufacturers Association, which represented 1,200 corporations across the state, argued that since the wartime emergency no longer existed that the child care centers were no longer necessary. It also maintained that "if they are to continue they should not be the burden of the statewide tax" and become the responsibility of local school districts.[82] Throughout the hearings the fiscally conservative senators representing rural areas were the most antagonistic toward child care services. They badgered witnesses about the feasibility of financing the child care program as well as the injustice of forcing the state to pay for services concentrated in four counties. Acting committee chair John A. Murdy Jr. from Orange County articulated the most forceful critique, attacking not just parent representatives and others outside the legislature but also the child care supporters within the assembly. A lima bean farmer and deeply religious man whose parents had migrated to Orange County from South Dakota early in the twentieth century, Murdy and his political views reflected his constituency. Orange County voters were overwhelmingly white, and many held a conservative Protestant outlook. These conservative churches took the lead in promoting antiliberalism in the region. By the 1950s, right-wing anticommunism had produced a political outlook defined by "a rejection of collectivism" in all its forms, including federal regulations and welfare provisions.[83] Murdy and his colleagues were preoccupied by the expenditure of public funds for child care. When the committee asked Lawrence Arnstein, testifying for the San Francisco Social Hygiene and Health Association, why counties without child care centers should help to pay for them, he replied, "The counties in which the centers do operate certainly contribute in taxes to programs which benefit the more rural counties."[84] Four days later, Fred Luke, a Los Angeles father and World War II veteran with three sons in the state's centers, voiced support for a permanent, education-oriented, child care program that would be available to all needy families, including those in rural areas. Murdy responded, "The thing that concerns me is where are we going to get the money? How would you finance a program such as you recommend?"[85] As a political tactic used successfully by opponents who came before him, Murdy insinuated that continued funding would be tantamount to expanding the program.

While Murdy questioned mothers and educators aggressively, his most hostile exchange took place with Carley Porter, a Democratic assemblyman who represented Los Angeles's working-class suburbs of Compton, Bellflower, and Lynwood. Porter, a high school and college history teacher, had supported the child care program since his election to the assembly in 1949 and spoke passionately about the child care needs of working women in his district. Year after year, those who operated presses and worked on assembly lines had written to him about how critical centers were to their families. After politely thanking Porter for his comments, Murdy dispensed with the niceties and attacked his position. He tried to get Porter to admit that permanent funding would lead to an expansion of the program into every county in the state and a major increase in social spending, in his mind the equivalent of "subsidiz[ing] the private income of a family." Senator Abshire (R-Sonoma) asked whether Porter and his constituents would be willing to pay for "a substantial increase" in taxes for these centers. Porter steadfastly reiterated his belief that public services such as child care centers should be funded by the state. When he told the committee that he always reminded constituents that "if you want service you are going to have to pay for it," Murdy angrily shot back, "We don't want child care centers in Orange County and we don't want to pay for Compton" to have them.[86]

At the hearing's conclusion the five members of the committee remained unconvinced that the state should continue financing child care centers, and the following day the *Los Angeles Times's* story was headlined "Child Care Hearing Ends on a Note of Disagreement."[87]

"Strength in Unity"

On January 5, 1955, the senate committee announced its recommendation "that the present program, wherein 86 percent of all child care centers are located in four counties, should not be continued with state funds."[88] Although the governor had not taken a public position on the issue, he had deleted from his 1955-56 budget the $4 million requested by the State Department of Education to run the centers. Newspapers warned that "Little Hope Held for Child Care Centers" and "Stiff fight Due on Child Care Centers."[89] The prospect of losing safe, affordable child care because of an apathetic governor and a hostile senate committee led to a flurry of activity. The coalition conducted a media blitz, worked to increase community involvement, and coordinated another letter-writing campaign. This effort relied almost entirely on the combined efforts of Mahler and Young to rally educators and mothers. The organizations they represented, NCANE and CPACC, formally united their political efforts because they believed there was "strength in unity" and in order to "save time, energy and money by the coordination of legislative activities."[90] They also turned to male allies, particularly the clever and well-connected Lawrence Arnstein. Once again, women leaders found themselves moving back and forth between the world of women's networks and institutions and the male-dominated arena of electoral politics.

The cause received a boost when the four major newspapers in San Francisco published editorials praising the state's centers.[91] Mary Young, as CPACC president, responded immediately with a letter to the editor of each newspaper, thanking them for the support and rebuking the Senate Interim Committee's recommendation. She asserted that "to withdraw support" for the centers would "in all likelihood be the death knell of the wonderful child care program that we all know" and force families to scramble to find other arrangements.[92] Many studies, including those by state agencies such as the Office of Vocational Rehabilitation, had shown that substitute care was scarce. Mothers inundated newspapers with letters to editors, many of which appeared in the *San Francisco Chronicle* and the *San Francisco Examiner* in late January and early February. The women told a familiar story, explaining that the centers enabled single mothers to work and support their children, reduced their anxiety because they knew "their children are properly cared for," and kept mothers from going on relief.[93] Women seemed most concerned with convincing Californians that the program kept their families off welfare. Mrs. J. Watson of Berkeley "resent[ed] very much [the] suggestion that I go on relief." She protested that "mothers with children in Child Care Centers pay for the care their children receive there. The State pays the difference . . . and the mother supports herself and her children." In an era rampant with mother-blaming, asserting that child care permitted working women to be good mothers was especially effective.[94]

Lawrence Arnstein sought endorsements from every major newspaper in the state and enlisted the assistance of Mahler and Young in this effort. Weary from the recurring battles in the legislature, he maintained that massive public support for child care would force resistant legislators to relent. He visited every editor of California's metropolitan newspapers in 1955, asking them to publish editorials expressing unqualified endorsement of a permanent child care system. Arnstein was an astute lobbyist and an effective agitator for progressive causes. Soon, thirteen or fourteen newspapers carried editorials criticizing the "ill-advised and short-sighted" recommendations to end state funding for child care services.[95] Only the conservative *San Diego Union* refused to publish an editorial. Arnstein had each editor send 136 copies of his editorial to Mary Young, who distributed them to all the legislators. The flood of favorable press continued throughout the 1955 legislative session, culminating with supportive articles from newspapers in rural parts of the state.[96]

Male and female leaders of the child care coalition campaigned vigorously against the committee's recommendations. By now the two networks depended on each other for political success. In 1954 Ernest Geddes, the moderate Republican assemblyman, who for years had sponsored child care legislation, tried to step down as chief negotiator in the legislature. He wrote to Mahler that he did not think he "should continually be regarded as the arbiter of C.C.C. legislation and if those interested can find some one else to carry the ball, I shall gladly yield both the laurels and the headaches."[97] Mahler, who had worked with Geddes for almost ten years, understood his importance to the cause as a political moderate and an accomplished statesman. She replied immediately, explaining how deeply his news had disturbed her and wishing her friend "good health so that you may continue to give us the guidance of your knowledge, and the courage of your fighting heart."[98] Geddes continued to guide child care bills through the assembly into the 1960s.

The close working relationship between Geddes and the women-centered coalition proved critical for securing permanent child care. Geddes turned to Mahler and Young to supply him with information from parents and mobilize supporters on the grassroots level. He asked both women to rally constituents to attend child care hearings, particularly if their senator sat on the Finance Committee. Geddes believed that the visible presence of constituents could "change a 'no' to a 'yes' vote."[99] At the same time, Mahler and Young needed Geddes to provide critical insights into the less public aspects of the legislative process. As the parents' association composed an informational pamphlet, Mahler and Young asked Geddes's advice on presenting their arguments, telling him that "we want to do everything possible to work this out according to what you think will be most effective."[100]

Mahler and Young drew on women's networks, including long-established women's groups, to involve a broader constituency in the cause. Mahler relied on her contacts in strong Los Angeles to help spread the message. When Arnstein wanted potential allies to learn more about the state's centers, for example, Mahler contacted the "southern gals": Irene Kline, director of the Los Angeles Centers; Elizabeth Woods, and Betty Bachman. She also enlisted Edith Story, the nursery school association representative from Fresno, to help secure an endorsement from the California Business and Professional Women (BPW). Although Story could not get child care on the official BPW platform, she did convince the organization to agree "as individuals through other groups" to "exert their influence for child care."[101] The California League of Women Voters (CALWV) had supported child care ever since the war, but in 1955 it removed the issue from its active platform. The League said it would endorse a permanent statewide program but argued that "further support of child care centers might well be left to the Parent Teachers Associations and to organizations like Business and Professional Women and trade unions whose members use the service." With so many legislative priorities and as a possible testament to the success of the parents' organization, the League decided to leave formal organizing to those whose membership they believed most directly benefited from the centers, an assumption that their membership did not include working mothers or those who might need public child care. The League continued to urge members individually to press for permanent child care in 1955 and 1957.[102] Mahler and Young spoke at the Non-Partisan Roundtable on Governmental Affairs, which sought to produce a unified legislative agenda among California's most prominent women's groups.[103] Reaching out to male-dominated civic organizations as well, they addressed labor unions and American Legion meetings. Through these speeches and their personal connections, the women helped sustain a wide base of support for the state child care centers.

By keeping child care in the public eye, Arnstein, Geddes, Mahler, and Young counteracted the influence of the senate committee's recommendations. After receiving negative press and a batch of disapproving letters from working mothers, Governor Knight publicly endorsed child care in early January.[104] In April the assembly voted 61–6 in favor of the child care legislation sponsored by Geddes on behalf of the coalition and supported by the State Department of Education. Then advocates redoubled efforts to convince the hostile Senate Finance Committee chaired by Ben Hulse, a Republican who represented Imperial County, an agricultural area in the southeastern corner of the state.[105] Over the years Hulse had gone to great lengths to stall or kill child care bills in the finance committee. Louis Sutton, who represented three counties in the Sacramento valley, responded to Mary Young's letter with a retort: "The child care program with its expenditure of State money is not of any benefit to the working mothers of my counties."[106] Senate leaders told Geddes that the price of passage was giving up the clause making the centers permanent and substituting another two-year extension. The senate voted in favor of a two-year child care program on June 7, 1955. The next morning San Franciscans awoke to the headline "Child Care Bill Passes."[107] Although advocates were disappointed that in two short years they would have to conduct another campaign, they counted the victory as a blessing.

Securing a Permanent Child Care Program

In 1957 the legislature finally acquiesced to the coalition's demands and established state child care centers on a permanent basis. After the drama and tension of the 1954 committee hearings and the 1955 legislative session, the passage of permanent child care legislation seemed a strangely quiet ending to years of tumultuous battles. In fact, 1957 capped a decade of struggle by mothers, educators, and a host of supporters to have temporary child care centers made permanent. Two days after CPACC's annual convention in 1955 Betty Bachman died suddenly from a brain tumor, leaving her husband to raise their son alone.[108] Mary Young, who had stepped down as president of CPACC, took over

Bachman's position because she was the only parent with extensive legislative experience. Within a few months it suddenly and surprisingly became apparent to Mahler and Young that they would have a smooth road toward securing permanent child care.[109]

Shifting political winds and the growing strength of the child care coalition contributed to this turn of events. When the 1957 session opened, lawmakers supportive of a permanent program considered "the legislative climate highly favorable."[110] In previous sessions child care legislation without a terminal date had passed on the assembly floor only to be stalled in the Senate Finance Committee. Hulse, a "main foe" of child care coalition, had retired the previous year. The new committee chair, Senator James McBride (D-Ventura), announced that he favored a permanent program. Mahler, Young, and their allies had waged an effective campaign, winning strong endorsements for permanent child care in every leading metropolitan newspaper in the state. They had used their well-honed skills as grassroots activists to persuade Governor Goodwin Knight to support the program. A decade of speaking at community meetings, testifying at hearings, and organizing letter-writing campaigns and petition drives finally bore fruit. On June 30, 1957, the governor signed the law extending California's child care centers indefinitely. Advocates breathed a sigh of relief. They no longer had to concentrate simply on saving the program. Now they could work to improve and upgrade the state's child care system—or so they thought.

Both leaders and supporters were well aware of the concessions they had been forced to make in order to save publicly funded child care services in the inhospitable climate of the cold war. As Betty Bachman told the Senate Interim Committee in 1954, "We have realized that it was necessary to accept compromises, and that it will be necessary to accept them in the future."[111] The program that survived in 1957 was not as robust as that hoped for by members of the coalition, but it was the only state-funded program in the nation. California was in an ideal position to take advantage of the federal government's new child care initiative in the 1960s. Whether federal funding would be good for education-based child care and low-income working mothers remained up for debate.

PART 3

The War on Poverty
and the Age of Protest

5

"We Do Not Consider Ourselves Welfare Cases"

*Education-based Child Care and
Low-income Working Families, 1958–65*

The passage of the Public Welfare Amendments to the Social Security Act in 1962 marked the first time since World War II that Congress had appropriated funds for child care services. These amendments were the first of many public preschool measures to be enacted in the 1960s. The goals of these new policies were twofold. First, lawmakers hoped to halt the rising cost of public assistance programs, particularly Aid to Dependent Children (ADC), which was later renamed Aid to Families with Dependent Children (AFDC). They saw funding child care as a way to encourage women welfare recipients to become self-supporting. Second, policymakers hoped that providing preschool education to poor children would furnish them with the skills to break the "cycle of poverty." Advocates across the country saw these funds as an important first step in placing child care to the national agenda. California's liberal legislators seized this opportunity to extend preschool to the state's poorest families.

Laudable as these goals were, federal funding for public preschool education had unintended consequences. Although the new federal laws did not explicitly connect child care to welfare, they required that the funds be administered through state departments of public welfare rather than education departments. Mothers feared that, whether or not they were welfare recipients, they would have to prove eligibility to caseworkers, exposing them to invasions of privacy and moral judgments. Eventually, the new laws irreversibly linked the state's child care centers with its welfare programs, which was precisely what California's child care advocates had worked for years to prevent.

Proponents feared that this association would change both the public perception and the practices of the state's centers and doom their hopes for a universal, education-based program. Nursery educators saw the introduction of federal funds as a threat to the high educational standards they had developed and to their control over the education of preschool children. Mothers reacted equally strongly to these shifts. The stigma attached to welfare intensified after the war, and by the early 1960s single mothers who sought public assistance found themselves vulnerable to the charge that they had "failed" both as wives and mothers and as workers and citizens. Working women with access to California's 324 publicly funded centers escaped such condemnation. They could live outside the boundaries of prescribed gender roles without being stigmatized as undeserving or dependent on the state. The centers enabled women to support their families. Equally important, the program gave them greater freedom to leave abusive or neglectful husbands and divorce those who had abandoned them and their children. Because the centers were administered by the Department of Education, the women were spared the intrusive, sometimes insulting, scrutiny of welfare department caseworkers. They did not have to justify their status as independent wage-earners and single mother status or fear the state's moral judgments on their life choices. Throughout the 1960s and into the 1970s they fought fiercely to maintain those opportunities.

The re-entry of the federal government into child care services pitted mothers and educators against some of their erstwhile allies, liberal state legislators. Lawmakers sought new federal funds regardless of their welfare stipulations, and advocates worked to keep child care aligned with public education. The campaigns engaged negative views of working women, degrading stereotypes of single mothers, and hostile images of welfare recipients. The legislative battles and resulting policy changes transformed the state's child care program, altering the nature and meaning of child care and reducing the political power of the child care coalition.

Persevering as Single Mothers

During the two decades after the establishments of California's child care centers, women's place in American society changed dramatically. By 1961 U.S. Department of Labor statistics revealed that 37 percent of all women between fifteen and sixty-five had joined the labor force, and the proportion of employed women who were mothers with children at home had increased from 11 to 38 percent between 1940 and 1960.[1] Rising divorce rates and increases in births to unmarried women meant that more and more working women were single mothers.[2]

The high cost of private child care and the dearth of publicly funded child care services forced many of the nation's single-parent families to turn to public welfare programs, especially ADC.[3] The longstanding negative attitudes toward those who received benefits from the government rather than "earning" them through employment intensified as unemployment rates declined during and after the war. The increasing number of single mothers, especially African Americans, on ADC rolls exacerbated the stigma attached to what began to be called "welfare dependency." When Congress passed the 1935 Social Security Act, legislators had assumed that most mothers who would benefit from ADC were white widows previously supported by their husbands, their misfortunes and "blameless" moral character making them exemplary objects of public charity.[4] ADC had faced little opposition because its basic tenets reinforced the prevailing assumption that mothers should stay at home with their children rather than enter the labor force. Nevertheless, the roots of the later demonization of ADC lay in the Social Security Act, which established the "two-channel welfare state."[5] Unemployment insurance and old-age pensions, which were also provided by the 1935 Social Security Act, came to be seen as employment-related benefits to which most workers were entitled. Although seen as an entitlement, the act excluded a significant portion of American workers, including "intermittent workers," agricultural workers, and domestic workers, which left out most black workers and an estimated 85 percent of employed black women.[6] Moreover, women who received old-age pensions based on their husbands' earnings received less than what their husbands' pension would have been. Public assistance for single mothers, by contrast, was based on need, which forced mothers to prove they were deserving.[7] Even more amazing, ADC as its name suggests, provided no assistance to mothers of dependent children; the federal government did not add such aid until 1950. ADC recipients found themselves at the mercy of caseworkers who had the power to decide whether they were worthy as well as needy, which entailed proving moral fitness as well as lack of resources and inability to secure employment.

The number of families using ADC, and the costs of providing aid for them, rose steadily after World War II. In 1940 the ADC program served 372,000 families; by 1960 that number had grown to 803,000. The cost of the program increased dramatically as well, rising from $133 million in 1940 to $904 million in 1960.[8] The massive migration of African Americans from the rural South into the nation's urban centers in the 1940s and 1950s made poverty more visible to white Americans.[9] The situation of women in California exemplifies this profound transformation. The number of working mothers with children under six rose from 27,500 in 1940 to 280,000 in 1960. In 1960 approximately 1.1 million California children under fourteen had working mothers.[10] The clientele of the state's child care centers reflected this shift. By 1955, 65 percent of families with children in the centers were headed by a single parent more than 75 percent of whom were divorced or separated rather than widowed.[11] By 1962, single parents made up 80 percent of the families using the centers in San Francisco and almost 99 percent of them were women.[12] Mothers using state child care services were more likely to be single and the sole wage earner in the family.

Barbara Gach and Ellen Hall's stories suggest the predicaments these women faced. Gach, a thirty-year-old single mother with a young son, moved from her home state of Iowa to San Francisco in 1957. She had raised her son, Jerry, without assistance for most of his life. Early in her marriage, she left her husband because of his drinking problem. It had not been an easy decision, particularly in a world that looked disapprovingly on single mothers. "It was one thing to cope with [his alcoholism] myself," Gach remembers. Jerry "didn't need to grow up under those circumstances so I took him. I left my husband and said, 'I don't want anybody to help me. I don't want alimony. I don't want anything. This is my child, I will bring him up my way.'"[13] When she decided to move to California, her brother said, "Okay, I'll go to San Francisco, and I'll go to San Francisco State and I'll live with you for one year while you figure out what you're doing and arrange—I'll help you take care of Jerry, we'll share his care, I will give you a year of my life."[14] As it turned out, Gach needed his help for only two weeks. Fortuitously, they moved into a rooming house located a few blocks from a child care center. Enrolling her son in the Frank McCoppin Child Care Center gave Gach the opportunity to secure a job as a secretary for the Air Force and avoid the stigma of welfare.

Ellen Hall, the daughter of a Presbyterian minister, found herself raising her four children alone during the early 1960s in southern California. Hall had not worked for pay since she gave birth to her first child in 1951, so she knew that when she left her husband for good she would have to secure employment in order to support herself and her children. She had met her husband, James Lawrence Hall, at church in 1950. In retrospect, that seemed to her like the "wrong thing." "Basically because that's what he came to church for. . . . he was in the Navy and he wanted to find some girl that was a Christian, but he wasn't." Hall cites their differing religious views as one of many reasons the marriage did not last. Fortunately, Hall found a job as an assistant in the Compton Child Care Centers. Because she could not place her children in the center where she worked, she enrolled them in the Burbank Child Care Center, an original Lanham Act facility in Long Beach. The centers "were a lifesaver as far as I was concerned. . . . I was better off having them in the child care centers than leaving them home alone. . . . I'd be much happier leaving them with the child care centers than" in most other places.[15] Hall managed to raise her four children without having to go on welfare and without having to worry about their safety. Hall's organizational abilities led Virginia Wisniewski, president of the Long Beach Parents' Association, to approach her to take an official role. "There are people who want to sit back and watch and you know, let everybody else do the work," says Hall. "And then there are other people that you ask to do something and they'll do it. And it's the old adage about you ask a busy person to do a job and you know it's going to get done. So I guess that's what [Virginia] saw because I was attentive and I went to every meeting, every parents' meeting that we had."[16] Over the next several years Hall found herself doing things she had never imagined she could.

Gach, Hall, and mothers like them dominated the parents' associations in the late 1950s and 1960s and formed the core group of activists who lobbied the legislature and local school boards to keep the child care centers under the State Department of Education and protect them from repeated attacks by those who wanted to scale back the program. Over the years, such women formed an increasing proportion of parent activists and worked together to support their vision of a child care program based on strong educational principles that was clearly distinguished from charity.[17]

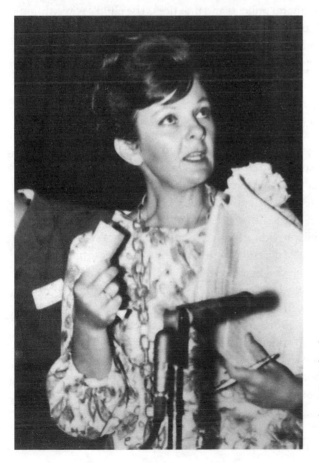

Figure 5. Ellen Hall at the California Parents' Association for Child Care Centers annual conference, around 1967. (Courtesy of the Center for Oral and Public History, California State University, Fullerton)

By the early 1960s advocates operated in a political climate dominated by liberals with an ambitious social agenda instead of the conservatives who had stubbornly opposed the program in the late 1940s and early 1950s. In the 1958 gubernatorial election, Democrat Edmund G. Brown defeated Republican William F. Knowland, a state senator nominated when the incumbent, Goodwin Knight, ran for the U.S. Senate. Knowland represented a more conservative element within the Republican Party than his predecessors. Earl Warren and Goodwin Knight had endorsed pro-labor legislation, but Knowland sought to undermine the power of organized labor by promoting a "right to work" policy that held that workers should not be required to join the union that had a contract with their employer.[18] Organized labor rallied its 1.5 million members to register and vote in unprecedented numbers. Democrats defeated Knowland and, for the first time in eighty years, took control of both houses of the legislature. This historic election transformed California's Republican-dominated, politically cautious state government; victorious politicians and newly appointed public officials embraced liberal policies and practices. The child care coalition's supporters in the legislature had either been voted out of office or had lost the political influence they once wielded. The coalition needed to find new allies in Sacramento. But first some parents and educators would have to fight a political battle closer to home.

Defending San Francisco's Child Care Centers

Advocates assumed that passage of permanent child care legislation in 1957 was a decisive step toward making the centers a regular service of the State Department of Education. Nancy Farrow, president of the San Francisco Child Care Parents' Association, stated in a letter to the editor of the city's major newspaper that the organization was "exceedingly gratified at the successful passage at this legislative session of the bill providing for a continuing child care center program. . . . we feel that we have passed a milestone in obtaining a measure of security concerning the future of the child care centers."[19] While a permanent program protected child care from yearly or biannual challenges to its funding, child care in California was still far from available to all working families. Moreover, rather than being able to relax its efforts, parents and educators discovered that they still had to defend publicly funded child care. In 1958, funding for both the state program and the program in San Francisco faced serious challenges.

Many state and city political leaders viewed the program primarily as a custodial service, so the coalition centered its campaign on its educational benefits. Conservative state legislative auditor Alan Post made a last-ditch attempt to eliminate child care funding from the state budget and revived the old argument that centers addressed "an urban problem, and should therefore be financed by the metropolitan communities."[20] The proposal was defeated before it made any headway in the legislature. Within days the child care coalition had placed editorials in local newspapers and written to legislators. Familiar with the coalition's dogged persistence and record of success, the politicians did not want to be bombarded by parents' letters and a negative press. Most had endorsed permanent child care the year before and wanted to avoid appearing indecisive or capricious by reversing their position.

After staving off this threat, mothers with children in San Francisco's twenty-five centers were greeted with alarming news when they opened their newspapers to the metropolitan section on Mother's Day, May 11, 1958. Harold Spears, the city's superintendent of schools, intended to cut $75,000 from the city's child care budget by closing five of its centers.[21] Spears blamed the centers' high cost per child, $875, on a low child-to-staff ratio. While the superintendent praised the program's high standards, he decided to save money by closing five centers and redistributing the children among the remaining twenty. His recommendation ignored educators' expertise in early child development and the standards they held. Spears argued that "with our knowledge of the pupil-teacher statistics in the elementary and secondary schools, it seems reasonable to expect an increased ratio in the Child Care Centers."[22]

What worked for older children, however, was not sufficient for preschoolers. Spears disregarded Theresa Mahler's evaluation of the centers' staffing needs even though he mentioned it in his report. Mahler emphasized the importance of small classes in order to maintain a "program conducive to the learning and development of children during this important period of their growth."[23] She endorsed a child-teacher ratio of 9.5 rather than the twenty customary in elementary schools. Spears's proposal pushed these ratios well above the recommended guidelines. Adding insult to injury, he informed the school board that he would look to Mahler, the program's director, to recommend which centers to close. After devoting the previous fifteen years to saving them, the prospect of having to close any centers was anathema to Theresa Mahler.

San Francisco parents quickly mobilized against this attack. Nyda Young, president of the Child Care Parents' Association of San Francisco, observed astutely that "the trend has been that, whenever economics are considered in the budgets, state or city, the child care program always seems to head the list of those to come under the axe."[24] Some public officials insisted that the centers provided more a babysitting service than an educational program.[25] Aware that the quality of the San Francisco program was once again under siege, Young urged immediate action. Parents had only nine days to convince the city of the centers' vital importance to working mothers and their educational value to children.

Nyda Lucille Napier was born on Februrary 20, 1924, in Seattle to Frances Lucille Summers and Russell Dodge Napier, who separated when she was two.

Napier spent much of her childhood bouncing between relatives, spending the longest stretch with her grandmother, Maud. When she graduated from high school in 1941, Napier's mother offered to pay for her to go to college. Strong, intelligent, and independent-minded, Napier, chose instead to set out on her own. In May 1942 she married her boyfriend Dick Vrooman, a newly enlisted private in the army. The couple remained married throughout the war years, Nyda living in San Francisco and working for IBM and as a nightclub photographer and Dick stationed in the Pacific. They reunited briefly after the war and separated in late 1946. Nyda returned to California, first to Los Angeles and then back to the San Francisco Bay area, where she met and married a World War II veteran, David Allen Young, in 1950. Their son, Karl, was born in 1951.[26]

By the time Nyda Young became a leader in the San Francisco parents' association, she and David Young had separated. In 1958 this single working mother with a school-aged son mobilized the citywide network of parents' councils and longtime supporters, including organized labor and the League of Women Voters. Bulletins went out to every center in the city spelling out the steps parents should take to "Save Child Care."[27] Parents were primed to respond to this call to action, and letters to the editor "poured into the [city] papers by the carload."[28] The *San Francisco Examiner* and *Call-Bulletin* published letters from the many mothers (and one father) who wrote in opposition to Spears's recommendation. Letters also landed on the desks of board of education members and other civic leaders. Parent representatives on the council worked long into the night, sending out postcards and contacting supporters. They brought their children along, sharing child care duties and involving them in organizing.[29] Mothers wrote and rewrote speeches. To be sure they made their points clearly and eloquently, they read the speeches "into a tape recorder, played back, corrected, timed, and finally printed" them in order to hand out copies at the school board meeting on May 20. Working collaboratively on many levels, parents deployed a sophisticated system of political organizing.[30]

Activists in the parents' association had become accustomed to the fact that responsibility fell on them to speak for the centers. Barbara Gach, whose gratitude for the centers led her to participate in the citywide parents' council and eventually to become president of CPACC, attended board of education meetings. "We would go, two or three of us, would go to every single board of education meeting there was in San Francisco," she recalls. "When we'd come home from work, after dinner, we'd get on the bus, go downtown, go sit in the front row, at least three of us, listening to every thing, showing an interest, occasionally speaking if something, anything, came up that was relevant to the child care centers. Just letting them know: we were here, we were interested in the education of our children."[31] Gach's memories represent the group's approach: consistent and sustained activism inspired by a sense of rights and responsibilities, which ultimately earned them respect, expertise, and political clout. The political strength of the parents' association reached its peak in 1958.

Accustomed to seeing just a few mothers at each bimonthly meeting, members of the school board were surprised by the huge crowd that arrived to protest the closing of five child care centers. On May 20, several hundred packed the school board hearing room. Parent Association representatives, mothers, rabbis and ministers, labor leaders, the National Association for the Advancement of Colored People (NAACP), and the San Francisco League of Women Voters (SFLWV) spoke against curtailing the program. In a resolution released two days after the hearings, the San Francisco Labor Council warned that the budget reduction could not be accomplished "without injury to the children using the centers, their mothers, and the employees of the facilities."[32] The SFLWV, in its usual measured fashion, asked the board of education to hold off its decision until a detailed plan had been laid out and urged the city to investigate "the availability and convenience of public transportation from each proposed discontinued center to the proposed consolidated centers." Without careful study, the League argued, the board should not take any action that would endanger the welfare of children.[33]

The Child Care Parents' Association of San Francisco and parents' council representatives argued more forthrightly for the centers' educational benefits. Mothers praised the high quality, education-oriented care their children received. "We are extremely proud that San Francisco's Child Care Program is acclaimed throughout the world as one of the finest in its field," Nyda Young told the board.[34] The program's success flowed from its low child-teacher ratio. The manageable size of the centers ensured that children separated from their parents for most of the day received the attention they deserved. Spears's recommendation to increase the number of students to between a hundred and 110 threatened the high standards that had been established.[35] Young drew on experience to emphasize her point: "I had my son, for a brief time, in a facility of this size, and it was nothing short of terrifying. The children all but have to stand in line to breathe."[36] Parents' representatives emphasized that the centers' proximity to their homes eased their dual role as workers and mothers and contended that moving a child to a center outside of his or her neighborhood could create additional hardship for a woman juggling children and jobs. Mothers might have to "take three buses to the Child Care Center and two more to work twice a day" or even be forced to withdraw children from the centers, leaving them to roam the streets during the day. Others would be compelled to quit their jobs and go on public relief. San Francisco's single mothers, who had survived without a second wage-earner or avoided ADC because of state-supported child care, could not afford to lose five centers. Indeed, they cited recent statistics to demonstrate that they needed additional centers not fewer. In 1958, for example, 1,319 children were enrolled in child care centers, but some 12,400 parents who had applied for enrollment had been turned away. Such a pressing need for child care made reducing the number of centers unfair and irresponsible.[37]

Despite the overwhelming testimony in opposition to closing the five centers, the school board voted 5-2 to slash the child care budget by $75,000 and left it up to the superintendent to figure out how to make the cut "without injuring the program."[38] Fortunately for the parents, Spears had been swayed by the public outcry and decided to save $50,000 by eliminating vacant positions and getting rid of temporary personnel. San Francisco parents had turned back another challenge to their valued social service.[39]

The success of the city parents' association served as testament to the learning process that many working mothers had undergone. Women who might have enrolled their children in child care centers without thinking about their civic duty or, for that matter, any form of political activism now regularly participated in public life. As Barbara Gach recalls her formative experiences organizing on behalf of the centers, "It was early on, and you didn't think about being an activist. You did what you could for your child care centers, and you were always polite and courteous because you didn't want to cast a bad name on them. . . . But we were there, plugging away. Driving up to Sacramento, attending the meetings where they were gonna vote."[40]

Civic activism became a regular aspect of many single mothers' lives. Reflecting on the battle with Spears and the board of education, parent representative Joan Salit Fernandez reported to the state convention that "we showed that we are a group of professional intelligent individuals willing to fight for our quality child care program. We hope that the experiences of the San Francisco Child Care Parents have, in some way, shown the potential of an organized child care center parents group and a City Council."[41] Child care offered these women independence and freedom from the scrutiny and intrusiveness of welfare case workers; participating in political battles like these taught them how to be effective participants in the democratic process.

By the late 1950s and early 1960s parents and nursery educators had well-established methods for encouraging members to become active citizens. Mary Young, who served as legislative chair of CPACC from 1955 on, worked hard to keep successive groups of mothers engaged in activism on behalf of child care. As she remarked at the 1961 statewide convention, "There is a constant turnover of parents using the centers, and it is a problem to educate those new parents concerning the history and development, and maintenance of our program."[42] Young encouraged mothers—and some fathers—to involve themselves in local parents' groups the moment they enrolled their children in the centers. "Without your support, interest, active participation and a little elbow grease" parents' groups would not be effective, she reminded them.[43] Young believed that parents would benefit from these organizing activities as well. "I have yet to meet a parent active in the Child Care Parent Association work who has not gained by his or her experience," she said. "I'm sure it has made better citizens of all of us."[44] Similarly, in a 1962 speech entitled "The Individual as an Activator in Legislation," Theresa Mahler raised the bar for members of the child care coalition. She tried to dissuade teachers and parents from shirking the "responsibility [of taking action] because they believe themselves to be confused or insufficiently informed when it comes to expressing opinions and ideas about legislative proposals."[45] Her experience had convinced Mahler that the citizen "who writes a concise, pertinent letter, addressed to his own legislative representatives and sent at the right time, can have a very real part in shaping that particular measure, and in the long run, the laws of the land."[46] CPACC and its local counterparts, the Northern and Southern California Associations for Nursery Education, and the Child Care Directors and Supervisors' Association gave working mothers and educators the tools with which to speak and protect these services. Advocates encouraged the community and the larger society to take an interest in educating young, economically disadvantaged citizens.[47] Generations of parents and educators learned the importance of combining activism with teaching or placing a child in the state's centers. Mahler and Young relied on them as the political terrain shifted over the next decade.

Enter the Federal Government

As advocates in California fought to keep the country's only remaining publicly funded child care program alive, other state legislatures as well as the federal government remained indifferent to women's growing child care needs. Aside from California's 235 centers, a 1960 Children's Bureau report found only forty-one other centers nationwide that enjoyed any level of public funding.[48] Private child care was available, but high fees put these services out of the reach of most low-income working mothers; many faced a choice between leaving their children unattended or quitting their jobs and going on welfare. Throughout the 1950s, advocates on the East Coast sought federal funding with little or no success. Even the Korean War did not result in a renewal of federal child care funds. National advocates did secure a child care deduction in the 1954 revision to the income tax code. Although the Republican-sponsored measure did not address the widespread need for affordable, adequate child care, it signified an important shift in the focus of the federal government's stance toward poor mothers. Rather than providing more women with incomes that would enable them to stay at home, as the Aid to Dependent Children program did, the government now offered them a deduction if they entered the workforce and used child care. Some policymakers began to view child care services as a way to reduce the welfare rolls and lift struggling families out of poverty by sending women into the labor force.[49]

New theories of child development helped to shift attitudes toward child care centers during the 1950s and 1960s. Two influential studies, J. McVicker Hunt's *Intelligence and Experience* and Benjamin Bloom's *Stability and Change in Human Characteristics* crystallized an emerging understanding of the importance of early childhood education.[50] Both maintained that children's early years were even more critical to their development than experts had originally thought and supported the idea that society had a responsibility to educate its children at an early age. With the election of John F. Kennedy, advocates finally found a sympathetic ear in Washington. Just before his inauguration, Kennedy promised Elinor Guggenheimer, a prominent day care advocate, federal money for child care. In 1960 Guggenheimer had helped to organize the National Conference on Day Care for Children, the first of its kind since World War II. Reflecting the new thinking regarding the importance of early childhood education, the president-elect wrote, "We must have provision for day care centers for children whose mothers are unavailable during the day. Without adequate day time care during their most formative years, the children of the nation risk permanent damage to their emotional and moral character."[51] Even more important in convincing Congress to include child care provisions in the amendments to the 1962 Social Security Act was Kennedy's emphasis on child care as a way of getting mothers off welfare and into the workforce. Funding for this effort remained quite limited, $5 million the first year and $10 million each year thereafter.

The new views of the importance of early child education shaped Lyndon B. Johnson's War on Poverty. Under the Economic Opportunity Act of 1964, the Johnson administration adopted Head Start, the most famous preschool program of the 1960s. According to proponents, preschool programs for poor children enhanced their development, prepared them for academic success, and improved their life chances. In 1965, Congress passed the Elementary and Secondary Education Act, which allocated federal funds for compensatory education programs to the states. Like nursery educators in California, federal policymakers claimed that early childhood education would reduce juvenile delinquency and help lift children out of poverty. Compared to skimpy child care grants in the 1962 Public Welfare amendments, these education programs were backed with generous funding. Finally, preschool education and child care had gained a national audience.

California's child care coalition and the state's liberal lawmakers welcomed federal funding for preschool services. They viewed the passage of the 1962 amendments to the Social Security Act and the 1964 Economic Opportunity Act, which funded Head Start, as opportunities to expand the child care programs in the state's neediest communities, especially urban ghettos and rural areas that had been underserved. These funds, the coalition and legislators believed, would "encourage establishment of day-care centers for children of working mothers" throughout the state.[52] Addressing the child care needs of farm workers marked the state's first attempt to develop a cooperative program in which they used federal funds to expand centers into rural school districts.[53] Of the two million women employed in California, approximately thirty thousand worked in agriculture in 1961, a low estimate that did not include migrant workers. State officials estimated that between seven thousand and 12,400 women farm workers, both migrant and resident, needed day care for their young children. A fourteen-county study conducted by the state found that child care needs had become critical in rural areas. Many women left their children unattended while they toiled in fields and packing houses. Federal grants appeared to be the welcome solution to a long-neglected problem. State officials had been aware of the need for at least a decade. In 1951, the state had opened a center for children of farm workers in Fresno. The executive secretary of the legislative committee studying child care in 1951 reported that "only a small portion of families in the rural areas are being served although there is evidence of considerable need for such services."[54] Stockton, situated in the middle of the fertile San Fernando Valley, had operated a center since World War II, but it was far from the section of town that housed most farm workers, migrant or otherwise. The state's reluctance to expand child care had blinded it to farm workers' needs until 1963, when the Department of Education recommended that the state allocate funds for five year-round centers and three seasonal centers in rural areas, partially funded by new federal money.[55]

Emma Gunterman, an activist who spent most of the 1960s securing and expanding child care services for agricultural laborers, wanted to model centers in rural areas after the state's existing program because its services were oriented toward education and not welfare. Born in Amsterdam to a Dutch father and American-born mother, Gunterman participated in the peace movement in the 1930s and came to California when she married fellow pacifist Joseph Gunterman. The Guntermans settled in Gridley, where they advocated for farm laborers. In 1962 Gunterman had first learned about the centers at the second annual statewide conference on Families That Follow the Crops. She remembered that "you did not have them anywhere where there were farm workers. . . . In addition, you certainly did not have them at the hours that the farm workers needed them." "And it isn't just that they would be safe, or away from accidents—because often there are accidents to little children on the farms, but they got education, they got nutrition."[56] Gunterman encouraged the state to open rural centers with the infusion of federal funds and pattern them after the centers that had been serving urban areas for almost twenty years.

Advocates welcomed the expansion of child care without much concern over the strings that came with accepting federal funds. Initially, the fact that the money would be administered by the State Department of Social Welfare was of little concern. Even with financial assistance from Washington, the legislature was slow to approve child care in rural areas. In the summer of 1963 the state opened a center at the Gridley Farm Labor Camp with Gunterman as its supervisor. A year later Governor Brown, with a little pressure from the coalition, signed a bill approving state matching funds for additional rural centers. As the state's liberal legislators looked to expand preschool funds to impoverished urban areas, advocates' concerns about the association of federal funds with the welfare department intensified.

Education, Not Welfare

When the 1965 session of the California legislature convened, early childhood education had captured the attention of national advocates of the War on Poverty as well as state political leaders. In the first two months of the session legislators introduced twenty-five bills to improve preschool education, legislation that tapped into federal funds for early childhood education and child care. The Social Security Act of 1962, the Economic Opportunity Act, and Titles I and II of the Elementary School Education Act offered California lawmakers the opportunity to assist preschool children without expending state funds as they had for the past twenty years.

The bills that created the most confusion and drew passionate objections from the state's child care coalition came from two members of the assembly who dedicated their careers to assisting California's neediest citizens. Mervyn Dymally, an African American second-term assemblyman representing one of Los Angeles's most impoverished districts, introduced Assembly Bill (AB) 1423, the Child Care and Pre-school Centers Act, in 1965. This law would increase the number of child care centers located in poor and predominantly African American neighborhoods.[57] Dymally's legislation was an "attempt to expand and improve the California child care centers."[58] Federal law mandated that the department that supervised the AFDC program administer these funds. Because of this stipulation, Dymally proposed that supervision of the state's child care centers be transferred from the Department of Education to the Department of Social Welfare. With this administrative change, California could qualify for federal funds to expand its child care program. Even though he asserted that "there is no intent to change the existing child care centers in AB 1423" and that "no child, no teacher, no center will be displaced," the proposal alarmed parents and educators involved with the state's centers.[59] Loath to forfeit independence, parents opposed any legislation that would give the Social

Welfare Department the authority to "approve [mothers] use of the centers."[60] For educators, ceding administrative control to the department represented a threat to the education-based child care program they offered.

Dymally was an unlikely target of the coalition's ire. In 1963, his first year in the assembly, he introduced legislation that would have allocated $2 million in state funds to procure sites and construct buildings for child care centers. Improving facilities had been a central goal of advocates since the centers gained permanent status. Many centers were still housed in the deteriorating "temporary" structures constructed during the war. CPACC immediately passed a resolution supporting his legislation. In 1965, CPACC, SCANE, NCANE, the American Association of University Women (AAUW), and the California Child Care Directors and Supervisors' Association, for which Theresa Mahler served as the northern section legislative chair, applauded Dymally's renewed effort to secure $2 million for structural improvements to the centers. In the next breath, however, they condemned him for trying to undermine the educational emphasis of the child care program.[61] Dymally was taken aback by the attack. In a memorandum written before he introduced AB 1423, he deplored the state's inadequate provision of services for the state's neediest children. In 1964 and 1965 only a handful of welfare recipients—an estimated 150 out of twelve thousand—used the centers.[62] To Dymally, expanding the child care program to families on AFDC went hand in hand with using state funds to construct new centers and renovate dilapidated buildings; the newly available federal funds, after all, made expansion possible.[63] As his predecessor, Augustus Hawkins, and the coalition itself could attest, the state had no intention of pouring more of its own money into the centers.

The Unruh Preschool Act, introduced by Los Angeles Assemblyman Jesse M. Unruh and intended to "establish an entirely new preschool program," also drew a negative reaction from child care advocates. Like the Dymally bill, the Unruh Preschool Act proposed an educational program centered in the state's most impoverished neighborhoods. In order to take advantage of the federal funds available under the Social Security Act, the bill mandated that these preschools would be open only to children of welfare recipients. The Department of Welfare would apply for federal funding and then contract with the Department of Education to carry out and oversee the preschool program. Advocates feared that linking preschool education with welfare would undermine the centers' educational emphasis as well as reserve them for the most impoverished families rather than for the working mothers they currently served.

"It seems ironic," Theresa Mahler told a newspaper reporter, "that just as the whole country is ablaze with enthusiasm for something we have been doing in California for more than two decades, bills are brought in to [the legislature] that change it."[64] Mahler praised the foresight of postwar policymakers who had placed the child care program under the Department of Education when the state took control. Referring to child care as welfare or charity would curtail the educational benefits of a preschool program intended to help the state's poor children. "Yet it seems strange," Mahler admitted, "that the proposal is to set up programs with the stigma that they are for the 'needy' attached, when we have been saying that what we want to do for these children is to end their being different, and bringing them into the mainstream."[65]

Mahler and the coalition promoted child care as an entitlement for California's low-income working mothers, regarding it as akin to kindergarten and elementary school. They believed that assigning the Department of Social Welfare to oversee child care would transform single working mothers from beneficiaries into dependents.[66] With the assistance of their moderate supporters in the 1940s and 1950s, advocates had avoided the stigmatization of those who used the centers. As Arnstein put it, "Here are a group of women who are willing to work all week to keep off the relief rolls and pay one-third of the cost, if we will only take care of their children while they are at work."[67] This culturally respectable image of working mothers and the educational benefits of the child care program lay at the core of the coalition's opposition to any connection between the state's centers and the welfare department. That link threatened to strip women of their identities as wage-earners and align them with impoverished mothers whom society labeled "undeserving."

The conflict that pitted single, working-class mothers against women and children who lived below the poverty line was a singularly unfortunate turn of events. Much of the blame can be placed on the double standard that had plagued the U.S. welfare state since the New Deal, which structured programs such as unemployment insurance that served full-time, nondomestic employees, a group composed predominantly of men, as an entitlement, and programs such as AFDC, that primarily served single women, as an unearned handout. Child care advocates had fought long and hard to keep the state's centers separate from this stigmatized part of the welfare system, emphasizing working women's value as contributors to the economy and as good mothers seeking education for their preschoolers. Many low-income working mothers did not want to be associated with women regarded as the "unworthy poor." Others worked to protect the child care centers because they knew from experience what it was like to be stigmatized as a recipient of AFDC. All defended the right of working mothers to continue to place their children in a child care program associated with education rather than with welfare.

Working mothers never directly mentioned race in efforts to distinguish themselves from welfare recipients, yet racist attitudes shaped the contours of the debate. By the early 1960s, "welfare mothers" had been coded black. A 1965 study of the rise in the number of AFDC recipients pointed to black families as responsible for two-thirds of the increase between 1948 and 1961.[68] Policymakers blamed black single mothers for rising welfare costs and held up black women on welfare as examples of the evils of unwed motherhood and divorce.[69] At both the state and local levels, 1965 was fraught with racial tensions. In San Francisco, civil rights leaders accused the school system of discriminating against black teachers and students. Later that year a protracted race riot engulfed Watts, an impoverished Los Angeles neighborhood, destroying businesses and leading to four thousand arrests. In this atmosphere, CPACC members' attempt to distance themselves from mothers on welfare had obvious racial implications. Indeed, the CPACC explicitly reinforced negative stereotypes of welfare mothers when it told policymakers, "We hold our heads high because we choose to be self-supporting rather than take the easier route of Aid to Families with Dependent Children."[70] These women wanted to preserve their status as productive citizens, which meant separating themselves from welfare, which was closely connected with black women.

With these tensions hovering in the background, the coalition plunged into a campaign against the Dymally and Unruh bills. As they had for twenty years, letters poured into the offices of legislators, the governor, and other state leaders. CPACC issued its usual call to action in March, asking parents to speak out to halt these "disastrous bill[s]" that would put an end to "our present wonderful child care program."[71] The perceived association with welfare elicited the most fervent responses. A Long Beach mother informed Dymally that she thought the Department of Social Welfare would fundamentally change the centers. "I am self-supporting and have a limited income," she declared. "I would rather pay my weekly fee to the child care center for the type of service I have been receiving for the past year and a half, than pay higher taxes for an inferior service which would have the added stigma of 'welfare' or 'charity' attached to it."[72] Marjorie Hughes, a single mother who had recently found a place for her daughter in a San Francisco center, which had allowed her to "take a job and get off ADC," shuddered at the thought of child care administered by the Department of Social Welfare because of her own negative experiences as a recipient. "I am so glad to be getting away from the Welfare Department to be a free citizen again," she wrote. "Though it is based on economic need, there is a completely different attitude in the Day Care Centers."[73] Hughes reinforced the notion that working mothers who enrolled their children in preschools deserved governmental assistance. The centers enabled this class of mothers, teetering precariously just above the poverty line, not only to remain or get off of public assistance but also to avoid having caseworkers and bureaucrats determine their eligibility for services.

Margaret Pignatelli, president of CPACC in 1965, reacted to the Dymally and Unruh bills with the passion of a woman who did not want to return to state aid as well and adhered to the increasingly prevalent argument that mothers who did not go out to work and relied on AFDC were choosing a less respectable way to raise their children. Pignatelli, a single mother with three sons, had used child care centers since her husband of twelve years deserted her. When he left in 1957 she moved to a public housing project and raised her three sons alone. Eventually, Pignatelli found a job and secured a place for her children in the state's centers. With an earned income and subsidized child care, she moved her family out of public housing and into an apartment, hoping never to return.[74] Pignatelli responded to the Dymally bill as a mother who knew the stigma that accompanied need-based public assistance programs. She joined many low-income working mothers' efforts to distinguish themselves from those who were "dependent" on the state. Pignatelli and other mothers expressed a genuine desire to expand the state's services for the children of mothers on welfare as well as those of low-income working mothers. She argued that "we are NOT trying to keep pre-school education our sole domain. We, better than most, are in a position to know the advantages of pre-school education for our children and adult-education classes for the parents."[75] As Mary Young put it, "We had no quarrel with the desires of the Social Welfare Department. If they could see a chance to help more people who needed it, we were all for it. The catch, as far as we were concerned was that, to help [the state's neediest families], these federal funds had to be administered through the Department of Social Welfare."[76] Marjorie Hughes, having been on welfare herself, proposed that the ideal way to achieve both the liberal legislators' and the parents' goals was to extend public child care services to all of California's neediest families. She told Dymally that "Day Care is Education, not Welfare. . . . I think it would be a wonderful thing if nursery schools were available to more children, whether their mothers were earning money or not."[77] Unfortunately, neither mothers nor the state were given that option. Federal funds were to be distributed through the State Department of Welfare, which in the minds of these mothers would compromise the quality of care or exclude working mothers from child care in favor of welfare recipients.

Expressing her frustration with the position in which CPACC found itself, Pignatelli composed a letter to Lyndon Johnson. The parents' association had not turned to the president since 1945, when the federal government had announced the closing of Lanham Act centers. She told Johnson that "many of us have been at one time or still are within the 'poverty group.' We had hoped that with the funds available through the Economic Act, the 1962 Social Security Act, and with the emphasis on combating poverty through education that our program could be expanded." Moreover, she underscored the way child care parents viewed themselves stating, "we do NOT consider ourselves welfare cases." She closed her letter by emphasizing, "We believe most sincerely, as you do, that the poverty cycle must be broken; we also believe, as you do, that education for both children and parents (as provided under our present program) is the answer. Why then cannot the California Child Care program remain under the auspices of the Department of Education? Is there any way you can implement changes so that all of these funds need not necessarily be channeled through Social Welfare?"[78]

The coalition's conflicts with state legislators became distressingly evident in a series of hearings held in April and May 1965. Without an assemblyman such as Ernest Geddes to represent their views in the legislature, the parent representatives were quite vulnerable. In April, a delegation of two dozen mothers "felt deeply enough about [the Unruh bill] to risk jobs and lose wages by making the trip to Sacramento, only to find that time ran out and they could not be heard."[79] Tensions were palpable between the parents and educators who wanted to preserve the program's existing structure and the liberal assemblymen and Department of Education officials who wanted to expand California's centers through federal funds. Only Margaret Pignatelli, CPACC president, and Fannie McFall, president of the San Francisco Child Care Parents' Association, questioned the committee, and many of their concerns were either ignored or addressed perfunctorily. When Pignatelli asked whether the bills laid out priorities for who had access to the child care centers and preschool program, no one answered. Later, she asked the committee, "If a local [school] board uses existing facilities for compensatory education, will priority be give[n] to [the] sole parent or parent[s] under Social Welfare?"[80] Ronald Cox, associate superintendent and chief of the Division of Public School Administration, responded by accusing her of "double talk." Cox had grown visibly impatient with the parents' and educators' concerns about plans to draw up a contract between the departments of Education and Social Welfare. In his mind, it was not a foregone conclusion that child care would be restricted to welfare recipients. He told parents that policymakers "hope to use money to expand facilities to care of all."[81] He believed that opposition to linking the education and welfare departments would only exclude poor children from these beneficial programs. The animosity between Pignatelli and Cox continued to build throughout the legislative session. Pignatelli felt ignored, and parents' complaints irritated Cox. In May, when Pignatelli returned from a trip to Sacramento, she told Mary Young that she "was so angry with Dr. Cox that when she left [the hearings] she wouldn't even look at him." She informed Mahler and other parent leaders that mothers who were currently using the centers had "been sold down the river completely."[82] The needs of California's low-income working mothers had taken a back seat to expanding the program to meet the needs of AFDC recipients.

Theresa Mahler was concerned that the legislative session had ended "in a blaze of heated acrimonious controversy, rather than a blaze of glory."[83] Mahler wrote to Assemblyman Leo Ryan, chair of the Subcommittee on Compensatory

Education, about the "difficult situation" in Sacramento the previous afternoon. "It must have been distressing to you, as it was indeed to us," she observed, that parents who had taken time off work had not been given a chance to speak at the hearings.[84] Struggling to remain courteous, Mahler continued, "I must confess that I, too, was somewhat distressed and discouraged." Although she appreciated being able to submit her statement to the committee, it did not "provide the same impact as might have been achieved in a presentation." Her remarks were not meant as "carping comment," Mahler assured Ryan. She asked his advice about how advocates could express their views effectively. In his reply, Ryan articulated his displeasure with the tone and attitude advocates had displayed. After encouraging parents to lobby individual members of the assembly personally, Ryan tactfully reminded Mahler that mothers "should attempt to convince by facts, rather than threats or belligerence."[85]

The 1965 legislative session ended as ironically as it began. The Children's Center Act, passed by both houses of the legislature and signed into law by Edmund G. Brown in July, changed the purpose of the child care centers from "care and supervision" to "supervision and instruction," a recommendation Mahler had made on behalf of the California Child Care Directors and Supervisors' Association in October 1964.[86] In addition, the new legislation renamed child care centers "children's centers" to remove any association with custodial care. Mahler and other educators believed that, "while the framework is not that of the traditional classroom or school, the program or curriculum, in both nursery and school-age centers, is educational in nature."[87] Having the centers officially associated with education was critical to Mahler, given her perspective as a professional early childhood educator. At the same time, however, the legislation authorized a contractual agreement between the Department of Education and the Department of Social Welfare so that the state could qualify for federal funds. With this agreement, children of families receiving public assistance would be approved for child care services by the welfare department and placed in the children's centers operated under the education department. Paradoxically, just as the program's educational merits received formal recognition, the legislature set in motion a move toward welfare-oriented goals. The statement of purpose and even the name chosen for the children's centers were contradicted by their placement within the state welfare bureaucracy. Child care advocates discovered that federal money came with many strings attached. The most problematic was the knot connecting child care with welfare.

6

A Different Kind
of Welfare State

*California's Child Care Coalition
in the Age of Protest, 1966–71*

In the fall of 1970, Lynne Monti and Willie Mae Addison composed a letter rallying the mothers in the California Parents' Association for Children's Centers (CPACC) to action. "This has been a bad legislative year for Children's Centers in Sacramento," wrote the two activist mothers. Association members needed to do more than send in dues; they needed to motivate other parents in their centers to rejoin the fight for child care.[1] The letter was occasioned by an impending major defeat for the child care coalition: the passage of a bill that moved the centers into the Department of Compensatory Education and gave enrollment priority to former, current, and potential welfare recipients. Monti and Addison were both divorced, single mothers. Monti was white, and Addison was black. Both had spent short stints on welfare before taking the helm of CPACC. Both worked for community agencies created with War on Poverty funds and had become involved in a political movement that reached beyond child care, Monti in the women's movement and Addison in the welfare rights movement. Both saw child care as central to poor women's quest for autonomy, dignity, and equality.

To take advantage of new poverty-related federal child care funds, California legislators proposed legal and administrative changes to the children's centers. The coalition vociferously fought the shift to federal funding in the late 1960s and early 1970s. Whether as a result of well-intentioned but underfunded War on Poverty programs, or of politicians wanting to reduce the welfare rolls, federal child care funds threatened a unique segment of the social safety net that had persisted in California into the 1960s. This alternative vision grew out of a public assistance philosophy that put women at its center and assumed that the key to keeping women and their children out of poverty was affordable, good-quality child care. Early childhood educators believed (and rightly so) that the shift to federal funds and the welfare policy priorities connected to these funds would undermine their professional status and the quality of the centers. Federal child care funds had two goals: employment for welfare recipients and serving the greatest numbers at the lowest cost. As a result, the state's working poor feared that access to child care would be limited to welfare recipients. Most working mothers did not see themselves as fundamentally different from those on welfare (many, in fact, had been forced onto welfare for short periods of time themselves), but they desperately did not want their child care program to be viewed as a welfare service. Unfortunately, fears of a stigmatized welfare identity, whether applied to the mothers themselves or their children's centers, made it difficult for the working poor to navigate the volatile political vortex of the late 1960s and early 1970s.

The explosion of social movements in the period meant that mothers in CPACC were no longer the only voice of poor mothers in political debate. A generation of poor women had been galvanized by the War on Poverty's Community Action Program (CAP), which encouraged "maximum feasible participation" from poor people and drew many of the nation's impoverished citizens into politics and activism. Others took political action because of the degrading nature of the welfare system. As a result, the nation's poorest women began speaking for themselves and forming welfare rights organizations. They pressed for increased public assistance while establishing child care alongside other community services. Concurrently, middle- and upper-middle-class women, many of whom had participated in other movements for social change, began to speak out for women's rights and women's liberation. They also made demands for child care, although they did not focus their efforts on public child care legislation. Yet even with new activism from welfare recipients and middle-class feminists, the front-line advocates for publicly subsidized care remained those who benefited from the state's centers—working mothers and the teachers who cared for their children. Despite the experience and political savvy of the child care movement, the unique welfare vision that had persisted in California fell victim to change in the late 1960s and early 1970s: generational shifts in the child care coalition, new ideas about child care that emerged from the War on Poverty and the women's movement, and increasing hostility in the state and the nation toward welfare recipients.

A Leadership Transition

By the mid-1960s, early childhood educators and teachers in the child care coalition were seasoned advocates. For almost two decades Theresa Mahler had been the chief legislative organizer for the California Children's Centers Directors and Supervisors' Association and had the support and assistance of other veterans such as Winona Sample, Violet Steiner, and Docia Zavitkovsky. Mahler was an astute and sophisticated lobbyist. During each legislative session she wrote trenchant analyses of bills and distributed her summaries to educators across the state. She also employed a well-practiced system for rallying educators as well as parents with children in the state's centers. As other public preschool and compensatory education programs proliferated, the directors and supervisors took on the role of extolling the positive benefits of the children's centers and emphasizing in particular their "*educational* advantages."

The Parents' Association faced a bumpier road in the late 1960s but survived into the 1970s because there was, as Lynne Monti recollected, "a structure in place."[2] Mary Young, whose daughter had long ago "graduated" from the child care centers, had wanted to retire as CPACC's legislative advocate for some time. As her daughter, Deborah Young, recalls, "I remember her saying once that she couldn't find anybody to take her place. Nobody seemed to step forward and she couldn't leave the child care in the lurch by just saying, 'I can't do this anymore.' So until they found somebody to take her place, she stuck with it. She was loyal. Even if it meant more sacrifices."[3] Mothers active during this transition period remember Young as the legislative mastermind for the parents' group. Fay Love, one of the mothers to infuse energy into the parents' association in the 1960s and early 1970s, reflected on what Young meant to CPACC and organizers in San Francisco: "She was a whiz. . . . Mary would open her home up to us. . . . She was the one who taught us about the bills, what bills we should support and what bills we don't support. . . . She introduced us to a lot of legislators. And she taught us letter writing. You didn't only go to Sacramento; you also had to write letters and spread [the word] among your parents so they would know what was going on." Young's influence stretched across the state. Ellen Hall of Long Beach, president of CPACC in 1967, recalled that Young "would get the word down to the different areas to say, 'Write, write, write because they need to know that you want that center open. And as a parent, you're the only one that can do that.'" Young's successor had big shoes to fill.[4]

Despite the changing clientele and turnover in leadership, the Parents' Association continued to recruit mothers committed to the organization and who could be tutored in child care advocacy. Moreover, the centers themselves preserved the collective memory of a movement that relied on a new cadre of activists every few years. Fliers about local, citywide, and statewide parents' association meetings were plastered on center bulletin boards, teachers watched children while the parents held their potluck dinner meetings, and Theresa Mahler continued to mentor parents in the art of advocacy.[5] The retirement of CPACC's seasoned lobbyist did not go unnoticed, however. At the Northern Section of the Directors and Supervisors' Association meeting in December 1966, participants conferred about the need for "reactivation of parent groups throughout the State." With the turnover in leadership there was "not the same enthusiastic activity in regard to legislation as in the past."[6]

While the level of parent activism waned momentarily, a new group of mothers and a handful of fathers soon emerged who believed that parents must maintain a voice in the political process. In 1966, Sharon Godske, a mother from San Francisco, volunteered to replace Young as legislative advocate for CPACC. Godske, a University of California at Berkeley graduate with a B.A. in political science, was the mother of two. She had returned to work outside her home in 1963 so her husband, Michael, could finish college. In order for Michael to focus on his studies, the Godskes enrolled their two daughters in the Argonne Children's Center located in the city's Richmond District, a neighborhood known for its Russian, Irish, Chinese, and Japanese immigrants and for its cool summer temperatures. Like most parents, the Godskes selected the center because it was close both to San Francisco State University, where Michael was finishing his degree, and to the University of California, San Francisco, where Sharon worked in the continuing education department.

When asked how she ended up as CPACC's legislative advocate, Godske initially responded, "I don't remember." After a moment of thought, she said, "I think it's because nobody else would do it. I really do. Plus the fact that I had a background in political science and I was aware of what was going on politically. I knew where Sacramento was. I knew the difference between the Assembly and the Senate and I knew what a Senate Bill or Assembly Bill was."[7]

Godske picked up where Young left off, helping to organize letter-writing campaigns, speaking at hearings, and meeting with local assemblymen such as John Vasconcellos (D-San Jose), thirty-four and recently elected, who immediately identified himself as a friend of the state's child care program.[8] Over the next five years the legislative advocate job changed hands many times. After a year of traveling the state, writing letters, and talking to legislators, Godske turned her efforts back to her family and a troubled marriage. As she recalls, "I didn't give it as much as I probably could have. And now I probably would be able to give it a lot more time and effort and energy. At that time, my voices were too scattered to do as good a job as I would have liked to have done."[9] Godske's marriage dissolved in 1968, and she, like the majority of parents in the state's centers, became a single mother.

Although Godske did not remain as legislative advocate for long, she was part of a cohort of dedicated parents who filled the leadership vacuum that Young's departure created and included Willie Mae Addison, Fay Love, Bettie Keesee, and Lynne Monti. These parents, and the teachers who organized alongside them, continued to articulate their vision of a welfare system that not only served the state's most impoverished citizens but also offered affordable, educational child care for the working poor.

Compensatory Education and Welfare to Work

In the late 1960s the War on Poverty continued to have a profound influence on the children's centers and the national perception of child care. Initial funding decisions for Head Start had a long-term impact on the federal government's most famous compensatory education program, and the ripple effect influenced state officials' approach to all public preschool programs. During Head Start's initial 1965 eight-week Summer Program, for example, some early childhood education experts determined that the government should spend $1,000 per child. Jule Sugarman, deputy director of Head Start, settled on a dramatically lower amount, $180 per child, which the administration announced without evaluating or trying to compromise with the higher funding suggestions. As a result, once the Johnson administration proclaimed the Summer Program a success, it became difficult for experts to lobby for additional funds. Behind this decision lay Lyndon Johnson's conviction that it was more important to create a "massive" health and education program than one that "served a smaller number with a higher level of care."[10]

A similar dilemma shaped debate over the children's centers. The focus on child care for the poor and disadvantaged brought much-needed national attention to early childhood education but propagated the assumption that public programs should serve only the neediest families. Theresa Mahler expressed the concerns of those who had long touted the educational merits of the centers in a speech she delivered at the twenty-fifth anniversary conference of the Children's Centers Directors and Supervisors' Association:

> I must continue to emphasize how unfortunate it seems to many of us who are interested in education that all preschool programs are considered by the general public to be for the disadvantaged only. The publicity given to programs like Head Start created this impression. Therefore all preschool is considered to be Compensatory Education by the general public and most of those in the field of education who have no actual experience with nursery or preschools. . . . Right now the chief interest appears to be in how to get the most children into a preschool program for each dollar spent, with a woeful inattention to the quality of the educational program offered.[11]

Despite educators' best efforts, both policymakers and the public increasingly equated child care with compensatory education.

In the late 1960s, after decades of neglect and inattention by the nation's politicians, child care became a prominent item on the congressional agenda. In 1967, for example, members of Congress introduced eight child care-related bills.[12] Five aimed to improve the educational standards for child care, and the other three amended the Economic Opportunity Act of 1964 to expand child care so that poor mothers could enroll in job training and employment programs. None of these modest bills passed. The bill with the most profound impact on the Children's Centers, however, was not explicitly about child care but rather welfare reform. The bill, which became law in 1967, amended the Social Security Act and authorized federal funds to purchase child care services for past and present welfare recipients and even for those deemed likely to go on welfare in the near future. The federal government offered these funds to states on a three-to-one matching basis, and initially without restraint on the amount of child care funds a state could request, although very little money was actually appropriated under the new law.

What proved to be most notable about this welfare reform bill was its mandatory work requirements for AFDC recipients, known commonly as the Work Incentive (WIN) Program.[13] Any welfare client who turned down employment or a job training program—"females and males alike, mothers as well as fathers, even in single parent, female-headed families"—would be refused government aid.[14] For mothers with young children the law signaled a major departure from the original premise of AFDC, which had insisted that mothers stay at home to care for their children. A state, however, could not force a mother to work unless the state established child care, and because most states did not have well-established child care programs, welfare mothers with young children could not participate in the WIN Program. Without child care, WIN job training and placement offices would turn these women away.[15] Ironically, for those who had fought to preserve the Children's Centers' educational function, the state best poised to take advantage of these new child care funds was California.

This fixation on welfare-to-work policies was a direct response to the swelling welfare caseload during the 1960s and to a growing public association of welfare with racial and ethnic minorities. In 1960 close to 3.1 million Americans received ADC; by 1970 the number had soared to approximately 8.4 million.[16] Female-headed households made up 75 percent of all AFDC cases. In California, the number of welfare recipients had risen from 375,000 in 1963 to close to 1.6 million in 1970.[17] By 1960, although whites still made up the largest single group receiving Aid to Needy Children (California's welfare program), people of color—primarily blacks and Hispanics—made up 60 percent of recipients.[18] The "new state's rights rebellion brewing in the West" took "welfare fraud [as] its rallying cry."[19] Appealing to the racism of white working- and middle-class constituents, politicians spoke in coded language about the "undeserving poor" wasting honest taxpayers' money. With the rising numbers of welfare recipients, fiscally conservative members of Congress and California's newly elected governor Ronald Reagan focused on programs that were punitive and aimed at reducing the size and cost of AFDC. For those in the California legislature who had grudgingly supported child care over the years or wanted to reduce state spending, newly available federal funds seemed like a perfect way to shift social costs away from Sacramento and move families off welfare at the same time.

The Conservative Response

An argument for financial independence became increasingly important as white, property-owning Californians led a major anti-welfare tax revolt.[20] Since counties paid for one-third of the state's welfare budget and property taxes for homeowners rose considerably during this period, some blamed the easiest available target: rising welfare costs. Despite the relatively small proportion of the welfare budget allocated to ADC nationally, it received a disproportionate amount of the hostility.[21]

This climate elevated Ronald Reagan, the anointed leader of a grassroots conservative movement that emerged in the late 1950s, to lead the assault on welfare from the state house. The Democrats' triumph over the Republicans in the 1958 state elections turned out to be a Pyrrhic victory, fueling a right-wing resurgence that steadily gained strength. When two-term Governor Edmund G. Brown decided to run for an ill-advised third term, the state was no longer the liberal stronghold it had been in the early 1960s.[22] Berkeley's free speech movement, the Watts riots, and the farm workers' movement all contributed to some Californians' sense that the state was out of control. Reagan, a former Democrat who supported Helen Gahagan Douglas's senatorial candidacy against Richard Nixon in 1950, was perfectly positioned to lead the assault and spearhead a conservative resurgence. Speaking against the radicals on college campuses, promising to control or contain inner-city violence, and pledging to reform the state's outdated welfare system, he won the governorship in 1966. In his inauguration speech delivered on a sunny but brisk January morning, the newly elected governor made his views on welfare clear. "We are a humane and generous people," he said, "but we are not going to perpetuate poverty by substituting a permanent dole for a paycheck. There is no humanity or charity in destroying self-reliance, dignity, and self-respect."[23] Reagan's views of the state's welfare recipients resonated with lower-middle-class homeowners who had watched their property taxes rise well above the national average. These Californians frequently pointed to "welfare" and the state's undeserving poor as the causes of their high taxes. They blamed not only welfare recipients themselves but also the generosity of liberal legislators in the state's capitol.[24] Ronald Reagan sounded like the man to reverse this spending trend.

With antiwelfare sentiments running high, advocates continued to emphasize that the children's centers permitted working mothers to be financially independent. The growing suburban backlash went hand in hand with a larger reaction against the War on Poverty. It surfaced not only in wealthier suburban communities in the San Francisco Bay Area and in Orange County but also in Los Angeles's working-class suburbs—and even among some of the working poor who took advantage of the state's child care program. Some mothers worried that the lack of attention to keeping child care affordable reflected the poverty-focused policies of Governor Brown and other liberal Democrats, and a few joined the backlash against spending on social programs that aided the poor, especially African Americans.[25]

In April 1966 Grace J. Angstman composed a letter to Assemblyman Corley Porter (D-Compton), the South Los Angeles County legislator who had been a vocal supporter of child care since the late 1940s. Angstman touched on themes that mothers had been emphasizing since the end of World War II: "I am only an ordinary mother trying to be assured of competent supervision of my minor children so I can support them and work without the constant worry of their running loose and, possibly getting into trouble." At the same time, her letter also reflected the shifting political landscape of the late 1960s. Angstman was aware of the unsettling events around her: local and national race riots, War on Poverty programs perceived to be prioritizing services for African Americans, and increasingly violent clashes between antiwar demonstrators, the police, and National Guard. She could not contain her anger as she wondered where a white, low-income working mother's child care needs fit in this racialized political context. After politely thanking Porter for his continued support of child care, Angstman asked, "Must we desperate parents move to Watts, create a riot, loot, and be directly or indirectly responsible for deaths (and be colored), in order to even be heard, let alone receive any consideration? To date, it appears, unless one breaks the law, gets arrested, causes untold expenses (the National Guard), yet, claims emotional strain—perhaps shoplifts—and makes headlines, he or she cannot be heard. . . . if one creates anarchy, the Governor is nothing but sympathetic with 'the plight of the poor people' and the world is their oyster."[26] Although Angstman had benefited from a state-sponsored social program of subsidized child care, she drew clear distinctions between herself and African Americans who benefited from War on Poverty programs and other forms of government aid. The letter reflects the discontent felt by some white working people who voted for Ronald Reagan that year.

Black Women Speak Out

Angstman represented the perspective of some white working-class women in the children's centers, but her views by no means reflected those of the majority. Indeed, many active mothers believed that parents' groups forged interracial understanding. As Marjorie Caro, an immigrant from England with a son in one of the centers, described it, "I find the best example of racial/social integration that works. . . . The mothers are from differing ethnic groups and widely differing social backgrounds, but we have one thing in common—we are determined to do the very best we can for our children, and we work as hard as we can to that end, both in our jobs and in our homes."[27] Caro and long-time leaders of the coalition stressed commonalities rather than differences.

Angstman's and Caro's comments came as more and more African American women, both in the California Parents' Association for Children's Centers and in the welfare rights movement, began pressing for improved social services for themselves and their families. Fay Love was one of the increasing number of black women in CPACC. By the late 1960s, she recalls, "most of the leaders were black." Lynne Monti described the parents' association as "pretty mixed . . . my recollection is it was primarily black and white but a fairly substantial mix. . . . I don't remember anything but real partnership."[28] The number of African Americans using the centers increased throughout the postwar period, first as the centers began serving more single mothers and then after they began accepting welfare recipients in the late 1960s. By 1974, black children made up 27 percent of those enrolled.[29]

Love, a single mother with two daughters, left her husband in 1962 after five years of marriage. Born and raised on a farm in Shaw, Arkansas, a rural community approximately thirty miles southwest of Little Rock, Love was the youngest girl of thirteen children born to Loretta and Ed Turner. Ed Turner occupied a place in the southern rural economy that receives little attention. He was an African American landowner who harvested a variety of crops on his two hundred–acre farm. Love grew up aware of segregation and inequality but does not remember experiencing racial discrimination until she came to California. As a young woman, she admired her father's business sense and her mother's community involvement; her mother served as treasurer of the local PTA for forty years, long after her last child had graduated.

The Turners encouraged their children to pursue their education; all eleven who survived childhood finished high school, and a majority of them graduated from college. After high school, Love's parents gave her a train ticket west. Her older sisters had moved to the San Francisco Bay Area at their parents' suggestion because, Love remembers, they "really wanted us to move forward, to get the best that we could get." Moving to California "was one of the ways of doing it." In Oakland, she met her future husband, Sam Love, who worked for the railroad, a job that afforded black men a certain amount of status in the 1940s and 1950s.[30] In 1952 Sam joined the military and became one of the six hundred thousand African Americans who served in the Korean War. While he was away, Love's mother became ill, so she returned to Arkansas to be close to home and attend Philander Smith College in Little Rock. After Sam returned and Fay finished college, the two were married at her sister's house in Oakland. They purchased a home in the Fillmore District of San Francisco, one of the city's predominantly African American neighborhoods, and joined the 35 percent of blacks in the United States who owned homes.[31] Love settled into married life, working at the post office until she gave birth to Deborah in 1957 and Beverly in 1959.

As it turned out, Fay and Sam had different visions of what it meant to have children and a family. Sam wanted to continue living a carefree life and spending as he pleased, while Fay believed the children should come first in terms of their attention and finances. These differences could not be overcome, and the couple separated. Fay and her two girls moved into a flat in 1962. As she recalls the transition, "When I paid the moving van, I had three dollars and sixteen cents. But my kids were happy. I was happy and we still are. Because I had made up my mind, I can do this! My mom would have taken my girls until I got fairly situated. No, I kept my girls with me and I survived."[32] Love never regretted her decision, but like most single mothers she had to juggle multiple responsibilities to make it on her own.

Initially, Love relied on her niece to help with child care, but eventually her niece needed a higher paying job and, as her daughters started getting older, Love wanted care that was a "little more constructive." She happened upon the San Francisco child care centers in her search for an education-based program. Immediately, Love realized how good the centers were for her daughters and for her. In addition to being in a structured educational environment, her daughters learned how to cook and sew, were taught healthy eating, and were exposed to "democratic principles and democratic ways."[33] Love viewed the centers as a blessing because the teachers were sympathetic to the difficulties faced by single working mothers. "Children's Centers and Mrs. Mahler. . . . they helped me out so much. Because they worked with me with an understanding: this woman is trying, she's trying. They gave me a lot of breaks, you know . . . The perks were like maybe I could be fifteen minutes [late] because I had to ride the bus. I had no car. And maybe it took me a little long."[34] Like her mother, Love believed deeply in education and community service. At her very first parents' meeting at the John Muir Child Care Center, when the president of the council planned to step down, there was no logical replacement because most parents in the group were new. The head teacher pointed to Love and announced, "She'll do it." Love agreed and stayed involved for almost a decade.

Just as Love was assuming an active role in CPACC, 350 miles to the south in Compton's Nickel Garden Housing Project, Johnnie Tillmon, also an African American migrant from Arkansas, began organizing poor mothers on Aid to Needy Children. The biographies of the two women are strikingly similar. Both were children of Arkansas farmers, both valued hard work, and both claimed not to have experienced racial discrimination until they moved to California. With the death of her father in 1960, Tillmon, a single mother of six, moved to

Los Angeles to be close to her brothers. She spent most of her adult life working in laundries, both in Arkansas and in southern California and took pride in the fact that she could support her family and be self-sufficient. In many ways all that separated Love and Tillmon was luck. Love suffered a debilitating back injury while jumping from a second-floor window to escape an apartment fire but was back in the workforce after a year. In 1963, Tillmon's arthritis and other physical ailments forced her to quit working permanently.

At first, Tillmon resisted the idea of public assistance. "One of the reasons I didn't want to go on welfare," she recalled, "was the attitude I heard people talk about . . . not in Arkansas, but here."[35] Once on welfare, she noticed that people treated her differently. She was politically active before she went on ANC, serving as shop steward for her union and secretary of a local Democratic Party club. Given that experience, and frustrated by the negative attitudes toward welfare recipients, Tillmon organized a group that eventually became Aid to Needy Children Mothers Anonymous, one of the first grassroots organizations founded and sustained by welfare mothers.[36] Tillmon encouraged women like herself to become politically active and work to improve community programs for their children. ANC Mothers Anonymous advocated not just for welfare rights but also for education, job training, and child care programs that would allow mothers to move off welfare and become self-sufficient. She later became the first woman president of the National Welfare Rights Organization. In a 1972 article in *Ms.* magazine, Tillmon declared boldly, "Welfare Is a Women's Issue."[37]

For Fay Love, working in the Children's Centers Parents' Association, and Tillmon, an emerging leader in the welfare rights movement, the critical issue was the same: Poor women with young children must have child care. Despite their similar biographies and the razor-thin economic margin separating them, Love was praised for her independence and survival skills whereas Tillmon and mothers like her were vilified as lazy dependents of the state. The demonization of welfare drove an artificial wedge between welfare mothers and the working poor, making it difficult for these natural allies to work together toward a common goal. Nevertheless, especially at the local and regional levels, there were important points of contact between the child care and welfare rights movements and between working women and welfare recipients.

Tillmon's organization represented one of many welfare rights groups emerging across the country that opposed work requirements, the invasiveness of welfare regulations, and the power of caseworkers. In 1967, under the leadership of George Wiley, a former leader in the Congress of Racial Equality, a national convention was held to pull together these disparate groups. The National Welfare Rights Organization (NWRO) provided a unified voice for the grassroots efforts of hundreds of welfare rights groups and helped these organizations coordinate demands for better services. While national and regional groups had similar goals, local activists had more diverse interests such as establishing child care centers, job training offices, youth programs, and health clinics. They viewed such services as part of their "own war on poverty."[38]

Willie Mae Addison, an African American mother of four who divorced her husband in 1962, embodied both movements. Addison had been forced to go on welfare for a short period of time in 1966 and understood what it meant to depend on assistance from the state. Employment and affordable, high-quality child care had allowed her to stay off welfare since then. She became involved with CPACC when she became president of the Jane Addams Center's Parents' Association in 1964, and by 1968 her passionate advocacy and leadership skills had gotten her elected president of CPACC. At a meeting of the Directors and Supervisors' Association in 1969, Addison informed the audience, "I think the Children's Centers is the greatest program I know of." She continued forcefully, "We're going to the moon, we're going everywhere else; let's take some of the money and build Children's Centers."[39]

For Addison, advocating for state-sponsored child care and welfare rights went hand in hand. She founded three welfare rights organizations in the South County communities of Carmelitos, a housing project in Long Beach, the Central Area, and Hawaiian Gardens, and was active in many other community groups. Whether she was working for child care or welfare rights, her goal was to improve services for the poor and enable them to achieve financial independence.[40] Addison had honed her activist skills in the National Adult Participation Program (NAPP), funded by the Office of Economic Opportunity as a means of insuring "maximum feasible participation" of community members like Addison. Trained as a social worker, she worked for a short time as a teacher's aide in a Head Start Program and was hired as a supervisor by the North Long Beach Neighborhood Center in 1968.[41] Funded by the Office of Economic Opportunity, the center operated a twenty-four-hour crisis center; sponsored a Big Brother and Big Sister program; and provided free food, clothing, and furniture for the city's neediest.[42] Reflecting on her efforts, Addison said, "It's rewarding work. . . . Poor people—kicked down by other agencies—come here and are surprised to find that we really care about them and are willing to help."[43] As California waged its child care battles in the late 1960s and early 1970s Addison and others like her who straddled the gap between the welfare rights movement and CPACC spoke to the importance of child care for poor women's ability to provide for their families, educate their children, and increase their opportunities.

The California Commission on the Status of Women

The importance of child care both to women on welfare and to the working poor emerged in a series of hearings held by the California Commission on the Status of Women in October 1968. When John F. Kennedy created the President's

Commission on the Status of Women in 1961, he did so at the suggestion of the newly appointed head of the Women's Bureau, Ester Peterson, and Secretary of Labor Arthur Goldberg. While the commission obligated the president to study the problems confronting women rather than promote specific policies, it represented the first government-sponsored organization to examine women's status in American society. Its 1963 report, *American Women*, did not advocate dramatic changes in women's roles; in fact, it reinforced women's responsibilities as wives, mothers, and homemakers while ignoring welfare policies and other issues relevant to single mothers.[44] At the same time, commission researchers amassed statistics and facts that supported some of the "complaints and problems" reported by housewives and women workers.[45] Most important, the commission acknowledged that a growing number of women were working outside their homes. Their children, the report argued, needed affordable quality child care.[46]

Despite California's progressive tradition the state was among the last to establish a Commission on the Status of Women, in part because political leaders believed women faced few inequities in the "golden state." In 1965 two black Democrats in the legislature, Mervyn Dymally and Willie Brown, provided the leadership behind the proposal for a state commission.[47] The California commission took a much stronger position on child care than the president's commission had done. In its second report, published in March 1969, the commission declared that "it is safe to say that the single biggest problem of the working mother—*at all economic levels*—is adequate care of her children while she is on the job" [emphasis in the original].[48]

From its inception the commission conducted surveys and held conferences to expose the "sharp disparities in opportunity between men and women in a wide variety of areas" and recommended policy changes so that California women could make "their maximum contribution to the society."[49] The commission compiled statistics about women's place in the workforce, their lack of political power, and their educational opportunities. Working women with small children made up 11 percent of the state's female labor force, which meant that 256,000 families needed child care. Female-headed households made up 10 percent of all California families, and 62 percent of them were below the poverty level with incomes below $3,000 a year. In its starkest examples the commission cited statistics from South Los Angeles, including the nationally famous black neighborhood Watts. In South Los Angeles in 1965, 26 percent of families were headed by a single mother; in Watts alone, 110,000 children needed child care.[50] Finally, the commission echoed an argument long made by parents and other child care advocates: With 80 percent of the children in the children's centers from single-parent households, it was "clear that were the centers not available so that the parents can be self-supporting, state or local government would have to provide far more costly assistance at a greater total tax load."[51]

California's next governor, Ronald Reagan, showed little enthusiasm for the Commission on the Status of Women. He discouraged its members from making recommendations that required state money and instructed them to look to the private sector for solutions. Indeed, the governor, like many in the male-dominated legislature, only grudgingly supported the commission. In an era when national and state attention began to focus on women's equality, most agreed to sponsor the continuation of the commission because they knew it would not be smart politics to vote against the "women's committee." Vern Sturgeon, Reagan's legislative liaison, scribbled across an internal Governor's Office memorandum: "Nobody likes it but only a few have the nerve to vote against it. This is a subject that members joke about but almost all are afraid to vote against."[52]

Despite the governor's indifference, the commission moved forward with its agenda. In order to investigate Californians' child care needs in more depth, the commission held hearings with the senate and assembly Social Welfare Committees in San Francisco on October 17 and 18, 1968. The commission made it clear that although they understood that many preschool education programs existed in the state, the hearings' purpose was to survey state services that provided "care of children which takes place all day, primarily to meet the needs of working parents." Reminded of the governor's words, the hearings would facilitate a blueprint for the "future of day care services by both public and private bodies."[53] As had been the case since the legislature held hearings on child care starting in 1945, a diverse array of voices from powerful government officials, early childhood education experts and social workers, and employed mothers spoke to the issues. Marking a definite shift from normal committee hearings, the commission held an evening session in order to accommodate the schedules of working mothers. Lending credence to Vern Sturgeon's view that legislators did not take the commission seriously, most members from the Senate and Assembly Social Welfare Committees did not attend and sent members of their staff to stand in their place.

Sensing the gravity of the shifting political context, Theresa Mahler realized that the state's poorest women were being pitted against each other. She pleaded with the commission not to overlook the working families struggling to stay off public assistance in their effort to focus on providing child care for welfare recipients. "In our desire to establish all kinds of programs for those who are in WIN, or are on AFDC," Mahler contended, "we should not lose sight of the needs for expanding programs for parents who are doing their self support, because otherwise we are moving these parents in and tossing the others out. I am hoping that all over the state consideration will be given to the fact that there are many families, not exactly living in the ghetto, but just one notch above, and it only takes a hairs breadth of their not being able to continue to get services or not being able to get in."[54] Mahler believed that the state should fund child care for all these needy families. Having watched single mothers teeter precariously just above the poverty line and having listened to their personal stories, Mahler spoke both as a child care expert and a direct observer of what the children's centers had meant to the more than 600,000 children who had come through the program since 1943.[55] Her historical view of the children's centers, especially her memory of the elimination of Lanham Act centers in 1945, led her to caution state officials that reliance on federal funds would compromise the "continuity, the security it gives parents to know this is an ongoing program."[56]

Espanola Jackson, president of California Welfare Rights, followed Mahler and state education officials. Like Mahler, she grasped the importance of child care for poor women, whether working or on welfare, but she did not see education-based care as the ultimate solution. Her views reflected those of California Welfare Rights and her San Francisco neighborhood, Bayview–Hunter's Point. In the early 1960s, Jackson's Merchant Marine husband had abandoned her and their six children. After she failed in efforts to force him to pay child support, Jackson had no choice but to go on welfare.[57] Jackson, who had resided in the city's oldest African American neighborhood since the 1940s, represented just one of many in her community forced onto public assistance. She remembered that as young as six she wanted to be like her grandmother, a preacher and community leader, and "go around and help people." In 1966, after five days of rioting in Hunter's Point, precipitated when police fatally shot a black teenager in the back, community members gathered to express growing frustration over the economic inequality between blacks and whites in San Francisco.[58] Jackson attended a meeting at the Economic Opportunity Board office, a War on Poverty–funded organization, at which someone started talking about welfare rights. After that meeting she mobilized women in her neighborhood, encouraging them to think of public assistance as a right and not a privilege. At the first gathering of representatives from the state's more than one hundred welfare rights groups in 1968, Jackson was elected president.[59] Having been given a job by a Community Action Program and seeing the benefits of maximum feasible participation in her neighborhood, Jackson applied that approach to child care as well. In her testimony, Jackson spelled out the community control perspective. "Our number one goal," she maintained, "is to employ welfare recipients, not others, in our welfare centers, child care centers, as well as any other centers that involve our mothers' children. I've been sitting here as everyone talked about 'we' as though 'we' in this hearing are ready, but we have to give mothers of those in need rather than mothers that are wealthier the jobs in our day care centers in order to be useful and get off the welfare rolls."[60]

To Jackson, community control of social service programs ensured that those initiatives met the needs of poor people. Poor citizens had founded their own children care program through Community Action Programs; Jackson was less concerned about a child care worker's level of training than whether she came from a neighborhood in need. Women on welfare sought jobs that paid them enough to feed and clothe their families and cover child care while they were at work. Like Mahler and other women in the child care coalition, Jackson recognized that child care was key to keeping women off public assistance. "Right now," she observed, "there are still mothers dropping out of their [job training] programs because of not having child care centers in the communities in which they live."[61] Jackson represented women whose perspective was shaped by race and position near the bottom of the economic ladder, a place not far from that occupied by advocates in CPACC.

Soon after Jackson spoke, Bettie Keesee stepped up to the microphone to represent the California Parents' Association for Children's Centers. In 1968 Keesee, whose daughter had been in the centers for eleven years, followed Ellen Hall as president of CPACC. Keesee, a service clerk at a linen company in Oakland, had struggled to raise her daughter and make ends meet. Described by another mother active in CPACC as "really smart and really hard working," she had become politically savvy during her years in the organization.[62] She struck just the right tone as a passionate mother advocating an expansion of the state's program to include those coming off welfare; at the same time, she reinforced that centers remained essential for low-income workers like herself. "I'm a concerned mother," Keesee began. "The name is not important—perhaps you could call me Mrs. Statistic." Keesee emphasized that not only was she "speaking as one of the 85 percent of parents with children in the centers from one-parent families" but she was also there "to speak for the parent and child who are not as fortunate. . . . I'm here to speak for the waiting child!"[63] Like an earlier generation of child care activists, Keesee viewed her personal child care needs as part of a larger struggle that many mothers like her faced.

What might Jackson and Keesee have said to each other as they sat waiting before or after testifying? Single mothers separated by race and the slimmest of economic margins, they proposed different types of child care for poor families. It is possible that they talked about poor mothers' collective needs. Perhaps Keesee tried to convince Jackson that teachers in the state's child care centers took excellent care of both black and white children. Keesee had advocated alongside black mothers in CPACC and seemed to understand the needs of poor mothers, whether employed or on public assistance. Jackson might have talked to Keesee about organizing an interracial poor people's movement, "because," as she put it, "when you're poor you're all in the same boat."[64] It is equally possible, however, that they might not have exchanged a word.

More sharply divided by the politics of a stigmatized and racialized welfare state than by their actual needs, the child care coalition and welfare rights groups did not always agree on what kinds of services they desired. Yet both supported the Child Care Construction Act of 1968. Jackson and Tillmon preferred a community-controlled program, but with such desperate need for safe, affordable care they welcomed the prospect of new children's centers in poor neighborhoods across the state. In this they resembled the black activists who twenty years earlier had pushed to create the privately funded Avalon Child Care Guild and for state-sponsored care at the same time. Introduced by Senator Mervyn Dymally (D-Los Angeles) and Assemblyman Alan Sieroty (D-Beverly Hills), the Construction Act provided funds to build new child care centers for the first time since World War II. Sieroty, an eager first-term legislator from the west side of Los Angeles, one of the wealthiest districts in the state, had asked Venice, the one impoverished community he represented, what he could do for its neediest residents. He recalled that "there was a lot of disagreement about things. But the one thing they did agree on was child care."[65] Sieroty was also influenced by the powerful women in his district who, two months later, formed Neighbors of Watts, "a group of women motivated towards some measure of narrowing and bridging the social and economic gaps between these two communities"—Beverly Hills and Watts.[66] The group's primary goal was to assist the organization Johnnie Tillmon helped form, ANC Mothers Anonymous of Watts, with the seed money and eventual funding for the child care center they had been trying to create since 1963.[67] To ensure success in the senate, Sieroty partnered with Dymally, elected the state's first black senator in 1966 and a seasoned advocate for child care.

The coalition mobilized quickly around the measure. With overcrowded school districts taking back child care facilities for elementary school classrooms and the increasing number of mothers with children under the age of six in the labor force, both educators and parents understood the pressing need to fund new centers. In San Francisco, Theresa Mahler let her legislators know that without additional state money for operation, the new children's center slated to open in Bayview–Hunters Point, which had been built with city funds, would have to keep its doors closed. She wrote state Senator George Miller (D-Contra Costa) that "this becomes more and more difficult to explain to the many, many parents needing the service."[68]

At first glance it seems surprising that Ronald Reagan, the governor who touted reducing the cost and size of government as a key goal of his administration, signed a bill to allocate $2.8 million in additional funds to children's centers. Knowing Reagan's position on social spending, Mahler and other advocates framed child care as a means of keeping women off of welfare. When Agatha Cohee, a leader in the Directors and Supervisors' Association, wrote to Reagan regarding the importance of centers to the working poor, she openly catered to the governor's conservative views: "You might see it also as a means by which families can help themselves to be financially independent instead of relying upon welfare."[69] When Mahler composed her letter to Caspar Weinberger, who supported the program both when he was in the state legislature and then as the state director of finance, she emphasized the coalition's longstanding argument about self-sufficiency: "No other program served the needs of families of working mothers who are doing everything they can to remain self-supporting and independent, and off the public assistance rolls."[70] Dymally had inserted an amendment to the Child Care Construction Act that allowed California to take advantage of the federal government's Work Incentive Program (WIN) child care funds, which covered 75 percent of costs. The Department of Health and Welfare emphasized the workfare aspects of the measure. The Construction Act would provide child care so parents could, as Reagan emphasized in his inaugural address, turn a "relief check to a paycheck," ultimately "reducing current cost for social benefits for some of these people."[71]

When Reagan signed the Child Care Construction Act he approved the first capital outlay for the program in twenty-five years. In all, the state built twenty new centers. The Venice School District, which inspired Sieroty's legislation, submitted plans for a children's center to serve 125 children.[72] In the early summer of 1969, the San Francisco Children's Center Parents' Association held a special program celebrating the opening of the first of two new centers in Bayview–Hunters Point, the Burnett Children's Center. Many leaders of the parents' association attended the ceremony, including Fay Love, Bettie Keesee, and Willie Mae Addison, who flew up from southern California. They invited new parents and members of the community. Perhaps Espanola Jackson was in attendance.[73] Under the aegis of the Department of Education, the center served seventy-five children in one of San Francisco's neediest communities.[74]

Child Care and the Women's Movement

While black and white poor mothers organized in CPACC and around welfare rights, a more visible women's movement developed among predominantly the white middle class. In 1966 the National Organization for Women (NOW) emerged out of frustration over the government's unwillingness to enforce Title VII of the 1964 Civil Rights Act, which made discrimination by sex as well as by race illegal. Formed by Betty Friedan, author of *The Feminine Mystique,* and other leaders of state and national commissions on the status of women, NOW spelled out its main goals as "to take action to bring women into full participation in the mainstream of American society now, assuming all the privileges and responsibilities thereof in truly equal partnership with men."[75] With seasoned women's rights, labor feminists, and a few black women at its helm, NOW quickly moved to the forefront of the struggle for women's equality.

From its founding, NOW identified universal child care as one of its primary goals. The organization's original statement of purpose advocated for "a national network of child-care centers and other social innovations to enable more women to work while raising a family." For members of NOW, child care would relieve women of the sole responsibility for childrearing. They could enter the workforce and simultaneously begin sharing parenting responsibilities with men, and child care centers would eventually be seen as an essential public service, similar to public schools.[76] Despite its demand for universal child care, however, NOW devoted the bulk of its energies to winning abortion rights and advancing the Equal Rights Amendment.[77] It did not assume a leadership role in federal or state legislative campaigns. Indeed, the head of National Task Force on Child Care bemoaned the fact that women in her own NOW chapter were more interested in employment discrimination and pay equity than in child care.[78] As Aileen Hernandez, president of NOW in 1970, remembers it, "In the very early days of NOW, there were some excellent 'papers' on a variety of subjects and one of them was on child care. My impression from those days was that while NOW identified child care as an issue, it never became a real national priority, although some local chapters took it on."[79]

At the same time, younger women in major cities formed women's liberation groups. Unlike NOW, which stressed legal and political equality, they focused primarily on equality in the private realm. The groups, as Sara Evans writes, "had little use for formal politics or detailed policy discussions for the first year or two."[80] These predominantly white women, many of whom had been active in civil rights, antiwar, and New Left organizations, realized that as they worked for the liberation of others they needed to address inequalities they personally experienced that were based on sex. They formed consciousness-raising groups and criticized women's roles in the family much more readily than the President's Commission on the Status of Women or NOW had done. Espousing democratic principles and practices in much the same way that black women advocates of community control did, many groups focused on self-help and building alternative institutions rather than legislative solutions. San Francisco Women's Liberation, a feminist coalition, held a mass meeting in May 1970 and began distributing a newsletter soon thereafter. By the end of the year, the publication had 1,400 subscribers. The newsletter raised the topic of child care but did not highlight it as an issue for immediate action. The issue was suggested as a future workshop topic as the newsletter reported on parents working to establish a center at San Francisco State College and proposed a babysitting exchange to meet members' immediate child care needs.[81] In short, an affordable, quality public child care program did not hold the same urgency for these young, single women as it did for the working poor and women on welfare.

NOW chapters were established in both San Francisco and Los Angeles by 1967. Although local chapters developed their own priorities, funding child care for the working poor did not make the top of their lists. San Francisco NOW did not have a contact person for child care issues until late 1969 and did not establish a child care committee until June 1970. In 1971, San Francisco NOW finally identified child care as one of the chapter's three top priorities, but by then the children's centers had already faced their most serious challenges. It is equally unfortunate that the policies and initiatives on which NOW concentrated did not address poor women's needs. On the national level as well, NOW members interested in the issues surrounding poverty had a difficult time rallying the membership to the cause.[82] The women who joined San Francisco NOW seemed to have no idea that many women in their own city had been working for child care for more than twenty-five years. The chapter committed to providing child care for membership at meetings and described doing so as a step toward "getting the ball rolling for free day care centers everywhere." Although they began to organize a child care committee and listed it as a major goal of the chapter in 1971 there is no evidence that the NOW membership actually took action on a state level before 1973.[83]

By the early 1970s, however, NOW and other women's movement organizations had begun conversations with the child care coalition. The evidence suggests that during CPACC's final years, working-class parents made an effort to collaborate with women in NOW. For example, *The Covenant,* the CPACC newsletter that parents began publishing in February 1972, included information on the National Organization for Women in a section on organizations working toward similar goals. CPACC notified its membership that "COVENANT draws your attention to the activities within this group devoted solely to legislation affecting children, child care centers, and single parents" and urged parents to look past the "flamboyant if not downright 'nasty' newspaper articles" about NOW.[84] Lynne Monti, active in both movements, was the driving force behind CPACC's move to connect with the women's movement.

Just as the women's movement gained momentum in 1965, twenty-one year-old Monti drove back to San Francisco in her Nash Rambler packed with her possessions and her two young children after deciding to separate from her husband. Confident she had made the right decision but deeply concerned about how she would support her family, Monti began searching for a well-paying job that allowed her to "make as much money as a man." She had no job skills; "the only thing, honestly, I knew how to do was nothing."[85] That summer, however, Monti was one of two women accepted into Safeway's grocery checker training program. With a job lined up, she began the search for affordable care for her children. Eventually, she found her way to the San Francisco Unified School District's Francis Scott Key Children's Center. Monti faced more than just the nine-to-five worker's dilemma. As a grocery checker, she often had to work nights and weekends, making it necessary to cobble care at state centers with more expensive and less reliable in-home care.

Born to Thomas Hicks Beeson Jr. and Viola Ana Christina Hansen Beeson on July 25, 1943, activism was Monti's heritage despite her initial resistance to it. Her grandfather was a socialist who had joined the farm holiday movement in Madison County, Nebraska, during the Great Depression. The Farm Holiday Association often intimidated potential buyers at farms repossessed by banks and put up for auction by staging "penny auctions" so association members could purchase farms for a few dollars at most and return them to their original owners.[86] Monti's mother, Viola Beeson, "was sort of raised in politics and passionate about it." She had a sporadic relationship with the Communist Party and in 1946 ran for the Omaha School Board on a child care and integration platform and with strong support from the black community. She did not, however, win. That same year she also traveled with three-year-old Lynne to Washington, D.C., as part of a grassroots effort by women from across the nation to demand the continuation of price controls after the end of the war.[87] In the early 1950s she headed up the Ethel and Julius Rosenberg Defense Committee in Omaha. Eventually, the Beeson family fled Nebraska in 1953 because of Viola's political activities. They settled in San Francisco and initially lived in a predominantly African American neighborhood where Monti was one of only two white students in her class. We "moved to the Western Addition, near the Fillmore," she recalls. Her mother "really did it because I think philosophically her identification with the oppressed was so great that she wanted to live in the ghetto."[88]

Rebellious and independent as a young woman, with a mother who worked long hours, Beeson navigated the city without much supervision. She met her future husband, Thomas Monti, in Mountain Lake Park when she was only thirteen, and the two youngsters bonded through their love of the outdoors. They had dated for three years when Beeson became pregnant during her senior year in high school. She told her sister, and they discussed abortion, but the couple decided to marry and have the baby. They were too young to marry without parental consent, so, Monti recalls, "we falsified our IDs . . . and got married the next day at City Hall in San Francisco at seventeen." After their daughter, Lisa, was born in 1961, the Montis moved to Nebraska, to a farm close to where Lynne had spent her childhood. They tried farming for a year, and then Thomas enrolled at the University of Oklahoma. By that point Beeson "was really wildly unhappily married." After confronting her husband about his extramarital affairs she decided that she needed to leave, wrote him a note, and headed to California with their two children.[89]

After securing employment and child care, Monti joined her center's parents group. Bold, straightforward, and driven by a strong sense of social justice, she quickly developed into one of the San Francisco parents' association's key activists. "The people who emerged as leaders in the parents' association," she reflects, "were very confident, probably hard-working, capable, upwardly mobile, leadership, strong leadership. You know, you had to want to do it. They couldn't make you do it. You can go to a meeting and be quiet, but . . . the people who emerged were very sophisticated, outspoken, capable people." Monti served as the organization's legislative advocate starting in 1969, held numerous other positions, and was elected president of CPACC in 1971. Like many mothers before her, she was mentored by Theresa Mahler, who taught her how to navigate the legislature, conduct herself as a lobbyist, and inspire and motivate other parents. She used these skills both in CPACC and for other organizations and causes related to child care.

Monti traversed between many worlds in the late 1960s: her job as a grocery checker, her life as a student at San Francisco City College, and her child care activism as well as her responsibilities for two young children. At City College, she and other mothers pushed the administration to establish a child care center. In order to pursue her college degree, Monti decided to go on welfare. When asked about that experience she responded, "Being on welfare—I was already poor. But to have time and to be twenty-seven years old and to go to school . . . I just thought I'd found heaven. I had more time with my kids. I could study. I had more flex-

Figure 6. Lynne Monti, president of the Parents' Association for Children's Centers, addresses a child care protest meeting held at the First Unitarian Church in San Francisco, May 13, 1971. (Fang family *San Francisco Examiner* photograph archive negative files, BANC PIC 2006.029:42520.04—NEG, the Bancroft Library, University of California, Berkeley)

ibility in my schedule. They were happier. . . . I just felt so lucky. I also happened to have a social worker that was very supportive of me and really believed that women should get an education."[90] That positive experience may well have had something to do with skin color; as a white woman, Monti did not face the same negative stereotypes from caseworkers that black mothers did. By the late 1960s some caseworkers could not have helped internalizing what they had been told about black welfare mothers being immoral, irresponsible, and undeserving of financial assistance.[91] Yet in many ways Monti's situation resembled that of black single mothers on welfare who had children while married and then either left or were abandoned by husbands. Unfortunately for black women in a position similar to Monti's, many white people were predisposed to see them in a one-dimensional fashion, as women who had illegitimate children, bore additional children to increase welfare checks, and lacked the desire to work.

Soon Monti joined the rapidly expanding women's movement in the Bay Area. As she describes her feminist viewpoint, "I think I've always been a feminist, I mean, in my heart of hearts. I am an independent person. . . . My grandmother drove tractors; she liked to be outdoors. I was raised by a single parent and my mother very much was a feminist long before it was an ideology." Monti's feminist child care activism won her a place on the advisory board of the state Commission on the Status of Women, and in 1971 she attended her first meeting of the Bay Area Women's Coalition. Formed in 1969 by representatives of more than thirty women's organizations, ranging from Women's Liberation to the AAUW and NOW to the National Negro Business and Professional Women, they agreed on nine key issues for the coalition to address and placed "developing government sponsored child care" first on the agenda.[92] Monti eventually chaired the child care committee for the coalition. She described the coalition of educated, professional women and their tacit support of child care:

> Although for a long time . . . I couldn't quite figure [it] out, I've reflected on . . . why child care didn't seem to be more embraced as a feminist issue. I think the reason was that they were very supportive. I participated all the time, went to all the meetings, was a regular member, but I was the child care person. If I brought an issue, they'd pass it. They trusted me. . . . They were supportive of that. But they weren't part of the childcare movement. They really were not part of the child care community. They were supportive of it, but in general, at least in San Francisco, . . . they tried to break through the glass ceiling in professorships and law offices, and affirmative action and businesses, in government jobs. Most of them, many of them, did not have children and it wasn't a gut issue for them in the same way. Many of them, frankly, were better educated . . . not working class, not poor women. . . . If you asked them to do anything, they'd do it. [But child care] wasn't their issue.[93]

Under the best of circumstances the differing needs of middle-class feminists and poor working women remained a barrier to a unified women's movement that could rally around universal child care. Individuals like Monti, especially those rooted in feminism and the left politically, were a bridge between the two movements.

Tying Child Care to Welfare

Monti was pulled into child care organizing for CPACC. She observes that "it was a big deal to go lobbying. . . . it's hard when you work all day and sometimes even two jobs and then you try to do this and you still have kids and we didn't ever really have any staff support." Monti's legislative baptism took place during one of the biggest challenges the child care coalition had faced since the centers had become permanent in 1957: mobilizing against legislation to move the children's centers into the Office of Compensatory Education.

In the spring of 1970, Jerry Lewis, a Republican assemblyman representing San Bernardino, introduced AB 750 with the "legislative intent that maximum federal reimbursement be obtained" for child care.[94] AB 750 would consolidate all preschool, custodial day care, and children's centers under the state Office of Compensatory Education. Simultaneously, in anticipation of the new federal welfare funds and at Governor Reagan's suggestion, the State Department of Finance recommended a $4 million cut in children's center funding. Since 1965 children's centers had been permitted to enroll children of welfare recipients, but the law did not require them to do so. This bill directed the Department of Education (DOE) and the Department of Social Welfare (DSW) to enter into a contract whereby federal child care funds for welfare recipients would be paid by the DSW and the DOE would continue to oversee the state's preschool programs. Most educators and parents viewed Lewis's bill as fundamentally altering the "administration, eligibility, and the funding of the Children's Centers."[95] For the directors and mothers, the proposed transfer represented a move away from education as a priority toward welfare-oriented goals. Sharon Godske maintained that this administrative shift would mistakenly lump the families with children enrolled in the centers with "disadvantaged" families. Godske contended, "While our children may be economically deprived, they are not culturally deprived and in need of the special help offered by any of the Compensatory Education programs."[96]

For Theresa Mahler, the changes represented a step toward reliance on federal funds, a threat to local control, and a move away from supporting the employed single mothers whom the centers had been serving since the 1950s. Mahler saw placing the children's centers under compensatory education as formalizing the public's association of child care with antipoverty programs such as Head Start and community centers.[97] Docia Zavitkovsky, whose perspective was also shaped by having lived through the federal government's cuts to Lanham Act funds, said, "My personal feeling is that if you can possibly operate a quality day care program without federal funds, don't ask for trouble by getting them."[98] Godske agreed, pointing to recent cutbacks in Head Start funding.[99] As Monti recalls, "There were really two legitimate positions about accepting or not accepting federal funds." Theresa Mahler "was against federal funds because she had seen . . . what had happened when federal funds were cut off overnight to the state of California and child care centers were closed overnight." Mahler also feared a loss of "control over the quality of the program."[100] Others favored taking more child care funds, no matter where they originated, in order to expand the service to more families.

AB 750 exposed a divergence of opinion among members of the child care coalition as well as their liberal supporters in the legislature. A number of educators and policymakers from southern California held a different view from that of Mahler and CPACC. For those in Los Angeles who had witnessed the Watts riots and the problems of urban poverty firsthand, "the possibility for huge expansion" of child care trumped keeping the centers funded by money from Sacramento. Los Angeles reported twelve thousand children on waiting lists every year from 1968 through 1970.[101] In its report on the Watts riots, the Los Angeles Police, Fire, and Civil Defense Committee noted that "the need for child care centers was one of the most frequently expressed needs of the community as heard by this Committee."[102] Dorothy Snyder, the recently appointed director of children's centers for Los Angeles City Schools, understood the concerns voiced by opponents but supported AB 750 because of the heavy demand and long waiting lists in her district.

Mahler rallied the Northern California Directors and Supervisors as well as the parents' associations to oppose this legislation. A pamphlet went out to parents with the headline *Children's Centers Are in Jeopardy*. The flyer implored parents, teachers, and friends of the program to write to their legislators and the governor and plead with others in the community to do the same: "TIME IS OF THE ESSENCE—WRITE NOW!!!" Editorials appeared in the *San Francisco Chronicle* and the *Sacramento Bee* maintaining that "Children's Centers Should Not Be Cut" because they "have proved themselves from the economic standpoint. They also have permitted families to be self-supporting without the stigma of accepting welfare. A cut and trim pen in this area is not good economics nor is it good humanity."[103]

The Northern and Southern California Sections of the CPACC converged in Sacramento to encourage members of the assembly and senate to vote against AB 750, and both Fay Love and Lynne Monti remember vividly Mahler's rallying cries to incite parents to walk the legislature's halls or attend an upcoming hearing. Thinking back fondly, Love describes the parents' activities:

When [the] legislature was in session and according to how many bills were introduced, sometimes [Lynne and I] went twice a week. Sometimes we went every
week for weeks. . . . Ms. Mahler would call me at three o'clock in the morning if
she found out something that she thought we should [know]. Because she knew
at the time what I was doing, I could get away a little bit better than others, you
know. And especially she knew when I was in the post office, if it was my off
day. My off day belonged to Theresa Mahler. . . . Because she knew I had a good
friend who could pick up the girls for me.[104]

Love, Monti, and anyone else they could rally piled into Monti's old Volkswagen
and drove the eighty-plus miles from San Francisco to Sacramento, leading
a caravan of two or three cars full of parents. The coalition's scanty financial
resources coupled with the mothers' straightened circumstances to make lobbying a challenge. Monti struggled to finding the proper attire. As she says,
"When I went up [to Sacramento] the only two kinds of clothes that I had at that
time were grocery checking clothes and what I called my Cinderella clothes.
My mother had made me the most exquisite evening clothes . . . my hot pink
French *peau de soie* mini skirt and matching coat. And that's what I wore to
Sacramento!"[105] Each parent was assigned to a legislator and given marching
orders. Lawmakers had become accustomed to the invasion. Mervyn Dymally
would exclaim, "Look! Here comes Theresa and all of her gang" when coalition
lobbyists entered a hearing room.[106] Parents from CPACC fanned out across
the capitol to try to solidify support and attempt to change the minds of those
who favored the bill.

Such tactics had little impact on legislators. Neither Republicans nor Democrats understood the coalition's objections to the bill, given that it allowed California to provide child care for a larger constituency. AB 750 passed both houses
of the legislature by an overwhelming margin. When it landed on Governor
Reagan's desk, many in his cabinet recommended that he veto the measure.
He seemed swayed, however, by the bill's main sponsor, Assemblyman Jerry
Lewis, who pointed out that "Republicans have long talked about the need for
efficiency in government. We have demanded that something be done about
cracking the welfare cycle. AB 750 will be a significant step in our effort to accomplish both of these objectives."[107] Reagan signed the bill into law on September 20, 1970, officially transferring the administration of children's centers
to the Office of Compensatory Education and, in effect, making public child
care a workfare program.

The final bill did include some compromise provisions pushed through by
child care advocates and their legislative supporters. The modifications intended
to ensure that the centers' new structure, priorities, and focus on AFDC mothers should not eliminate "families of working mothers who receive no welfare
assistance—the families for which the service was instituted so many years

ago."[108] Fiscal concerns, however, soon supplanted this provision. By October 1971, children's centers directors and supervisors began complaining about limits on attendance for children of the working poor who did not qualify under federal welfare-related funds. The DOE explained these limitations as based on budgetary concerns and the mandate to "maximize federal participation" in the program. Supervisors also reported that some parents refused to be certified eligible for child care by the welfare department because they regarded certification as an invasion of their privacy. The working poor, whose children were already in children's centers, resented having to be classified as "as former or potential recipients" by a welfare caseworker.[109] It was akin to being stamped with the stigma of welfare.

AB 750 had a very personal impact on the child care coalition, displacing John Weber, the statewide children's center supervisor since 1946, and leading to the retirement of Theresa Mahler. Reagan signed AB 750 into law while Weber was on a two-week vacation in Mexico. When he returned, all of his files and his entire office had been moved into the Office of Compensatory Education and placed under the control of Jeanada Nolan, chief of the Bureau of Compensatory Educational Programs. Nolan, a former social worker and director of the Sacramento Parent Participation Preschools, had been hired by the DOE when the Bureau of Compensatory Education was established in 1965. Nolan had faced her own struggles with finding child care as a single mother in Sacramento. As she recalled, "I used to take [my son] by streetcar out to Sutterville to the Children's Home and leave him and then take a streetcar down to work by eight o'clock in the morning. That's not easy. And then [back] again at night." With a degree in social work from Fresno State and a master's in early childhood education, Nolan had excellent credentials for the job. She knew, however, that those in the child care coalition who had worked with John Weber over the years would not welcome her presence. Nolan remembers, "This was a very painful time for a lot of people. I think it was probably less painful for me than for John. It was terrible for John. I know that Docia and Theresa were completely supportive of John. They probably felt terrible about it. Who's this upstart? Me. I mean, John didn't lose anything; he just didn't get the promotion that he would have liked, which would have been the Chief of the Bureau. His co-workers saw him as the logical person, and he wasn't selected and I was. Needless to say, that didn't make it easy for me to be there."[110] Weber wrote to Lawrence Arnstein, "I will admit this all came as a severe shock to me after having served as children's center supervisor for the past twenty-four years."[111] Weber remained with the Department of Education for a few more years as the director of child care food service and then quietly settled into retirement earlier than he would have liked.

The passage of AB 750 was also a devastating blow for Theresa Mahler. Reliance on federal funds and prioritizing welfare over education signified the destruction of the child care vision Mahler and the child care coalition had fought so hard to preserve. By 1971 she had been supervisor of the San Francisco centers for more than twenty years and had devoted her free time to lobbying legislators in Sacramento and mobilizing educators and parents closer to home. She retired the next summer.[112] Many in the city and across the state saw this as a great loss for California's poor families. Letters and cards poured into Mahler's office. Lorna Logan, a head teacher at a San Francisco center, captured the sentiments of teachers and parents. "I will always remember our long struggle together," she wrote, "and I shall always be grateful to you that you wouldn't give up, so I was helped not to give up either! But the community owes so much to you in the many ways you have helped to bring child care to its poor families."[113] The coalition lost its longtime leader.

The legislation marked a substantial shift in the centers' clientele. Children benefited from the expansion; enrollment rose from approximately 17,300 in 1969 to 23,300 by June 1971. In the six years since the Social Security Amendments of 1967, however, the program was transformed from a service for the working poor to a welfare provision. In April 1968 AFDC families made up 14 percent of children in the state's centers; by 1973, current, former, or potential AFDC recipients made up 87 percent.[114] Many single working mothers no longer qualified. Sharon Godske understood that access to the children's centers had provided her family with opportunities that they would not have had otherwise. Placing their children in the center gave the Godskes "peace of mind to go on and do what we had to do and know that the kids were being taken care of and not costing us an arm and a leg. . . . I don't know that we would have made it without going on some sort of public assistance. . . . There's no way we would have been able to do it."[115]

Across the nation, the liberal architects of the War on Poverty overlooked the working poor. Policymakers failed to realize that requirements they placed on child care would alter local programs and favor mothers on public assistance over those with low-wage jobs and young children. White, middle-class feminists in California overlooked poor working mothers as well. They focused efforts on alternative child-rearing methods and "universal child care goals," not recognizing a program and coalition of activists operating in their backyard. In California, the option of being a poor, working mother without being subjected to scrutiny by a welfare caseworker disappeared. Child care advocates nationwide suffered crushing defeat when Richard Nixon vetoed the Comprehensive Child Development Act in December 1971, which would have provided care on a sliding scale for any family that needed it.

Conclusion

On November 13, 1971, the California Parents' Association for Children's Centers (CPACC) held its twenty-third annual conference in San Francisco. It was CPACC's first meeting since AB 750 had "change[d] the thrust" of the children's center program and since the retirements of John Weber and Theresa Mahler. The organization struggled to readjust to the new political landscape, the loss of its experienced leaders and allies, and a changing clientele. As it had for decades, the parents' association attracted enthusiastic people who understood the importance of the children's centers and wanted to mobilize mothers to have a strong political voice. Ironically, just as the parents' association was struggling to keep the membership engaged and active, it received statewide recognition as a vital preschool interest group. A week after the annual convention, CPACC President Lynne Monti received an invitation from the governor's office to nominate three parents to serve on the recently established statewide Advisory Committee of Preschool Educational Programs. State political leaders had watched what one observer described in 1952 as a "wacky, amateur parent pressure group" sustain diligent political action for child care for more than twenty-five years and assumed it would continued to do so.[1]

As the small cohort of parent leaders tried to reinvigorate the organization at the convention, they searched for improved methods to communicate with members and mobilize them. The presentation on motivation was presented by Farida Melendy, twenty-nine and a single mother of three, who had just been elected president of the Parents' Association of the Lincoln Child Development Center in Santa Monica as well as a statewide officer. She described the Lincoln Center's success in recruiting active parents over the past year and reported on strategies that worked. She was also aware of the movement's history: "When we understand the beginnings of the children's centers in the war years and learn how interested parent groups were able to make their voices heard in Sacramento so their centers were able to receive funding and continue in operation and also to grow in number, we can see our place in a long chain of parents and thus are able to feel the responsibility of our position at this time."[2] Melendy most likely appreciated the program's history because the Santa Monica centers were still under the direction of Docia Zavitkovsky, a child care director who had been working alongside parents since World War II and imparted to this new generation of parents her knowledge of successful strategies: supplying babysitting at parent meetings, holding meetings after work and providing dinner, and assigning parents the responsibility to train newer participants and help them become active members.[3]

Lynne Monti, too, was determined to rejuvenate the statewide parents' group. Having gained experience and a reputation as legislative advocate for the previous two years, in November 1971 Monti became CPACC president. When she took the helm Monti knew the organization needed to rebuild. Soon after assuming office, she wrote to Assemblywoman Yvonne Braithwaite, seeking assistance and advice. "The organization is weak, but the potential for educating large numbers of women is great," she explained. "We are a group of twenty thousand women and a few men who are primarily single parent low-income people struggling to make ends meet."[4] Monti met with Jeanada Nolan, who oversaw the children's centers and served as bureau chief for Preschool Education Programs, and corresponded with the president of the California Children's Centers Directors' and Supervisors' Association about the parents' desire for "having closer relations with administrators."[5] Finally, she strategized with many CPACC executive board members. In a letter to David Michaelis, an executive board member and leader in the Long Beach parents' group, she declared, "I am certain we will all be able to work together and put the organization on the map."[6] Well trained by Theresa Mahler in the legislative process and acutely aware of CPACC's importance to preserving child care for poor single mothers, Monti did everything she could in northern California and across the state to keep the organization viable.

Despite the best efforts of Melendy, Monti, and other dedicated parents, however, the statewide parents' association disappeared from the political landscape sometime in 1972.[7] Individual parents and local parents' groups remained active, but by the time a crisis over federal child care funds ensued in 1973, parents were still speaking out but no longer as members of CPACC. How did this happen? From historical evidence it seems that parents demonstrated and organized as part of citywide efforts but not statewide. On many policy issues they had to appeal to Washington, D.C., which was not a brief commute. Moreover, the coalition that had so long sustained activists had lost some of the keys to its success: long-term leadership among parents and educators, allies in the state

Department of Education, and a seasoned activist to help train and strategize with new generations of parents. Organizing now fell solely on single mothers struggling to make ends meet, raise their children, and be politically active. Keeping their efforts local may have been easier.

The California Parents' Association was not active to oppose the new federal welfare regulations that reportedly would cut 40 to 50 percent of children from government-sponsored child care centers, but local parents groups, individual mothers, and educators protested and spoke out against the proposal. The formal organization had disappeared, but the wellspring of the child care movement remained consistent and strong. Mothers in 1973 emulated many tactics used by parents and educators over the previous three decades, suggesting that social learning continued to occur in the centers themselves. On March 16, the *Los Angeles Times* featured a story on a gathering of single mothers who planned to protest against the federal cuts that coming Saturday in McArthur Park. Thirteen women showed up at Marion Schneider's apartment. All were divorced, many had been on welfare, all were workers, and most chaired the parents' groups at their child care centers. As the reporter put it, "They were about to become, for the first time in most of their lives, out-and-out, noisy, demanding, activists."[8] Lynne [Monti] Beeson describes similar efforts by San Francisco parents to organize a march from Union Square to the Civic Center in front of the federal regional office buildings.[9]

In addition to staging protests in San Francisco and Los Angeles, parents across the state bombarded U.S senators and House members with constituent mail, and, as in the past, they composed thoughtful, individual letters. Martha Campbell, special assistant to Senator John Tunney, told the *Los Angeles Times*, "This isn't an organized form-letter campaign, these are just little people who are sitting down writing letters." Ron Dellums (D-California) received more than a thousand letters, most of them from mothers, about the impact of proposed federal welfare regulations on California's child care and preschool programs. One correspondent asked what by then had become a twenty-eight-year-old question: "Will you please tell me as a mother and sole support to my family, what am I going to do if the day care centers are discontinued?" She further informed Dellums, "I have not been on welfare for some months . . . I get no support from parents, ex-husband or any other source. Now, you tell us (mothers that are now using the centers) what the hell are we to do?"[10] The letter represents one of thousands that landed in the offices of Dellums and other members of California's congressional delegation as well as the state's two U.S. senators, Governor Ronald Reagan, and other public officials.[11] In fact, a legislative assistant to Representative Robert Leggett (D-Vallejo) proclaimed, "We have mounds and mounds of mail. . . . It's as heavy—if not heavier than the mail we received in December about the U.S. bombing of North Vietnam."[12]

This letter-writing campaign marked the second time that California women had mobilized to save child care services threatened by federal funding cuts, the first time being at the end of World War II. In both cases the child care coalition convinced California to fund the state's centers—if and when the federal government withdrew its support. After nationwide protests in March 1973 the federal government postponed indefinitely the proposed changes in federal child care regulations, and thus the state avoided having to provide additional funds. Although the statewide association no longer existed, the tactics and methods its members had used lived on in children's centers and parents' councils. The written, heartfelt pleas for child care made by working mothers and their supporters reveal a striking continuity between arguments for child care in the 1940s and those in the 1970s. Child care needs, as defined by these working-class women, changed little despite dramatic changes in the political climate—from the possibility immediately after World War II to the repressive cold war era that began in the late 1940s to the War on Poverty and the modern women's movement in the 1970s. What remained a constant was that working mothers demanded safe and affordable care for their children.

How, then, should we view this story of women's grassroots efforts for child care in California? Some might consider a story that ends with the disbanding of an effective statewide organization and another threatened reduction in child care services available to the working poor as a depressing and dismal end to a postwar movement. Although this is a story with its share of disappointments, it is also one filled with successes. First, the women activists who emerged after the war sustained a movement that lasted and endured for as long as the most prominent postwar social issue, civil rights. Driven by the desire to improve their lives and those of other women in a similar position, California's low-income working mothers and educators saved public child care. The services the coalition preserved were only for a small percentage of California's working families, mostly female-headed households, but theirs is an inspiring story about the importance of women's activism to public policies. Such efforts kept public child care alive in California as it vanished across the nation, leaving a one-of-a-kind program between World War II and the War on Poverty. Given the relative powerlessness of rank-and-file single mothers and child care teachers as well as their political inexperience and turnover, the fact they sustained the movement for more than twenty-five years is remarkable. Moreover, the cross-class, cross-race coalition emerged from shared necessity. For many, child care meant the economic survival of their family and their ability to work and care for their children. The coalition believed that by taking action it was helping preserve a program that "was a leg up for those of us who were working and who were trying to stay off of welfare and not have any government subsidization and whatever just do it on your own. And it was a great thing because you could afford it and still have quality care and education."[13] Unfortunately, such care still eludes many of America's families.

While California's child care centers provided women with a valuable service, they also produced a few generations of active democratic subjects, women who realized a need beyond their own and took political action. For some, activism was short-lived, but for others, such as Mary Young, Lynne Monti, and Fay Love, it lasted well beyond their children's years in the children's centers. In 2006 Fay [Love] Williams shared her reasons for staying involved as long as she did. She was "just hoping that I could help somebody else's child. You know I thought if I just stayed around then that would maybe show this parent that it's not so bad. You know and when you are doing something for your children, nothing is too much. And I think it did help some. I think it did help some."[14]

Whether for a year or two or a decade, women who participated in the movement learned how to express their political rights. Ellen Hall Mitchell recalled on a warm February afternoon in 2006 that she gained understanding of why it is important for women to have a political voice. "What I learned about politics: only that you basically, if you wanted something done, you definitely had to have somebody up there in Sacramento that was in favor of what you wanted done. . . . But what I learned about politics only that you know, you got to speak up. That's it!"[15] Some of the women were leftists or members of labor unions but for most, joining parents' councils or the statewide association was their first foray into the world of politics. The modern women's movement was in part about giving women a political voice that would allow them to influence legislators, governors, and others with political power, so this movement, and others like it, must be included in that history for the contributions of the parents' organization and the democratic subjects and women leaders it created.

Furthermore, the child care movement empowered those who participated in it. The movement allowed Mary Young to discover a talent for lobbying that she did not know she possessed. When asked in 1998 what she was most proud of, she replied, "Well, I suppose getting the parent groups organized. . . . That's how they campaigned to get me elected to the parent group presidency. I fought it all the way!" When asked why she resisted, she responded, "I just never thought I had it in me to do. And like I said, Mrs. Mahler drew me out."[16] Young went from a reticent leader to the CPACC's legislative authority for fifteen years. For Lynne [Monti] Beeson, participation in CPACC launched her career as advocate for children and child care. It meant, she recalled, "Everything. Everything. I mean it was my launching pad and one thing was a springboard to something else. It's so clear you know. From my activities in the parents' group to my involvement in citywide and statewide [child care struggles] and even national political things, to being sought out and asked to apply for a job further in child care. So you know, it's been a blessing in the sense that it took me through different stages in my life."[17] She continued to work as an advocate for child care long after her stint with CPACC, working for Model Cities Program (part of Lyndon Johnson's War on Poverty) and in the San Francisco Mayor's Office for Child Care. She remains passionate about the issue to this day.

These women did not succeed in providing child care for all of California's families, but their achievements and the program they preserved should be measured from the perspective of the activists themselves. As I asked these women what they valued most during their participation in this grassroots movement, or in the case of Young and Mahler when I asked their daughters, where some might see failure, the participants saw triumph. Long-time child care director and statewide advocate Winona Sample recalled, "I think my work with early days of child care was important, probably very important. Not very many people were doing it [child care] at the time and I think it did make a difference and that's what I like to do."[18] Sample continued advocating for child care and early childhood education working as a Head Start director and with migrant children in the late 1960s and early 1970s as well as working as an assistant to the Director of the state Office of Child Development. She later served as Chief of Indian Health Services for the state of California.

By the time I wanted to ask a similar question of Mary Young in 2005, she had already begun to suffer from dementia. When I asked Mary's daughter what her mother would want history to remember about her work with CPACC, she told me, "Probably the fact that they managed to keep them going. She helped a lot in keeping them going for as long as they did. I think she'd probably be proud of that. Because they were ready to fold after World War II. They kept them going for like another twenty, twenty-five years."[19] Long-time educator and advocate, Theresa Mahler's daughter, Jeanne Miller, said that her mother was most proud of "getting these centers accepted as a real physical part of the Board of Education in the San Francisco Unified School District, and not just some welfare thing that was set up for poor working mothers. That was the crux of what she believed in: that these centers belonged as part of education. That was it. If you wanted to put that on her gravestone, that would have been it."[20] Finally, when I asked Winona Sample what she valued most about the people she worked with during the child care battles, she responded, "I think that they were a wonderfully, intelligent, competent, caring group of people committed to doing the job that they wanted done. They were so committed that nothing else seemed to get in the way at the time. You know it was years . . . It wasn't a flash in the pan."[21]

Notes

Introduction

1. Maurine Jorgensen to Earl Warren, Jan. 13, 1947, Governor's Files, Child Care, 1947, Earl Warren Papers, California State Archives, Sacramento.

2. I am drawing on what Nancy Fraser terms the "politics of need interpretation." The battle for child care in California illustrates how ordinary women with children in the state's child care centers took their own definitions of their day care needs and directly challenged the interpretations of women's needs held by policymakers. Fraser, *Unruly Practices*, 144–60; Fraser, "Struggle over Needs," 199–225.

3. The term *underclass* emerged during the early 1960s and usually referred to those who could not sustain work and perpetually lived in poverty. Most used the term to describe the undeserving poor, who were blamed for their poverty and seen as not worthy of government assistance. Katz, "The Urban 'Underclass' as a Metaphor for Social Transformation," 3–24; Katz, *The Undeserving Poor*.

4. All the interviews conducted for this study, and Mary Young's Papers, can be found in the collections at the Center for Oral and Public History, California State University, Fullerton.

5. In 1965 the CPACC became the California Parents' Association for Children's Centers.

6. The working poor avoided (for the most part) the negative connotations that came along with being in the underclass. Consequently, the state deemed social services for the working poor, such as child care, as deserving while programs like ADC as undeserving. On a woman's wage as a "symbol of family degradation," see Kessler-Harris, *A Woman's Wage*, 3.

7. Gilmore, *Gender and Jim Crow*, 1. In her discussion of women's role in Atlanta's massive voting rights campaign in 1946, Kathryn Nasstrom makes a similar point about only evaluating an event's success by its result. With the election of black city officials in Atlanta in the early 1950s, the campaign's success became measured in terms of the political leadership of black men, thus erasing from memory the vibrant and crucial role

of women in the campaign. Nasstrom's research restores women's central role. Nasstrom, "Down to Now," 113–44.

8. Virginia Rose, interview with author, May 28, 1998, Oakland, Calif. On African American women in Philadelphia looking to local public institutions to improve the lives and future of their families, see Levenstein, *A Movement without Marches.*

9. For other examples of women using conservative arguments to achieve progressive ends, see Hall, *Revolt against Chivalry;* Higginbotham, *Righteous Discontent;* Swerdlow, *Women Strike for Peace;* and White, *Too Heavy a Load.*

10. These women were practicing what Holloway Sparks has termed dissident citizenship. This type of activism and direct challenge to the dominant publics, Sparks maintains, is essential to the democratic process. Sparks, "Dissident Citizenship: Democratic Theory, Political Courage, and Activist Women," 75; Sparks, "Dissident Citizenship: Lessons on Democracy and Political Courage."

11. These educators were most likely drawn to California for its large number of nursery schools. By 1930, close to a third of the nation's nursery schools were in California. In addition, the state had laboratory nursery schools at some of its major colleges and universities: the University of California at Los Angeles, Mills College, and the University of California at Berkeley. Christianson, Rogers, and Ludlum, *The Nursery School,* 264–68; Stewart, "Preschools and Politics," 47–55.

12. Reese, "Maternalism and Political Mobilization," 566–89.

13. For the war's impact on California, see Johnson, *The Second Gold Rush;* Lotchin, *The Bad City in the Good War;* Lotchin, *Fortress California;* Lotchin, ed., *The Way We Really Were;* Nash, *The American West Transformed;* Starr, *Embattled Dreams;* and Verge, *Paradise Transformed.*

14. May, *Homeward Bound,* xviii–xx ; Coontz, *The Way We Never Were,* 23–41.

15. *Public Papers of the Presidents of the United States: Lyndon B. Johnson, 1965–1969,* 704. As more recent scholars demonstrate, many on welfare worked for pay because most states provided welfare recipients much less assistance than they needed to survive. See, for example, Levenstein, *A Movement without Marches,* and Orleck, *Storming Caesar's Palace.*

16. Orleck, *Storming Caesar's Palace,* 4.

17. For connections between feminists on the left and the postwar women's movement, see Horowitz, *Betty Friedan and the Making of the Feminine Mystique,* and Weigand, *Red Feminism.*

18. Acklesberg, "Communities, Resistance, and Women's Activism"; Orleck, "'If It Wasn't for You I'd Have Shoes for My Children.'"

19. Kaplan, *Crazy for Democracy;* Kaplan, "Female Consciousness and Collective Action." For another study of motherhood as the basis of political activism, see Jetter, Orleck, and Taylor, eds., *The Politics of Motherhood.*

20. Tilly, "From Interaction to Outcomes in Social Movements," 264.

21. Evans and Boyte, *Free Spaces.*

22. In fact, that is precisely what the California Child Care Resource and Referral Network did when it launched its Parents' Voices project in 1995. According to the Website, "Parent Voices is a parent-led grassroots organization fighting to make quality child care

affordable and accessible to all families." Available from http://www.parentvoices.org, accessed Aug. 13, 2009.

23. On the decline of women's moral authority in the period after suffrage, see Cott, *The Grounding of Modern Feminism;* Lemons, *The Woman Citizen;* and Muncy, *Creating a Female Dominion.*

24. Freedman, *Maternal Justice;* Gabin, *Feminism in the Labor Movement;* Garrow, ed., *The Montgomery Bus Boycott;* Harrison, *On Account of Sex;* Nasstrom, "Down to Now"; Rupp and Taylor, *Survival in the Doldrums;* Ware, "American Women in the 1950s."

25. Meyerowitz's collection *Not June Cleaver,* by examining a racially, ethnically, and economically diverse group of women, begins to dismantle the notion of domesticity in the postwar United States. See also Cobble, *The Other Women's Movement;* Muncy, "Cooperative Motherhood"; Murray, *The Progressive Housewife;* Nickerson, "The Power of a Morally Indignant Woman"; Nickerson, "Women, Domesticity, and Postwar Conservatism"; and Weigand, *Red Feminism.*

26. On the persistence of reform in the postwar period, see the essays in Meyerowitz, ed., *Not June Cleaver;* and Freedman, *Maternal Justice* and "Separatism Revisited." On the rhetoric of the child care campaign in California from 1946–57, see Hassan, "Rosie Re-Riveted in Public Memory."

27. Many did not embrace the term *feminist* because they associated it with early-twentieth-century efforts for suffrage or support of the ERA. In the 1960s, some in the child care movement identified as feminists, but the majority equated feminism with protests against marriage and motherhood. Rupp and Taylor, *Survival in the Doldrums,* 52–55.

28. Kaplan, "Female Consciousness and Collective Action."

29. For discussions of the feminist label, see Cott, "What's in a Name?"; Freedman, *No Turning Back,* 7–9; and Gilmore, ed., *Feminist Coalitions,* 6.

30. Baxandall, "Re-Visioning the Women's Liberation Movement's Narrative"; Cobble, *The Other Women's Movement;* Davis, "Welfare Rights and Women's Rights in the 1960s"; Nadasen, "Expanding the Boundaries of the Women's Movement"; Ruiz, *From Out of the Shadows,* ch. 5; White, *Too Heavy a Load,* ch. 7.

31. Chappell, "Rethinking Women's Politics in the 1970s"; Gilmore, ed., *Feminist Coalitions;* Gilmore, "The Dynamics of Second-Wave Feminist Activism in Memphis"; Valk, *Radical Sisters.*

32. Michel, *Children's Interests/Mothers' Rights.*

33. In 1993 Mary Francis Berry's *Politics of Parenthood* argued that "mother care," the practice of holding women primarily responsible for child care, placed an unequal burden on working mothers and remained the main obstacle to the development of child care services in the United States. Rose, *A Mother's Job.* On the differing meanings of motherhood, see Glenn, "Social Constructions of Mothering."

34. Stolzfus, *Citizen, Mother, Worker.* Before the excellent scholarship produced since 2000, child care policy had been largely unexplored from a historical perspective. For many years Margaret O'Brien Steinfels's *Who's Minding the Children?* was the only study of child care that included a historical component.

35. White, "Listening across the Race Line: Conversations with Women in Project Head Start," 6.

36. MacLean, "The Hidden History of Affirmative Action," 46–48.

37. Putnam, "The Prosperous Community," 40–42; Skocpol and Fiorina, "Making Sense of the Civic Engagement Debate," 13.

38. On social learning see Korstad, *Civil Rights Unionism,* esp. 120–41; see also Orleck, *Storming Caesar's Palace,* and Orleck, *Common Sense and a Little Fire.*

39. Susan Lynn, in *Progressive Women in Conservative Times,* has referred to this period as the "bridge" that linked female progressive reformers before World War II with women's activism in the movements of the 1960s.

Chapter 1. Californians Secure Wartime Child Care

1. *Daily People's World,* June 23, 1943; *San Francisco Chronicle,* June 22, 1943; *McKinley* [School] *Newsletter* no. 4, June 1943, box 18, folder 8, Tillie Olsen Papers, Stanford University Libraries.

2. *Daily People's World,* July 22, 1943. For a similar situation in Seattle, see Anderson, *Wartime Women,* 130.

3. FBI File Report, 1949, box 18, folder 12, Tillie Olsen Papers; *Daily People's World,* June 21, 1943; *San Francisco Chronicle,* June 17, 1943.

4. Goodwin, *No Ordinary Time,* 416–18.

5. Braitman, "Partisans in Overalls," 217.

6. Cahan, *Past Caring,* 38; Kelley, "Uncle Sam's Nursery Schools"; Steinfels, *Who's Minding the Children?* 67.

7. Interview with Sadie Ginsberg in Hymes, *Living History Interviews,* 13.

8. Cahan, *Past Caring,* 39; "Report to International Congress on Mental Health from San Francisco Commission on Report of the Wartime Child Care Centers on Children of Working Mothers," Documents for International Congress—1948, Historic Files, Golden Gate Kindergarten Association [hereafter GGKA] Papers, San Francisco.

9. Quoted in Martha Chickering, *California Children,* March 15, 1943, Sacramento, Calif.: California State Deparment of Social Welfare, 9, folder 44, League of Women Voters of San Francisco [hereafter SFLWV] Papers, MS1270, California Historical Society [hereafter CHS], San Francisco.

10. In California a series of unregulated boarding homes had emerged in war production areas to serve families with working mothers. The horrendous conditions in these homes provided strong arguments for state-sponsored child care. For a more detailed discussion see Fousekis, "Fighting for Our Children," 48–50.

11. Close, "Day Care Up to Now," 197; Chafe, *The American Woman,* 169; Lichtman, "Women at Work, 1941–1945," 305–7.

12. Testimony of Thomasina Johnson, legislative representative, National Non-Partisan Council on Public Affairs of Alpha Kappa Alpha Sorority, in U.S. Congress, Senate, *Wartime Care and Protection of Children of Employed Mothers,* 78.

13. Quoted in Chafe, *The American Woman,* 170.

14. Lundberg, "A Community Program of Day Care for Children," 152–53. This requirement was also spelled out to local communities in a pamphlet: Regional Day Care Committee, *Policies and Procedures Governing the Day Care Programs of the Federal Gov-*

ernment: A Handbook for State and Local Agencies and Child Care Committees (Atlanta: Representatives of Federal Agencies Serving the States of Alabama, Florida, Georgia, Mississippi, South Carolina, Tennessee, 1943).

15. Nash, *The American West Transformed*, 59; Parker, "Strangers in Town," 170.

16. Johnson, *The Second Gold Rush*, 30.

17. Lotchin, *The Bad City in the Good War*.

18. Rawls and Bean, *California: An Interpretive History*, 364–66.

19. Johnson, *The Second Gold Rush*, 38.

20. Dewitt, *The California Dream*, 265. On black Los Angeles during World War II, see Sides, *L.A. City Limits*, 36–56.

21. U.S. Congress, House Committee on Naval Affairs, Subcommittee of the Committee on Naval Affairs, *Investigation of Congested Areas*, 78th Cong., 1st sess., 1943, vol. 1, pt. 3, 867.

22. Parker, "Strangers in Town," 170; see also Verge, *Paradise Transformed*, 107–10.

23. Johnson, *The Second Gold Rush*, 46.

24. "Women Workers for Victory," Women's Clubs 1943–44, Administrative Files, Earl Warren [hereafter EW] Papers, California State Archives [hereafter CSA], Sacramento.

25. Nash, *The American West Transformed*, 66; Jensen and Lathrop, *California Women*, 105–6.

26. "Eight-hour Orphans," *Saturday Evening Post*, Oct. 10, 1942, 21.

27. Meyer, *Journey through Chaos*, 152–53.

28. Elizabeth Hall to John Shelley, July 31, 1942, Committee on the Care of Children File, carton 41, San Francisco Labor Council [hereafter SFLC] Records, Bancroft Library [hereafter BANC], University of California at Berkeley. Shelley served as president of the SFLC.

29. Lichtman, "Women at Work," 323.

30. Gabin, *Feminism in the Labor Movement*, 5.

31. Cobble, *The Other Women's Movement*, 134.

32. Nationwide women's union membership increased from one to three million by 1943.

33. Los Angeles CIO Conference, Summary of Proceedings, June 28, 1942, Women Subject Files, 1940–49, Southern California Library for Social Studies and Research [hereafter SCL], Los Angeles.

34. Harry Bridges, speech at the sixth annual convention of the California CIO Council, Oct. 24, 1943, as quoted in *Women in the War* (San Francisco: California CIO Council, 1943), Women Subject Files, 1940–49, SCL, Los Angeles.

35. *Proceedings of the Ninth International Convention of the United Electrical, Radio and Machine Workers of America*, New York, Sept. 13–17, 1943, 221. See also Horowitz, *Betty Friedan and the Making of the Feminine Mystique*, and Cobble, *The Other Women's Movement*.

36. *CIO News*, Nov. 9, 1942.

37. *Daily People's World*, May 17, 1943.

38. *Daily People's World*, May 17, June 1, July 12, 1943.

39. Report of the Meeting of the Nursery–Child Care Committee, San Francisco

Labor Council, Sept. 3, 1942, carton 41, SFLC Records, BANC, University of California at Berkeley.

40. Elizabeth Hall to John Shelley, July 31, 1942, SFLC Records, BANC, University of California at Berkeley.

41. Report of the Meeting of the Nursery–Child Care Committee.

42. Susan Moore, "Report of Subcommittee on Areas Needing Assistance," May 1942, Social Welfare–War Services, Defense, Department of Social Welfare Records, CSA, Sacramento; California Committee for the Care and Supervision of Preschool and Primary Children, Child Care Survey, June 15, 1943, Alameda County Welfare Committee, Oakland History Room, Oakland Public Library.

43. Brief History of the Golden Gate Kindergarten Association, miscellaneous file, GGKA Papers, San Francisco.

44. Board Meeting Minutes, Sept. 20, 1943, Minutes of the Board of Directors, 1943–47, GGKA Papers, San Francisco.

45. Memorandum, 1944, Chinese Nursery School File, unlabeled box, GGKA Papers, San Francisco.

46. *Berkeley Day Nursery: A Daytime Home for Children*, 1945, box 2, file 4, Printed Brochures, 1925–54, and F. L. Koughan, "*Survey of the Berkeley Day Nursery*," 1924, box 2: file 5, clippings, Berkeley Day Nursery [hereafter BDN] Records, BANC, University of California at Berkeley. Evidence suggests that in Oakland the African American–run nursery school, the Fannie Wall Home and Day Nursery, also altered the type of care it provided during the war by taking more children in its day care center. The home, however, left very few written records. Fannie Wall Home and Day Nursery, *Building Fund Charity Program*, Dec. 9, 1946, series 2: California State Association of Colored Women's Clubs: box 3, folder 10, Northern Federation, Fannie Wall Children's Home, Colored Women's Association Collection, Northern California African American Museum and Library, Oakland.

47. Superintendent's Report, Feb. 1942, carton 2, folder 18, BDN Records, BANC, University of California at Berkeley.

48. Superintendent's Report, March 1942, carton 2, folder 19, BDN Records, BANC, University of California at Berkeley.

49. Hartmann, *The Homefront and Beyond*, 146–47; Hartmann, "Women's Organizations during World War II," 320–21.

50. This represented the League's view of its role in the child care debates. California League of Women Voters, *The Bulletin*, Feb. 1943, BANC, University of California at Berkeley.

51. Ibid.; League of Women Voters of California, Position on Child Care Centers, 1943, revised 1947, box 14, folder 37, Education: Child Care Centers, 1943–1957, SFLWV Papers, CHS, San Francisco.

52. Mrs. George Rourke Jr. to Marguerite Wells, July 18, 1943, MS3585, box 6, League of Women Voters of California [hereafter CALWV] Papers, MS 1268, CHS, San Francisco.

53. Resume, Harriet Judd Eliel Oral History, MS 954, CHS, San Francisco.

54. Recommendations by the Department of Government and Social Welfare of the Los Angeles League of Women Voters, 1942, part 1: series 1: Minutes of Meetings,

1920–75, box 5–12, Minutes Board of Directors, 1942; Minutes of the Executive Board, April 8, 1943, box 5–13, League of Women Voters of Los Angeles [hereafter LWVLA] Papers, Urban Archives Center [hereafter UAC], California State University, Northridge [hereafter CSUN].

55. Minutes of the Executive Board, Oct. 6, 1943, LWVLA Papers, UAC, CSUN.

56. Takaneshi interview in Stolz, *An American Child Development Pioneer.*

57. California Senate, Interim Committee on Economic Planning, *A Report on the Care of Children in War Time,* 1, 2.

58. Fraser, *Unruly Practices,* 157.

59. *Daily People's World,* Sept. 15, 1942.

60. California Senate, Interim Committee on Economic Planning, *A Report on the Care of Children in War Time,* 5, 6.

61. *San Francisco Chronicle,* Sept. 20, 1942.

62. *San Francisco Chronicle,* Sept. 17, 1942; *Daily People's World,* Sept. 17, 1942; Rhoda Kellogg's personal notes, Political Correspondence–State Child Care Programs file, Rhoda Kellogg Files, GGKA Papers, San Francisco.

63. California Senate, Interim Committee on Economic Planning, *A Report on the Care of Children in War Time,* 8.

64. *San Diego Herald,* Oct. 1942, scrapbook 12, carton 10, Robert W. Kenny Papers [hereafter Kenny Papers], BANC, University of California at Berkeley.

65. California Senate, Interim Committee on Economic Planning, *A Report on the Care of Children in War Time,* 10.

66. *Daily People's World,* Sept. 17, 1942.

67. Nasstrom, "Down to Now," 124.

68. *Recommendations from the Bay Area Council on Child Care to the State Senate Interim Committee on Economic Planning,* Political Correspondence–State Child Care Program, Rhoda Kellogg Files, GGKA Papers, San Francisco.

69. Unidentified newspaper, scrapbook 12, carton 10, Kenny Papers, BANC, University of California at Berkeley.

70. *San Diego Herald,* Oct. 1942, scrapbook 12, Kenny Papers, BANC, University of California at Berkeley.

71. Takaneshi interview in Stolz, *An American Child Development Pioneer.*

72. Stolz was one of the leaders of this new cohort of female professionals that can be seen as an extension of the "female dominion" examined by Robyn Muncy in *Creating a Female Dominion in American Reform.*

73. On Stolz's role in WPA nursery schools see Beatty, *Preschool Education in America,* 177; Fousekis, "Lois Hayden Meek Stolz," in *Notable American Women,* 617–19; Grant, "Lois Meek Stolz," in *Women Educators in the United States,* 475; "In Memoriam: Lois Meek Stolz," *Young Children,* Jan. 1985, Lois Meek Stolz, series 2: Research Files, 1921–86, box 6, folder 22, Rosalie Blau Papers [hereafter Blau Papers], UAC, CSUN; and Takaneshi interview in Stolz, *An American Child Development Pioneer.*

74. In the 1920s both Stolz and Dewey registered as socialists in New York City. Grant, "Lois Meek Stolz," 473.

75. "Women in War: Group Named to Cope with Wartime Child Care," *San Fran-*

cisco Chronicle, Nov. 2, 1942; Grant, "Lois Meek Stolz," 475; Stolz, *Lois Meek Stolz: An Interview by Margo Davis.*

76. *Daily People's World,* Sept. 21, 1942.

77. "Conference held with Oakland School Authorities and Others," Feb. 28, 1943, box 1/1, series 2–2, Investigating Material on Legislation, 1943–56, John R. Weber Papers, Marianne Wolman Archives, Pacific Oaks College, Pasadena, Calif. See also Stolz, *Interviews with Leaders in the Child Guidance and Clinic Movement.*

78. Beatty, *Preschool Education in America,* 75–80.

79. "A Tribute" to Dr. Elizabeth Woods, n.d.; Virginia Powers to Rosalie Blau, April 15, 1983; and biography of Elizabeth Lindley Woods. All in research notes, n.d., box 3, folder 1, Blau Papers, UAC, CSUN.

80. Woods to Chickering, Jan. 19, 1942, Social Welfare–War Services Bureau, Children, 1941–43, State Department of Social Welfare Records, CSA, Sacramento.

81. Woods to Chickering, Jan. 26, 1942, Social Welfare–War Services Bureau, Children, 1941–43, CSA, Sacramento.

82. Elizabeth Woods, "Civilization Moves Forward on the Feet of Little Children," scrapbook 12, carton 10, Kenny Papers, BANC, University of California at Berkeley.

83. *Daily People's World,* Oct. 25, 1942.

84. *Daily People's World,* Oct. 31, 1942; *San Francisco Chronicle,* Nov. 11, 1942.

85. Stolz, *Lois Meek Stolz: An Interview by Margo Davis.*

86. Office of Legislative Counsel, *Report on Assembly Bill No. 307,* Feb. 5, 1943, Governor's Chapter Bill Files, CSA, Sacramento; California *Statutes 1943,* ch. 16, 127.

87. Connecticut, New York, New Jersey, and Washington were the only others to approve funds.

88. Out of fifty requests received, the Council only acquiesced once, allocating $5,000 to Eureka.

89. A. Earl Washburn to Edith Fox, April 13, 1944, Administrative Files, War Council–Child Care Centers, 1944/45, EW Papers, CSA, Sacramento.

90. May 1, 1943, California State War Council Minutes, June-Aug. 1943, California State War Council [hereafter CSWC] Records CSA, Sacramento.

91. Remarks of Governor Earl Warren, May 1, 1943, California State War Council Minutes, June-Aug. 1943, 64, CSWC Records CSA, Sacramento.

92. Remarks of Lieutenant Governor Frederick F. Houser, May 1, 1943, California State War Council Minutes, June–Aug. 1943, 64, CSWC Records CSA, Sacramento.

93. Elizabeth Woods to Miriam Van Waters, March 18, 1943, and Woods to Van Waters, April 11, 1943, box 8, folder 282, Anna Spicer Gladding and Miriam Van Waters Papers, Schlesinger Library, Radcliffe Institute for Advanced Study, Cambridge, Mass.; Freedman, "Separatism Revisited," 176–78.

94. California State Department of Education, *Child Care by California School Districts,* 2.

95. Alma Winona Sample interview with author, transcript, Nov. 22, 2005, Folsom, Calif.

96. Diana Lachantere, "Interview with Katherine Stewart Flippin" in *Black Women Oral History Project,* ed. Hill, 38.

97. Virginia Rose interview with author, May 28, 1998, Oakland, Calif.; Butler, *Black Women Stirring the Waters,* 25.

98. California State Department of Education, *Child Care by California School Districts,* 2.

99. Ibid., 23.

Chapter 2. Postwar Hopes

1. "Meet One of Ten Thousand Door-Key Kids," *Daily People's World,* Aug. 29, 1945; California State Department of Education, *Child Care by California School Districts,* 2.

2. Steinfels, *Who's Minding the Children?* 70; Michel, *Children's Interests/Mothers' Rights,* 151; National Committee on Group Care of Children, *Community Planning on Group Care of Children,* bulletin 1, Legislative Files, Special Session, Legislation–Child Care Centers, 1945–46, Earl Warren [hereafter EW] Papers, California State Archives [hereafter CSA], Sacramento; Stolzfus, *Citizen, Mother, Worker,* 113–28. By 1950, however, all but those in California, New York, and Philadelphia had closed.

3. Nash, *The American West Transformed,* 222–23; U.S. Bureau of the Census, *Historical Statistics of the United States* (1975), 93.

4. Katcher, *Earl Warren,* 193; Putnam, "The Progressive Legacy in California," 258; Rawls and Bean, *California: An Interpretive History,* 377–79.

5. Sociologist Ellen Reese, who tallied the letters written to Earl Warren in 1945, found that 78 percent of those who contacted him were women and 18 percent were men; the remaining 4 percent could not be identified by gender. Reese, "Maternalism and Political Mobilization," 574–75. From my own count of parents who wrote to Earl Warren a year later in 1946, 96 percent were women and 4 percent were men.

6. Evelyn Schroettner to Helen Gahagan Douglas [hereafter HGD], Sept. 3, 1945, and Donna Fry to HGD, Aug. 24, 1945, box 17: Seventy-ninth Congress, General Files, 4a: Child Care Program, Helen Gahagan Douglas Collection, Carl Albert Center Congressional Archives, University of Oklahoma, Norman. Emily Stolzfus describes the similar anxieties of a Washington, D.C., mother in *Citizen, Mother, Worker,* 110.

7. Johnson, *The Second Gold Rush,* 185–97. For another look at the short-lived liberal alliance in Oakland, see Self, *American Babylon,* 62–76. On progressive optimism in the immediate postwar era, see Horowitz, *Betty Friedan and the Making of the Feminine Mystique,* 122–23; and Korstad and Lichtenstein, "Opportunities Found and Lost," 786–811.

8. Reese, "Maternalism and Political Mobilization," 567.

9. McEnaney, "Nightmares on Elm Street,"1268.

10. According to Kevin Starr, Communist Party literature between the war and 1948 had a "tone of optimism and confidence" about its platform, which supported labor, unions, and equality for African Americans. Starr, *Embattled Dreams,* 305–6.

11. "Child Care Projects for which Federal Assistance under the Lanham Act Was Being Provided as of August 31, 1945," State of California, box 141, General Reference Files: CIO Women's Council, HGD Collection, Carl Albert Center Congressional Archives, University of Oklahoma, Norman.

12. Cantril, *Public Opinion,* 1044.

13. United States Department of Labor, Women's Bureau, "Women Workers in Ten War Production Areas," 5.

14. Johnson, *The Second Gold Rush,* 210.

15. Tobias and Anderson, *What Really Happened to Rosie the Riveter?* 3.

16. Cantril, *Public Opinion,* 1044–45; Docia Zavitkovsky interview with author, July 28, 1998, Los Angeles.

17. For an excellent treatment of these postwar protests in Cleveland, Washington, D.C., and California, see Stolzfus, *Citizen, Mother, Worker.*

18. *American Aeronaut,* Sept. 7, 1945, International Association of Machinists, District Lodge 727, AFL-CIO, Urban Archives [hereafter UAC], California State University at Northridge [hereafter CSUN].

19. Ellen Reese observes that fathers did not mobilize around child care in California because they considered it a "women's issue." Reese, "Maternalism and Political Mobilization," 575.

20. National Committee on Group Care of Children, *Community Planning on Group Care of Children.* For protests in Cleveland and Washington, D.C., see Stolzfus, *Citizen, Mother, Worker,* 68–69. On Cleveland see also Johnson, "What Mothers Think about Day Care,"103–6. On protests in Philadelphia, see Rose, *A Mother's Job,* 182–83.

21. Los Angeles Parents Council Telegram to Earl Warren, Sept. 16, 1945, Legislative Files, Special Session Legislation, Child Care Centers, Aug.-Nov. 1945, EW Papers, CSA, Sacramento.

22. Beach Vasey to Earl Warren, Inter-office Memorandum, Aug. 29, 1945, Legislative Files, Special Session–Child Care, 1945–46, EW Papers, CSA, Sacramento; Welfare Council of Metropolitan Los Angeles, *Child Care News: Emergency Child Care Committee,* Newsletter 1, Sept. 28, 1945, Legislative Files, Special Session–Child Care, Aug.-Nov. 1945, EW Papers, CSA, Sacramento.

23. Beach Vasey to Earl Warren, Inter-office Memorandum, Aug. 28, 1945, Legislative Files, Special Session–Child Care, Aug.-Nov. 1945, EW Papers, CSA, Sacramento; "Child Care Emergency: Three Thousand Mothers Rally Neighborhood Fight; Official Call for Permanent Nurseries," *Daily People's World,* Sept. 1, 1945.

24. I have found no documents that break down the racial composition of the California Child Care Centers statewide, but I have been able to determine that some, particularly in Los Angeles and Oakland, were racially mixed. The children who attended at least two Los Angeles centers were African American. Chang, "Comparative Study of Child Day Care Centers in Los Angeles, California and Canton, China," 125–35, 246–54; Virginia Rose interview with author, May 28, 1998, Oakland, Calif.; "Oakland City Council Asks Action on Child Care Centers," *Daily People's World,* Aug. 27, 1945.

25. "L.A. Mothers Rally to Force Action," *Daily People's World,* Sept. 1, 1945; Parson, *Making a Better World,* 77–78. Parson reports (70) that in December 1945, 37.2 percent of Aliso Village's occupants were white, 23.4 percent black, and 39.5 percent were "Americans of Mexican, Japanese, Filipino, or Chinese descent." See also Sides, *L.A. City Limits,* 115–20.

26. "Child Care Right Spreads," *Daily People's World,* Aug. 30, 1945; "Continuation of Child Care Urged," *Los Angeles Times,* Sept. 26, 1945.

27. "How to Fight for Continued Child Care," *Daily People's World*, Aug. 27, 1945; "How to Keep Child Care," *Daily People's World*, Sept. 1, 1945.

28. The actual number of attendees must have been somewhere between 1,200 and 1,500. According to a Western Union Telegram from the Emergency Child Care Committee, 1,200 parents and two hundred community activists attended. The *Daily People's World*, however, reported the number as 1,500. "Child Care Discussed," *Los Angeles Times*, Sept. 7, 1945; "L.A. Parents Hold Kid Center Rally, *Daily People's World*, Sept. 8, 1945; Western Union telegram from H. F. Whittle, chair, Emergency Child Care Committee, to Earl Warren, Sept. 7, 1945, and Welfare Council of Metropolitan Los Angeles, *Child Care News*, Sept. 28, 1945, Legislative Files, Special Session–Child Care, Aug.-Nov. 1945, EW Papers, CSA, Sacramento; "Child Care Meet to Be Held Here," *California Eagle*, Aug. 30, 1945.

29. Beach Vasey to Earl Warren, Inter-office Memorandum, Aug. 29, 1945, Child Care, 1945–46, Legislative Files, W. T. Sweitgert Files, EW Papers, CSA, Sacramento.

30. Western Union telegram to Earl Warren, Sept. 7, 1945, EW Papers, CSA, Sacramento.

31. Lemke-Santangelo, *Abiding Courage*, 118; Lotchin, *The Bad City in the Good War*, 76; Sides, *L.A. City Limits*, 92–93.

32. "An Ounce of Prevention's a Pound of Cure," editorial, *California Eagle*, Sept. 20, 1945. See also "Child Care Guild Needs Support," *California Eagle*, Aug. 30, 1945; "In California," *California Eagle*, Sept. 20, 1945; and Letters to the Editor, *California Eagle*, Oct. 4, 1945.

33. Board of Supervisors, County of Los Angeles, "In Re Child Care: A Resolution Urging Federal Aid for Operation (91)," Sept. 18, 1945, box 63, B, Los Angeles County Government, 3, Services, 14, Welfare, folder 1, John Anson Ford Papers, Huntington Library, San Marino, Calif.; "The Southernaires," *California Eagle*, April 6, 1946; Marjorie Gordon Giles, president, Avalon Child Care Guild, to John Anson Ford, March 19, 1946, box 62/B III, 14B, bb (3), John Anson Ford Papers.

34. "One Hundred Make Plea for Child Care," *San Francisco Daily News*, Aug. 20, 1945, League of Women Voters of San Francisco, box 14, folder 44, Education: Nursery Schools, 1940–46, League of Women Voters of San Francisco [hereafter SFLWV] Papers, California Historical Society [hereafter CHS], San Francisco.

35. Bierman, "The Influence of Pressure Groups on Child Care Legislation in California," 5. There is also evidence that the Los Angeles Board of Education had "controversial discussions" about the continuation of child care. "School Board Answers Women Voters League," *Los Angeles Times*, Nov. 30, 1945.

36. *Oakland Tribune*, Aug. 29, 1945; "Berkeley Board Must Take Action," *Daily People's World*, Sept. 1, 1945.

37. "New Appeals on Child Centers," *Oakland Tribune*, Aug. 30, 1945.

38. Robert Reed, director, Child Care Centers, Antioch, to Mr. Karl Holton, California Youth Authority, Sept. 5, 1945, Special Session, Legislative Files, Legislation–Child Care Centers, 1945–46, EW Papers, CSA, Sacramento.

39. Minutes of Executive Board of the Golden Gate Kindergarten Association, Aug.

6, 1945, Minutes of the Board of Directors, 1944–47, Golden Gate Kindergarten Association [hereafter GGKA] Papers, San Francisco.

40. Minutes of the Board of Director Meeting, Sept. 24, 1945, Minutes of the Board of Directors, 1944–47, GGKA Papers, San Francisco.

41. Parent's Questionnaire, San Francisco Board of Education, June 1945, box 14, folder 44A, Education: Nursery Schools, 1940–46, SFLWV Papers, CHS, San Francisco; *San Francisco News,* Aug. 20, 1945; Emergency Child Care Committee, "Some Answers to Questions about Child Care Centers in Los Angeles," Oct. 1, 1945; Association for Nursery Education of Southern California, Survey, July-Aug. 1945, Legislative Files, Special Session, Legislation–Child Care Centers, 1945–46, EW Papers, CSA, Sacramento. Fact-gathering was a proven method to influence public policy in California. Putnam, "The Progressive Legacy in California," 249.

42. Association for Nursery Education of Southern California, Survey, July-Aug. 1945, Legislative Files, Special Session, Legislation–Child Care Centers, 1945–46, EW Papers, CSA, Sacramento; see also "Child Care Emergency," *Daily People's World,* Sept. 1, 1945.

43. "New Appeal on Child Care," *Daily People's World,* Aug. 30, 1945; "Child Care Fight Spreads," *Daily People's World,* Aug. 30, 1945; "Ten Thousand Kids in Eviction," *Daily People's World,* Aug. 24, 1945; "Civic Groups to Fight End of Child Care," *San Francisco Chronicle,* Aug. 28, 1945.

44. For an excellent discussion of the GI Bill's advantages for white male veterans, see Cohen, *A Consumer's Republic,* 137–51.

45. Earl Warren to H. F. Whittle, chair, Emergency Child Care Committee, Los Angeles, Legislative Files, Special Session, Legislation, Child Care Centers, 1945–46, EW Papers, CSA, Sacramento.

46. Cray, *Chief Justice,* 137; Helen MacGregor to Earl Warren, Sept. 11, 1945, Legislative Files, Special Session, Legislation, Child Care Centers, 1945–46, EW Papers, CSA, Sacramento.

47. T. H. Delap to Earl Warren, Aug. 29, 1945, Everett Burkhalter to Earl Warren, Aug. 24, 1945, and Kathryn Niehouse to Earl Warren, Aug. 30, 1945, all in Special Session Legislation, Child Care Centers, 1945–46, EW Papers, CSA, Sacramento. For more on Burkhalter see "Fifteen Valley Child Care Centers Periled," *American Aeronaut,* Sept. 7, 1945, International Association of Machinists, District Lodge 27, Los Angeles County Federation of Labor [hereafter LACFL], AFL-CIO, UAC, CSUN.

48. Earl Warren to Harry Truman, Sept. 12, 1945, EW Papers, CSA, Sacramento.

49. Extension of Remarks of Helen Gahagan Douglas of California, House of Representatives, Thurs., Sept. 19, 1945, box 17, General Files: folder 4a, Child Care Program, HGD Collection, Carl Albert Center Congressional Archives, University of Oklahoma, Norman. On Douglas's political career see Scobie, *Center Stage.*

50. Harry Truman to Speaker of the House of Representatives, Oct. 4, 1945, Legislative Files, Special Session, Legislation–Child Care Centers, 1945–46, and Philip Fleming to Earl Warren, Feb. 8, 1946, both in Federal Files, Federal Works Agency, EW Papers, CSA, Sacramento.

51. Helen Gahagan Douglas, press release, Oct. 1945, HGD Collection, Carl Albert Center Congressional Archives, University of Oklahoma, Norman; Stolzfus, *Citizen,*

Mother, Worker, 142. Clyde Doyle was one of the six California Democrats swept out of the House in November 1946 during the Republican landslide, when they captured fifty-six seats and gained control of the House. He would return to Congress in 1948 after ousting his opponent from two years earlier.

52. Earl Warren to Philip Flemming, Jan. 12, 1946, and Philip Flemming to Earl Warren, Feb. 12, 1946, Federal Files, Federal Works Agency, 1946, EW Papers, CSA, Sacramento.

53. Dorothy Clancy to Earl Warren, Oct. 22, 1945, Legislative Files, Special Session, Legislation–Child Care Centers, 1945–46, EW Papers, CSA, Sacramento; Welfare Council of Metropolitan Los Angeles, *Child Care News,* newsletter no. 2, Oct. 10, 1945, box 17: Seventy-ninth Congress, General Files, 4ab: Child Care Program, HGD Collection, Carl Albert Center Congressional Archives, University of Oklahoma, Norman.

54. Ware, "American Women in the 1950s," 281; Bierman, "The Influence of Pressure Groups," 42–46; "League Position on the Care of Children of Working Mothers," Sept. 14, 1945, box 14, folder 44A, Education: Nursery Schools, 1940–46, SFLWV Papers, CHS, San Francisco (emphasis in the original).

55. Interview with Marion Turner, Sept. 5, 1945, and tour of San Francisco child care centers, Nov. 13, 1945, SFLWV Papers, both in box 14, folder 44A, Education: Nursery Schools, 1940–46, League of Women Voters of California Papers, CHS, San Francisco. This strategy of encouraging community organizations, government officials, and legislators to visit centers as a way of showcasing their benefits would be used by child care educators throughout the state battles.

56. "Report on Child Care Center Policy," Nov. 12, 1945, box 14, folder 44A, Education: Nursery Schools, 1940–46, SFLWV Papers, CHS, San Francisco.

57. State Board Meeting Minutes, Dec. 5, 1945, MS 1269A: box 1, Board Meetings 1945–46, Agenda and Minutes, CALWV; "A Personal Reaction to the Subject—Nursery Schools," Nov. 27, 1945, box 14, folder 44A, Education: Nursery Schools, 1940–46, SFLWV Papers, CHS, San Francisco.

58. See Nelson Lichtenstein, "From Corporatism to Collective Bargaining: Oranized Labor and the Eclipse of Social Democracy," in Gerstle and Fraser, eds., *Rise and Fall of the New Deal Order,* 123–25.

59. On the CIO and World War II see Lichtenstein, *Labor's War at Home,* and Zeiger, *The CIO,* 141–252.

60. State Legislative Program, California CIO Council, 1945, Record Group 1: Los Angeles County CIO Council—Executive Secretary Files, 1939–52, series 1: Los Angeles County CIO—Administrative Files, box 1: California CIO Council: Jan.–March 1945, LACFL, UAC, CSUN; Bierman, "The Influence of Pressure Groups," 19–20.

61. Bierman, "The Influence of Pressure Groups," 52. Howard Dratch also claims that the "politically well-organized and influential" CIO failed to fight for public child care at the war's end. Dratch, "The Politics of Child Care in the 1940s," 202.

62. "Continuation of Centers for Child Care Urged," *Los Angeles Times,* Sept. 26, 1945; "Mothers Urge Interim Child Care Action by State," *Daily People's World,* Oct. 1, 1945.

63. Los Angeles Central Labor Council to Earl Warren, Oct. 4, 1945, Legislative Files, Special Session Legislation, Child Care Centers, Aug.-Nov. 1945, EW Papers, CSA, Sacramento; Law and Legislative Committee of the S.F. Labor Council, Minutes, Sept.

18, 1945, San Francisco Labor Council Records, Bancroft Library [hereafter BANC], University of California at Berkeley.

64. "Ten Thousand Shipworkers to Lead Huge Job Rally," *Daily People's World,* Sept. 19, 1945; "Giant Job Rally Planned for L.A." and "Child Care Centers to Be Aided," *Daily People's World,* Sept. 24, 1945; "Full Employment Rally Held Here," *Los Angeles Times,* Oct. 4, 1945.

65. On the increasing power of women in unions in the 1940s, see Cobble, *The Other Women's Movement,* 15–26.

66. *War News,* 1945, series 1: Los Angeles County CIO—Administrative Files, box 4, Los Angeles CIO Women's Auxiliary: newsletters; CIO Women's Auxiliary Council to Los Angeles CIO Council, Sept. 21, 1945, series 1: Los Angeles County CIO—Administrative Files, box 4, Los Angeles CIO Women's Auxiliary, LACFL, UAC, CSUN.

67. Proceedings and Action Program of Statewide Emergency Legislative Conference, Jan. 5–6, 1946, Record Group 1: Los Angeles County CIO Council—Executive Secretary Files, 1939–52, series 5: Non-Affiliate Organizations Files, box 22: California Legislative Conference: Statewide Emergency Legislative Conference, proceedings, 1946, LACFL, UAC, CSUN; "People's Conference is Top Political News," *Labor Herald,* Jan. 4, 1946; "Grassroots' Meeting Maps Program," *Labor Herald,* Jan. 11, 1946.

68. "Heat on as Legislature Opens Today," *Los Angeles Times,* Jan. 7, 1946.

69. List of Members, Statewide Emergency Legislative Conference Child Care Panel, 1946, and Proceedings and Action Program of Statewide Emergency Legislative Conference, RG 1, series 5, box 22: California Legislative Conference: Members, L.A. County Deputy, registrar, lists, n.d., LACFL, UAC, CSUN.

70. Ibid., 30; California League of Women Voters, *The Bulletin* (Feb. 1946): 1, BANC, University of California at Berkeley.

71. Because the legislature enacted new programs and debated nonbudgetary issues every other year, the only way the legislators could discuss programmatic issues in 1946 was by special order of the governor. Warren quoted in Katcher, *Earl Warren,* 193. Scholars and Warren's Republican critics have pointed to the governor's 1946 legislative agenda as an example of his liberalism.

72. Jack Tenney interview with Donald J. Schippers, *California Legislator;* "Message of Governor Warren before the California State Legislature, Extraordinary Session," Jan. 7, 1946, W. T. Sweitgert Special Files, EW Papers, CSA, Sacramento; "Warren Lists Tasks before Legislators," *Los Angeles Times,* Jan. 8, 1946.

73. Putnam, "A Half-Century of Conflict," 43.

74. "Tenney Alters Child Care Stand," *Los Angeles Times,* Sept. 20, 1945.

75. Jack Tenney interview with Donald J. Schippers; "Child Care Fight Just Beginning," *Daily People's World,* Feb. 25, 1946; Pritchard, "California Un-American Activities Investigations," 310–12.

76. *San Francisco Chronicle,* Jan. 23, 1946. For a transcript of the Assembly Interim Committee on Public Education hearings, see Assembly Interim Committee on Public Education, "Should Child Care Centers Be Continued in California—by Whom, for How Long, in What Manner?" Sept. 17, 1945, San Francisco California, Joint Legislative Budget Committee Files, CSA, Sacramento.

77. "Gus Hawkins Candidate for Re-Election," *California Eagle,* March 14, 1946.

78. Christopher, *America's Black Congressman,* 222; Smith, ed., *Notable Black American Men,* 522–23; Augustus F. Hawkins interview with Clyde Woods, *Black Leadership in Los Angeles;* Stewart, "Preschools and Politics," 88. Hawkins served in the California Assembly from 1935–62 and in the U.S. Congress from 1963–91.

79. "Child Care Fight Just Beginning," *Daily People's World,* Feb. 25, 1946; Beach Vasey to Governor Warren, Aug. 29, 1945, W. T. Sweitgert Special Files, 1945–46, EW Papers, CSA, Sacramento; *Daily People's World,* Sept. 1, 1945. For evidence of the progressive coalition's longtime support of Hawkins's legislative proposals for child care, see Vasey memo, Aug. 29, 1945, State Legislative Conference Agendas, and articles in the *Daily People's World.*

80. "Solon Sees State Aid for Child Care Centers," *Los Angeles Times,* Sept. 11, 1945.

81. "Bill for Temporary Child Care Centers Is Passed," *San Francisco Chronicle,* Jan. 26, 1946; Desmond quoted in Jack Tenney interview with Donald J. Schippers.

82. Chapter 35, section 4.5, *Statutes of California,* California Legislature, First Extraordinary Session, 1946, 59.

83. On development of the two-tier system, see Nelson, "The Origins of the Two-Channel Welfare State."

84. Gordon, *Pitied but Not Entitled,* 10–11.

85. *San Francisco Chronicle,* Dec. 15, 1946.

86. California Legislature, *Technical Staff Report to the Joint Committee on Preschool and Primary Training,* Jan. 17, 1947, 133 [hereafter *Technical Staff Report*]; *Southern California Wave,* Feb. 17, 1946, cited in Scales, "A Study of the Development," 199–20.

87. *Technical Staff Report,* 11.

88. Joint Executive Committee Meeting, Associations for Nursery Education, Northern and Southern California, San Francisco State College, April 12, 1946, Mills College April 13, 14, 1946, series 2, box 4:38, Rosalie Blau Papers [hereafter Blau Papers], UAC, CSUN.

89. Fundraising letter for the Association of Nursery Education of Southern California (SCANE), May 2, 1946, box 1:3, Biographical Data, 1946–49, Blau Papers, UAC, CSUN.

90. Fundraising letter for SCANE; membership application for SCANE, 1945 or 1946, box 1:2, Biographical Data, 1946-49, Blau Papers, UAC, CSUN.

91. Prescott, Milich, and Jones, *The "Politics" of Day Care,* 1:18. Many of the nursery school educators had studied early child development at Columbia Teacher's College during the 1920s and 1930s.

92. "How Women Won the Vote," *San Francisco Chronicle,* Aug. 26, 1970.

93. Rhoda Kellogg interview with Barbara Tate for the Golden State radio program, Feb. 26, 1946, Rhoda Kellogg Personal Files, 1946, GGKA Papers, San Francisco.

94. Annual Report of Supervisor to Board of Directors of the Golden Gate Kindergarten Association for 1946, miscellaneous information box, Annual Report 1946; Board of Directors Meeting Minutes, Jan. 21, 1946, Minutes of Board of Directors Files, 1944–47, GGKA Papers, San Francisco.

95. "A Report on Mrs. Kellogg's Visit to the Legislature," Jan. 16, 1946, Golden Gate Kindergarten Association History, Old Documents File, GGKA Papers, San Francisco.

For more on Vallejo's centers, see "Report to International Congress on Mental Health from San Francisco Commission on Report of the Wartime Child Care Centers on Children of Working Mothers, Part 2," Documents for International Congress—1948, Historic Files, GGKA Papers, San Francisco.

96. Recommendations to the Joint Legislative Committee on Pre-school Training, April 2, 1946, GGKA History, Old Documents File, GGKA Papers, San Francisco.

97. *Technical Staff Report*, 142.

98. Muncy, *Creating a Female Dominion in American Reform*, xiii.

99. Left feminists include women whom other historians call red feminists, labor feminists, or progressives. I have chosen the term *left feminist* rather than some of the others because it is the most inclusive. DuBois, "Eleanor Flexner and the History of American Feminism," 84; Storrs, "Red Scare Politics and the Suppression of Popular Front Feminism," 494.

100. Staub, "Labor Activism and the Postwar Politics of Motherhood," 104–9; "Tillie Lerner Olsen," Federal Bureau of Investigation File Report, Jan. 21, 1949, box 18, folder 12, Tillie Olsen Papers, Stanford University Libraries, Stanford, Calif.; Cobble, *The Other Women's Movement*, 134–35. Olsen quote from "Tillie Olsen Says: Back to the Slave Shops," *People's World*, June 6, 1946.

101. Lichtenstein, *Labor's War at Home*, 144–45.

102. Healey and Isserman, *Dorothy Healey Remembers*, 105.

103. Weigand, *Red Feminism*, 68–75.

104. *Child Care Centers: A Political Football*, 1946, Communist Party Files, 1946–53, Southern California Library for Social Science and Research [hereafter SCL], Los Angeles. On role of CP women in San Francisco's child care movement, see Louise Todd Lambert interview with Lucy Kendall, *Women in California Collection*, 1976, CHS, San Francisco.

105. Dorothy Healey to All Los Angeles Communist Clubs, Nov. 13, 1946, Communist Party Files, 1946–53, SCL, Los Angeles.

106. On the Congress of American Women, see Swerdlow, "The Congress of American Women," 296–312; Weigand, *Red Feminism*, 46–64. Gerda Lerner confirms the interracial make of CAW in her discussion of the Los Angeles chapter and its leadership in *Fireweed*, 258–62.

107. Lerner, *Fireweed*, 258.

108. *Save Our Child Care Centers*, Congress of American Women, 1947 or 1948, Los Angeles CIO Council Records, box 30: Child Care, LACFL, UAC, CSUN.

109. Swerdlow, "The Congress of American Women," 309.

110. *Technical Staff Report*, 141; Bierman, "The Influence of Pressure Groups," 36.

111. *Techinical Staff Report*, 145.

112. See, for example, Myron Jepson to Earl Warren, Jan. 14, 1946, and Elizabeth Thompson to Earl Warren, Jan. 8, 1946, Legislative Files, Special Session Legislation, Child Care Centers, Dec. 1945–Feb. 1946, EW Papers, CSA, Sacramento.

113. California Legislature, *Senate Journal*, March 17, 1947, 869.

114. Ernest R. Debs, *Minority Report*, Joint Interim Committee on Pre-School Train-

ing, March 17, 1947, box 4/1: Legislative Historical Data, Children's Centers, 1943–66, Theresa S. Mahler Papers, Marianne Wolman Archives, Pacific Oaks College, Pasadena.

115. Stolzfus, *Citizen, Mother, Worker*, 40; *Technical Staff Report*, 35.

Chapter 3. Child Care "Is a State Problem"

1. The quotation in the chapter title is from a resolution signed by many organizations and local governments. See, for example, "Resolution on Child Care Center Program" signed by the Fourth Congressional District Townsend Club, Legislative Files, Gen. Child Care Centers, 1948–49, Earl Warren Papers [hereafter EW], California State Archives [hereafter CSA], Sacramento. Other similar resolutions can be found in the same folder. Petition signed by thirty-four mothers, April 18, 1947, Legislative Files, Governor's Files, Child Care, 1947, EW Papers, CSA, Sacramento.

2. Mouffe, *The Democratic Paradox*, 96.

3. Greene, *Our Separate Ways*, 113–16.

4. Republicans also ousted other key child care supporters in Congress, Clyde Doyle from Long Beach and Ned Healey from Los Angeles. Doyle, however, was reelected in 1948.

5. Navasky, *Naming Names*, viii, 80–84; Starr, *Embattled Dreams*, 293–297; Rawls and Bean, *California*, 383.

6. Barrett, *The Tenney Committee*, 30–35; Pritchard, "California Un-American Activities Investigations," 311; Starr, *Embattled Dreams*, 281–82.

7. See also Storrs, "Red Scare Politics and the Suppression of Popular Front Feminism," 495–96, 523.

8. For anticommunism's effect on mainstream women's organizations, see Rupp and Taylor, *Survival in the Doldrums*, 136–44.

9. According to legislators, well-established organizations such as the League of Women Voters held political clout because of name recognition and a longstanding reputation. Bierman, "The Influence of Pressure Groups on Child Care Legislation in California," 41–42.

10. Fraser, *Unruly Practices*, 157–58.

11. Messer, *Who's Who on the Pacific Coast*, 637; Rosalie Blau, Biographical Data, 1940–45, Rosalie Blau Papers [hereafter Blau Papers], Urban Archives [hereafter UA], California State University at Northridge [hereafter CSUN].

12. Docia Zavitkovsky interview with author, July 28, 1998, Los Angeles.

13. For biographical information on Zavitkovsky, see Biography of Docia Zavitkovsky, Research Notes, n.d., box 6, folder 31, Blau Papers, UA, CSUN; "Day Care Pioneer Recalls '43 Program, *Los Angeles Times*, July 14, 1983; Docia Zavitkovsky interview with author.

14. For more on nursery educators, see Beatty, *Preschool Education in America*, 177–92, and Stewart, "Preschools and Politics," 60–67.

15. Membership application, Association for Nursery Education of Southern California, 1946 or 1947, box 1, folder 2, Blau Papers, UA, CSUN; Legislative Committee, Northern California Association for Nursery Education, Oct. 7, 1948, Theresa S. Mahler

[hereafter TSM] Papers, Marianne Wolmann Archives, Pacific Oaks College, Pasadena [hereafter POCP].

16. Docia Zavitkovsky interview with author.

17. For the early history of SCANE and NCANE, see Dorothy Hawes, "Guide/History of the Organization," 1983, Southern California Association for the Education of Young Children Papers, 1935–83, UA, CSUN.

18. Prescott, Milich, and Jones, The "Politics" of Day Care, 17–18.

19. Minutes of the first California Committee for Child Care Meeting, Oct. 25, 1947, Division of Public School Administration, Division Chief's Files, Child Care/Children's Centers 1947–51, Department of Education Records, CSA, Sacramento; Stewart, "PreSchools and Politics," 108–9; "New Group Plans Child Care Study," Labor Herald, Nov. 4, 1947.

20. Lovisa Wagoner to Ruth Howarth, Oct. 31, 1946, box 4/1: Legislative Historical Data [hereafter, LHD], Children's Centers, 1943–66, TSM Papers, POCP.

21. Docia Zavitkovsky interview with author.

22. Zavitkovsky quoted in Bothman, "Reflections of the Pioneers on the Early History of the Santa Monica Children's Centers and the Changing Child-Rearing Philosophies," 13, UA, CSUN.

23. Prescott, Milich, and Jones, The "Politics" of Day Care, 7.

24. Winona Sample interview with author, Nov. 21, 2005, Folsom, Calif.

25. Fraser, Unruly Practices, 157–58.

26. 1948 Charter of the Child Care Parents' Association of San Francisco in Marcus Whitman, "Child Care 1958: A San Francisco View," Mary Young [hereafter MY] Papers, author's possession; Bierman, "The Influence of Pressure Groups," 57.

27. For connections between women's activism and shared work culture, see Cobble, The Other Women's Movement, 28–32; Hewitt, Southern Discomfort, 203–6; Orleck, Common Sense and a Little Fire, 32–35; and Ruiz, Cannery Women, Cannery Lives, 30–44.

28. Lucie White, talk at the Humanities Institute, UNC-Chapel Hill, May 23, 1996, copy of audiotape in author's possession.

29. Fraser, "Rethinking the Public Sphere," 123.

30. Sara Evans and Harry Boyte argue that free spaces are situated "between private lives and large-scale institutions where ordinary citizens can act with dignity, independence, and vision." Evans and Boyte, Free Spaces, 17; see also Kaplan, Crazy for Democracy, 182–83.

31. Virginia Rose interview with author, May 28, 1998, Oakland; Skocpol and Fiorina, "Making Sense of the Civic Engagement Debate," 13–14.

32. Quoted in Prescott et. al, An Institutional Analysis of Day Care Program, 100.

33. Virginia Rose interview with author. Rose could not estimate the percentage of black children in Oakland's centers but recalled there being "just more and more" over the years.

34. Rosalie Blau and Docia Zavitkovsky in Annette Bothman, "Reflections of the Pioneers," 13; Winona Sample interview with author.

35. On social learning and grassroots activism, see Korstad, Civil Rights Unionism, esp. 120–41.

36. Bierman, "The Influence of Pressure Groups," 57; California Parents' Association for Child Care Centers Constitution and By Laws (before 1958) in Whitman, "Child Care 1958: A San Francisco View," MY Papers, author's possession.

37. This number is based on the correspondence found in Legislative Files, Governor's Files, Child Care, 1947, EW Papers, CSA, Sacramento.

38. Ibid. The 1950 calculations are based on letters in Legislative Files, Proposed Legislation—General, Child Care Centers, 1949–51, EW Papers, CSA, Sacramento.

39. Jessie Coles and Catherine Landreth, Child Care Centers in California, 1947, Department of Home Economics, UC Berkeley, Jan. 1949, box 1/1, series 3–1, History of Child Care Centers, 1945–69, John R. Weber Papers [hereafter Weber Papers], POCP. See also Fowler, "A Study of the Economic Status of Student Veterans of World War II Having Children in State-Supported Child Care Centers," 25. Oral interviews and some letters identify the writers' backgrounds, making it clear that women of color were present. See, for example, petition and cover letter from Chinese parents at Commodore Stockton Nursery School, Dec. 28, 1948, Legislative Files, Proposed Legislation–General, Education, Child Care Centers, 1948–49, EW Papers, CSA, Sacramento; Tarea Hall Pittman interview with Joyce Henderson, *Tarea Hall Pittman: NAACP Official and Civil Rights Worker;* and Virginia Rose interview with author.

40. "An Ounce of Prevention's a Pound of Cure," *California Eagle,* Sept. 20, 1945.

41. "W. J. Wheaton Says," *California Eagle,* Jan. 30, 1947.

42. Schlup and Whisenhunt, eds., *It Seems to Me,* 3; Sussman, *Letters to FDR,* 12–16, 135–38, 143–44; Hall et al., *Like a Family,* 309–16.

43. Thelen, *Becoming Citizens in the Age of Television,* 8–10.

44. For more on political letter-writing, see Frantzich, *Write Your Congressman,* and Thelen, *Becoming Citizens in the Age of Television.*

45. Federation of Parents for Child Care Centers, Jan. 8, 1947, Legislative Files, Governor's Files, Child Care, 1947, EW Papers, CSA, Sacramento.

46. "Housing: The Homeless Southwest," *Collier's,* Dec. 14, 1946, 22–29.

47. Mrs. T. A. Emmons to Earl Warren, Jan. 10, 1947, Legislative Files, Governor's Files, Child Care, 1947, EW Papers, CSA, Sacramento; Parents and Teachers, Manhattan Beach Child Care Center to Earl Warren, March 5, 1949, Legislative Files, Proposed Legislation—General, Education, Child Care Centers, 1948–49, EW Papers, CSA, Sacramento.

48. Irma Keal to Earl Warren, Jan. 10, 1947, and Maurine Jorgensen to Earl Warren, Jan. 13, 1947, Legislative Files, Governor's Files, Child Care, 1947, EW Papers, CSA, Sacramento.

49. Kathleen Davis Marco to Earl Warren, Jan. 15, 1947, Irma Keal to Earl Warren, Jan. 10, 1947, and Mrs. Lena Newman to Earl Warren, Jan. 20, 1947, all in Legislative Files, Governor's Files, Child Care, 1947, EW Papers, CSA, Sacramento.

50. Dorothy Patterson to Earl Warren, May 27, 1949, Legislative Files, Proposed Legislation—General, Child Care Centers, 1948–49, EW Papers, CSA, Sacramento.

51. Marjorie Richardson to Earl Warren, May 17, 1949, Legislative Files, Proposed Legislation—General, Child Care Centers, 1948–49, EW Papers, CSA, Sacramento.

52. Acklesberg, "Communities, Resistance, and Women's Activism," 302–4; Orleck,

"'If It Wasn't for You I'd Have Shoes for My Children,'" 115–16; Orleck, *Storming Caesar's Palace,* 100–101.

53. Kathleen Kay to Earl Warren, March 26, 1947, Legislative File, Governor's File, Child Care, 1947, EW Papers, CSA, Sacramento.

54. Mrs. Ann Owens to Earl Warren, May 19, 1947, Legislative File, Governor's File, Child Care, 1947, EW Papers, CSA, Sacramento.

55. Mary Jones Dmitrieff to Earl Warren, April 18, 1947, Legislative File, Governor's File, Child Care, 1947, EW Papers, CSA, Sacramento.

56. Solinger, *Wake Up Little Susie,* 78–81; Orleck, *Storming Caesar's Palace,* 70.

57. Eva Mack to Earl Warren, Dec. 5, 1945, Legislative Files, Governor's Files, Special Session—Child Care, 1945–46, EW Papers, CSA, Sacramento; Mrs. George Hughes to Earl Warren, Dec. 19, 1946, Administrative Files, Education, Child Care and Day Nurseries, 1946–48, EW Papers, CSA, Sacramento; Mrs. Lolita Power to Earl Warren, Dec. 26, 1946, Legislative Files, Governor's Files, Child Care, Jan. 6–Dec. 1947, EW Papers, CSA, Sacramento; Fifteen Mothers to Earl Warren, Jan. 10, 1947, Legislative Files, Child Care, 1947, EW Papers, CSA, Sacramento.

58. Sara N. Tiaxer to Earl Warren, Dec. 28, 1946, Governor's Files, Legislative Files—Child Care, Jan. 6–Dec. 1947, EW Papers, CSA, Sacramento.

59. Mrs. W. B. Robinson to Earl Warren, Jan. 10, 1947, Governor's Files, Legislative Files, Child Care, 1947, EW Papers, CSA, Sacramento.

60. Kathleen Kay to Earl Warren, March 26, 1947, Governor's Files, Legislative Files, Child Care, 1947, EW Papers, CSA, Sacramento.

61. By making demands on the state for child care, these mothers articulated what Temma Kaplan calls female consciousness: women's roles as the mothers and nurturers in society lead them to take political action. Kaplan, "Female Consciousness and Collective Action," 545–78.

62. Kerber, "A Constitutional Right to Be Treated Like American Ladies, 17–35; Kerber, "The Meanings of Citizenship," 838–41; Pateman, "The Patriarchal Welfare State," 231–60.

63. Mrs. Jean Ramsey to Earl Warren, Dec. 19, 1946, Administrative Files, Education, Child Care and Day Nurseries, 1946–48, EW Papers, CSA, Sacramento.

64. Mittelstadt, *From Welfare to Workfare,* 56.

65. Mrs. Eunice Shreve to Earl Warren, Jan. 29, 1947, Legislative Files, Governor's Files, Child Care, 1947, EW Papers, CSA, Sacramento.

66. Bell, *Aid to Dependent Children,* 60; Mittelstadt, *From Welfare to Workfare,* 41–43.

67. Beach Vasey to Earl Warren, Memorandum, June 27, 1947, Governor's Chapter Bill Files, Assembly Bill 1781, chapter 956, 1947, CSA, Sacramento.

68. "Delegates Leave for Sacramento to Press Fight for Child Care," *California Eagle,* April 24, 1947.

69. Beach Vasey to Earl Warren, Memorandum, March 1948, Assembly Bill no. 9, chapter 4, 1948, Governor's Chapter Bill Files, CSA, Sacramento; Inter-office Memorandum, Beach Vasey to Earl Warren, Jan. 26, 1948, Proposed Legislation, Legislative Files, Child Care Centers, 1948–49, EW Papers, CSA, Sacramento.

70. As quoted in Bierman, "The Influence of Pressure Groups," 61.

71. "Child Care Backers Go into Action," *Daily People's World*, April 24, 1947; "Parents Plead for Child Care," *Daily People's World*, April 25, 1947; "Delegates Leave for Sacramento to Press Fight for Child Care," *California Eagle*, April 24, 1947.

72. Docia Zavitkovsky quoted in Bothman, "Reflections of the Pioneers," 13; Docia Zavitkovsky interview with author; Tebb, *Thoughtful Reflections for Future Directions*, 20.

73. Tarea Hall Pittman interview with Joyce Henderson; Virginia Rose interview with author, May 28, 1998, Oakland, Calif., 58. See also Jensen and Lothrop, *California Women*, 112. Pittman remembers Asian, black, and white women represented in the group. As for Latinos, Pittman stated, "We were not hearing so much about the Chicano involvement. . . . I do not remember a specific Chicano name group." See also "Pittman, Tarca Hall," in Bakken and Kindell, *Encyclopedia of Immigration and Migration in the American West*, 2: 541–45. On the interest of African American women from northern California in the state's child care centers, see also Crouchett, Bunch, and Winnacker, *Visions toward Tomorrow*, 55.

74. *San Francisco Chronicle*, April 24, 1947; "Child Care Bills Are Studied," *Sacramento Bee*, April 24, 1947.

75. "Parents Plead for Child Care," *Daily People's World*, April 25, 1947.

76. *San Francisco Daily News*, Feb. 6, 1947, as quoted in Stewart, "Preschools and Politics," 114.

77. *A Brief Inquiry into the Need for a Child Care Program in California*, Dec. 1948, 3, box 5/1, Child Care Centers, Pamphlets, Convention Programs, 1948–62, TSM Papers, POCP.

78. Ibid., 5–6.

79. May, *Homeward Bound*, xxi.

80. *A Brief Inquiry*, 5–6. .

81. Mittelstadt, *From Welfare to Workfare*, 61. For a more detailed discussion see Leon Lefson, "Rehabilitating Public Assistance Clients," *Public Welfare* 11 (April 1953): 46–55.

82. Helen Christiansen and Barbara Greenwood, "The Western Share in NANE Beginnings: 1925–1935," *Journal of Nursery Education* (Fall 1958), box 4, folder 24, Blau Papers, UA, CSUN.

83. *A Brief Inquiry*, 8.

84. Ibid., 13–15. For the "traditional" family as a means of national security, see May, *Homeward Bound*.

85. *A Brief Inquiry*, 24–25.

86. The California Parents' Association for Child Care, Report of the Legislative Chairman, Feb. 26–March 16, 1949, box 4/1, LHD, Child Care Centers, 1949, TSM Papers, POCP.

87. Theresa Mahler, legislative chair, Nursery School Education of Northern California, Feb. 10, 1949; Minutes of the Legislative Committee Meeting, Feb. 24, 1949, box 4/1, LHD, Children's Centers, 1949, TSM Papers, POCP.

88. A copy of this film is located in the Marianne Wolman Archives, Weber Papers, POCP.

89. Draft of film script, 1947, box I/1, series 3–1, History of Child Care Centers, 1945–69, Weber Papers, POCP.

90. "Parents Plead for Child Care," *Daily People's World,* April 25, 1947.

91. For examples of reformers endorsing traditional values while simultaneously undermining them, see Hall, *Revolt against Chivalry,* especially chapter 7, and Higginbotham, *Righteous Discontent,* especially chapter 7.

92. Ernest R. Geddes interview with Enid Douglas, *Ernest R. Geddes: California Assemblyman;* Prescott, Milich, and Jones, *The "Politics" of Day Care,* 19; Docia Zavitkovsky interview with author; Stolzfus, *Citizen, Mother, Worker,* 147–48.

93. Pollack, "Schools That Save Families," 81, box 5/1, Child Care Centers, Pamphlets, Convention Programs, 1948–62, n.d., TSM Papers, POCP.

94. Birdice Phillips to Roxie Alexander, legislative chair, Northern California Association of Nursery Education, March 15, 1949, box 4/1, LHD, 1949, TSM Papers, POCP.

95. Mary Jones Dmitrieff to Earl Warren, April 18, 1947, Legislative Files, Governor's Files, Child Care, 1947, EW Papers, CSA, Sacramento.

96. Mrs. Barbara Morris to Earl Warren, March 9, 1949, Legislative Files, Proposed Legislation, General–Child Care Centers, 1948–49, EW Papers, CSA, Sacramento; Child Care Parents' Association of San Francisco, Special Bulletin, Dec. 1950, box 4/1, LHD, Children's Centers 1950, TSM Papers, POCP.

97. Theresa Mahler, personal notes, Aug. 18, 1949, and Theresa Mahler, president, Association for Nursery Education of Northern California to Senator Gerald O'Gara, June 1, 1949, box 4/1, LHD, Children's Centers, 1949, TSM Papers, POCP; Stewart, "Preschools and Politics," 136.

98. Gerald O'Gara to Earl Warren, Dec. 14, 1949, Legislative Files, Proposed Legislation, Child Care Centers, 1949–51, EW Papers, CSA, Sacramento.

99. Sam Yorty to Earl Warren, Feb. 21, 1950, and Fred H. Kraft to Earl Warren, Jan. 13 and Dec. 20, 1950, Legislative Files, Proposed Legislation, Child Care Centers, 1949–51, EW Papers, CSA, Sacramento.

100. Directors of Catholic Social Service and Education to Members of the California Legislature, Feb. 3, 1948, box 4/1, LHD, Children's Centers, 1947–48, TSM Papers, POCP.

101. For an overview of Catholic opposition, see Lawrence Arnstein interview with Edna T. Daniel, *Lawrence Arnstein: Community Service in California, Public Health and Social Welfare,* 116–17. See also Bierman, "The Influence of Pressure Groups," 36–40.

102. On minimal opposition to the closing of Lanham Act centers, see Earl Washburn to Beach Vasey, Dec. 31, 1945, Special Session Legislation, Child Care Centers, 1945–46, EW Papers, CSA, Sacramento.

103. M.F. Taylor to Earl Warren, Dec. 5, 1946, Child Care and Day Nurseries, 1946–48, Administrative File, Education, EW Papers, CSA, Sacramento; Elizabeth Thompson to Earl Warren, Jan. 8, 1946, Special Session Legislation, CCC, Legislative File, EW Papers, CSA, Sacramento.

104. California Legislature, *Technical Staff Report to the Joint Committee on Preschool and Primary Training* [hereafter *Technical Staff Report*] (Sacramento, Jan. 17, 1947), 44; California Legislature, Assembly, *Report on the Child Care Program by the Assembly Interim Committee on Social Welfare* (Sacramento, Jan. 1951), 17; "Report on Assem-

bly Bill No. 1781," June 20, 1947, Assembly Bill 1781, Chapter 956, 1947, Governor's Chapter Bill Files, CSA, Sacramento; California State Department of Education, *Survey of Families Requesting Service*, 6.

105. Gordon, *Pitied but Not Entitled*, 11–12.

106. As quoted in "Meeting of Special Committee to Determine Eligibility for Admission to Child Care Centers," March 30, 1946, box 1, series 2–1, Historical Legislation, Weber Papers, POCP.

107. Mrs. Doris Day Scott to Walter E. Dexter, April 1, 1946, Box 1, series 2–1, Historical Legislation, 1943–46, Weber Papers, POCP.

108. California Legislature, *Technical Staff Report*, 47; California State Department of Education, *Report of Child Care Centers Administered and Operated by California School Districts*, 5–8.

109. See also Stolzfus, *Citizen, Mother, Worker*, 174–76.

110. Koshuk, "Developmental Records of Five Hundred Nursery School Children," 135.

111. "The Need for Child Care in Bellflower," Feb. 1947, Legislative Files, Governor's Files, Child Care, 1947, EW, CSA, Sacramento.

112. Child Care Centers, Southern Section Meeting, Los Angeles City Board of Education, June 27, 1947, Division of Public Schools, Division Chief's Files, Child Care, 1947–1951, Department of Education Records [hereafter Ed. Records], CSA, Sacramento.

113. Ibid.

114. Parents' Council for Child Care Centers to Roy Simpson, Superintendent of Public Instruction, Education, Child Care and Day Nurseries, EW Papers, CSA, Sacramento; Western Union Telegram, Parents' Council for Child Care to Warren, November 2, 1946, Education, Child Care and Day Nurseries, 1946–52, EW Papers, CSA, Sacramento.

115. Richmond Child Care Council to Earl Warren, March 10, 1947, Legislative Files, Governor's Files, Child Care, Jan. 6–Dec. 1947, and Lynwood Parents' Council, Resolution on Child Care, Jan. 6, 1947, Governor's Files, Legislative Files, Child Care, 1947, both in EW Papers, CSA, Sacramento.

116. Mrs. Wanda Huish to State Superintendent of Schools, Aug. 15, 1947, Division of Public Schools, Division Chief's Files, Child Care/Children's Centers, Ed. Records, CSA, Sacramento.

117. Fowler, "A Study of the Economic Status of Student Veterans," 10.

118. For the advantages the G.I. Bill gave some veterans, see Cohen, *A Consumer's Republic*, 137–45.

119. Frank M. Wright to Lela M. Carbonell, July 21, 1947, Division of Public Schools, Division Chief's Files, Child Care/Children's Centers, 1947–51, Ed. Records, CSA, Sacramento.

120. For state distribution of nursery schools and child care centers in 1950, see "A Directory of Nursery Schools and Child-Care Centers in the United States," 1951, as cited in Michel, *Children's Interests/Mothers' Rights*, 179.

121. For a similar argument see Greene, *Our Separate Ways*, 210–15.

Chapter 4. "We Need to Stand Together"

1. Title quotation from the California Parents' Association for Child Care, *Legislative Bulletin,* March 16, 1954, Legislative Historical Data [hereafter LHD], Children's Centers [hereafter CC], Theresa S. Mahler [hereafter TSM] Papers, Marianne Wolman Archives, Pacific Oaks College at Pasadena [hereafter POCP]; Mary ElizabethYoung Arnold interview with the author, Oct. 7, 1998, Santa Rosa, Calif.

2. Fred Luke to Earl Warren, Dec. 13, 1950, Legislative Files, Proposed Legislation, General Child Care Centers, 1949–51, Earl Warren [hereafter EW] Papers, California State Archives [hereafter CSA], Sacramento; "Legislators Will Return to Their Yearly Problem of Child Care Centers," *Los Angeles Times,* Dec. 22, 1950, box 5/1, child care clippings, TSM Papers, POCP.

3. Freedman, "Separatism Revisited," 170–88.

4. Abramovitz, *Regulating the Lives of Women,* 319–29; Brown, *Race, Money and the American Welfare State,* 170–77; Mittelstadt, *From Welfare to Workfare,* 85–109.

5. California State Department of Education, *Survey of Families Requesting Service or Enrolling Children in Child Care Centers.* A list of the officers in each child care center's parents' group in San Francisco during 1958, for example, reveals eighty-one mothers and three fathers. Telephone book of parent representatives in San Francisco, 1958, Mary E. Young [hereafter MY] Papers, author's possession. See also Barbara Gach interview with author, July 2, 1998, Belvedere, Calif.; Mary Elizabeth Young Arnold interview with author; and Docia Zavitkovsky interview with author, July 28, 1998, Los Angeles. On SCANE and NCANE see List of Presidents, box 4, folder 24, Rosalie M. Blau [hereafter RB] Collection, Urban Archives [hereafter UAC], California State University at Northridge [hereafter CSUN].

6. Kathryn Kish Sklar observes that women reformers in the late nineteenth century depended on separate female institutions but "were able to realize the full potential of their collective power only by reaching outside those boundaries" into the male world of politics. Sklar, "Hull-House," 658–77.

7. Mary Elizabeth Young Arnold interview with author.

8. California Division of Labor Statistics and Research, "Womanpower in the California Economy," Feb. 1966, 3, box 8/1, California Child Care Centers, Directors and Supervisors' Association, 1966, TSM Papers, POCP.

9. Jack Harrison Pollack, "Schools That Save Families," *Nation's Business,* Sept. 1952, box 4/1, LHD, CC, 1952, TSM Papers, POCP.

10. Young, *Descendents,* ix; Mary Elizabeth Young Arnold interview with author; Reese, *South Dakota;* U.S. Bureau of the Census, *Fifteenth Census of the United States,* 843.

11. Mary Elizabeth Young Arnold interview with author. See also Stock, *Main Street in Crisis,* and Low, *Dust Bowl Diary.*

12. Mary Elizabeth Young Arnold interview with author.

13. Hartmann, *The Homefront and Beyond,* 31–48; Campbell, *Women at War.*

14. Kunzel, *Fallen Women,* 150.

15. Federal Security Agency U.S. Public Health Service, *Vital Statistics of the United*

States, part 1: *Illegitimate Births by Race: Birth Registration Area, 1917–46* (Washington, D.C.: U.S. Government Printing Office, 1948), xxxviii. These statistics did not include illegitimate births from fourteen states, including California, that did not require a statement of legitimacy of the child. It is likely the number of out-of-wedlock births would take a significant jump if these states were included in the statistics. Solinger, *Wake Up Little Suzie;* Kunzel, "White Neurosis," 304–31.

16. For a similar story see Lynne Beeson interview with author, May 2, 2006, San Francisco.

17. Mary Elizabeth Young Arnold interview with author.

18. Ibid.

19. *Mobil Travel Guide: California and the West* (New York: Rand McNally, 1975), 99.

20. California Legislature Assembly, *Report on the Child Care Program by the Assembly Interim Committee on Social Welfare,* Jan. 1951, 17.

21. Brief Report on the Annual Convention of the California Parents' Association for Child Care, Oct. 14, 1950, box 8/1: California Senate Interim Committee of Social Welfare, TSM Papers, POCP.

22. Frank Wright, associate superintendent of public instruction, to Lawrence Arnstein, Sept. 15, 1950, Division of Public School Administration, Division Chief Files, 1949–53, Department of Education [hereafter ED] Papers, CSA, Sacramento.

23. California League of Women Voters, 1950, California League of Women Voters [herafter SFLWV] Papers, California Historical Society [hereafter CHS], San Francisco.

24. James T. Lapsley to Earl Warren, Feb. 20, 1950, Legislative Files, Proposed Legislation, Child Care Centers, 1949–51, EW Papers, CSA, Sacramento; "Deaths," *Los Angeles Times,* Oct. 21, 1955.

25. On Betty Bachman, see Stewart, "Preschools and Politics," 114; Lawrence Arnstein interview with Edna Daniel, *Lawrence Arnstein: Community Service in California, Public Health and Social Welfare;* Mary Young speech, California Parents' Association for Child Care Centers, Thirteenth Annual Conference, Nov. 11, 1961, MY Papers, author's possession; and Mary Elizabeth Young Arnold interview with author.

26. "Child Center Law Praised as Progress: State Parents' Group Hears Speakers Call It Good Compromise," *Los Angeles Times,* Oct. 14, 1951.

27. For a similar experience in the suburbs, see Muncy, "Cooperative Motherhood," 259.

28. Ruth Lindquist, *Interim Newsletter,* California Parents' Association for Child Care, Child Care/Children's Centers, Division of Administration, Division Chief's Files, ED Papers, CSA, Sacramento.

29. Mary Elizabeth Young Arnold interview with author.

30. Ibid.

31. Theresa Mahler to David E. Weglein, superintendent of Public Instruction, Baltimore, May 5, 1945, box 1/1: Permits, Credentials, Schooling, Teaching, TSM Papers, POCP; see also Jeanne Miller interview with author, June 16, 1999, Kentfield, Calif.

32. On southern California's growth in the 1920s, see Starr, *Material Dreams.* On the growth of the film industry and its role in bringing the California dream to the rest of

the nation, see Starr, *Inventing the Dream*, 283–339. The 1920s marked the start of two decades of heavy migration to the Los Angeles area.

33. Jeanne Miller interview with author.

34. Ibid.

35. Helen Christianson and Barbara Greenwood, "The Western Share in NANE Beginnings: 1925–1935," *Journal of Nursery Education* 27 (Fall 1958), box 24, folder 4, RB Collection, UAC, CSUN.

36. See also correspondence with Docia Zavitkovsky, fall 1998, in author's possession; Letters of recommendation for Rosalie Blau by Elizabeth Woods, Sept. 11, 1941, box 1:2, and Biographical Data, 1940–45, RB Collection, UAC, CSUN.

37. Theresa Mahler to Marion Turner, April 24, 1946, box 1/1: Permits, Credentials, Schooling, Teaching, TSM Papers, POCP.

38. Jensen and Lathrop, *California Women*, 106.

39. Elizabeth Woods to Joel Burkman, Jan. 12, 1944, box 1/1, Permits, Credentials, etc., TSM Papers, POCP.

40. Theresa Mahler to Marion Turner, April 24, 1946; Theresa S. Mahler, Biography, Oct. 6, 1971, box 1/1, miscellaneous information, personal files, TSM Papers, POCP.

41. For more on Turner see the comments of Flora Jacobi Arnstein on the Presidio Open Air School of San Francisco and Progressive Education in Lawrence Arnstein interview with Edna Daniel, 248.

42. Jeanne Miller interview with author; California Children's Centers Directors and Supervisors' Association, box 2/1: Correspondence 1947/74 TSM Papers, POCP; Catherine Landreth to Distinguished Women Nomination Committee, Jan. 31, 1969, box 1/1, Personal Files, TSM Papers, POCP.

43. "Lawrence Arnstein: The Man with the Board of Directors," *Search Magazine*, Aug. 1952, 215–16, box 1/1, series 1–2, Arnstein Correspondence, John R. Weber Papers, POCP.

44. Lawrence Arnstein interview with Edna Daniel, 112.

45. Ibid.; "Lawrence Arnstein: The Man with the Board of Directors"; Stewart, "Preschools and Politics," 86–88.

46. Jeanne Miller interview with author.

47. Catherine Landreth to Distinguished Women Nomination Committee, Jan. 31, 1969, box 1/1, Personal Files, TSM Papers, POCP.

48. Winona Sample interview with author, Nov. 22, 2005; Loretta Juhas interview with author, Jan. 4, 2006, San Francisco.

49. Mahler to Woods, May 13, 1953, box 4/1, LHD, CC, 1953, TSM Papers, POCP. Woods, who retired in 1950 at the age of sixty-five, remained active in state and Los Angeles political circles until her death in 1975. Freedman, *Maternal Justice*, 346.

50. Lawrence Arnstein to Fred Luke, Jan. 19, 1953, LHD, CC, 1953, TSM Papers, POCP.

51. Lois L. Trevennen to Fred Luke, April 25, 1953, miscellaneous files, MY Papers, author's possession.

52. Jeanne Miller interview with author.

53. Larry Arnstein to Mary Young, Nov. 29, 1961, MY Papers, author's possession.

54. Young speech before the thirteenth annual conference, CPACC, MY Papers, author's possession; Mary Elizabeth Young Arnold interview with author.

55. Child Care Parents' Association of San Francisco, *Welcome to Our Child Care Centers*, MY Papers, author's possession.

56. California Parents' Association for Child Care, *Legislative Bulletin*, March 16, 1954, box 4/1, LHD, CC, 1954, TSM Papers, POCP.

57. Putnam, *Bowling Alone*, 18–20; Skocpol and Fiorina, "Making Sense," 13–16.

58. On Knight, see Rawls and Bean, *California*, 386–87, and Putnam, "The Progressive Legacy," 260–61.

59. California Legislature, Assembly, *Child Care Center Operations under the Geddes-Kraft Child Care Center Act*, March 1952, 9–10.

60. Results, State Child Care Center Questionnaire, March 1953, Division of Public School Administration, Division Chief's Files, 1949–53, ED Papers, CSA, Sacramento.

61. Stolzfus, *Citizen, Mother, Worker*, 128–33; Michel, *Children's Interests/Mothers' Rights*, 204–5.

62. Theresa Mahler to Fern Smith, Feb. 15, 1952, box 4/1, LHD, CC, 1952, TSM Papers, POCP. See also letters to Ruby Winzler in Eureka, Birdice Phillips in Napa, Barbara Gleason in Berkeley, and Ruth Howarth, March 3, 1952, all in box 4/1, LHD, CC, 1952, TSM Papers, POCP.

63. Theresa Mahler to Fern Smith, Feb. 15, 1952; Theresa Mahler to Ruth Howarth, March 3, 1952 (emphasis in the original).

64. "Your Reference for Writing Your State Legislators," box 4/1, LHD, CC, 1953, TSM Papers, POCP.

65. Ruth Howarth to Theresa Mahler, March 13, 1952, box 4/1, LHD, CC, TSM Papers, POCP.

66. Child Care Parents' Association of San Francisco, *What Our Employers Should Know about Child Care Centers*, May 6, 1953, miscellaneous file, MY Papers, author's possession; Child Care Report to Cabinet of Oakland Board of Education, Feb. 11, 1954, LHD, CC, 1954, TSM Papers, POCP.

67. Women made up 60 percent of the witnesses who spoke at both hearings. California Senate, Interim Committee on Social Welfare, *Report of the Senate Interim Committee on Social Welfare*, part 6: *The Child Care Center Program*, (Sacramento, 1955), 68–69.

68. Fraser, *Unruly Practices*, 157.

69. Theresa Mahler, Legislative Report, Sept. 23, 1954, box 5/1, Child Care Centers—Analysis, Reports, Meetings, Legislative Reports, 1951–61, TSM Papers, POCP. See also Stolzfus, *Citizen, Mother, Worker*, 177–79; Bierman "The Influence of Pressure Groups," 66–82; and "Senate Interim Committee on Social Welfare Public Hearings on Child Care Centers," San Francisco, Oct. 1, 1954, and Senate Interim Committee on Social Welfare Public Hearings on Child Care Centers, Los Angeles, Oct. 4–5, 1954, Joint Legislative Budget Committee, Transcripts of the Senate Interim Committee on Social Welfare, 1955–62, CSA, Sacramento.

70. Prepared Statement by Mary Young, Social Welfare Interim Committee hearing, San Francisco, Oct. 1, 1954, box 4/1, LHD, CC, 1954, TSM Papers, POCP.

71. Mary Young to Betty Bachman, Oct. 1, 1954, Governor of California file, MY Papers, author's possession.

72. Ibid.

73. Ibid. Colleen Norton, testimony in "Senate Interim Committee on Social Welfare, Public Hearings on Child Care, Oct. 1, 1954, San Francisco," 129–34, Transcripts of Senate Interim Committee of Social Welfare, 1955–62, Joint Legislative Budget Committee Files, CSA, Sacramento; Gutherie and Hutchinson, "The Impact of Perceptions," 382.

74. Mittelstadt, *From Welfare to Workfare*, 70–82.

75. Statement of Betty Bachman, 1954, box 4/1, LHD, CC, 1953, TSM Papers, POCP. These arguments were made on behalf of what Emilie Stolzfus has aptly labeled "productive citizenship." Working mothers, Stolzfus maintains, make their claims as citizens who make both domestic and economic contributions to society. Citizenship includes maintaining an independent household. Stolzfus, *Citizen, Mother, Worker*, 9, 188–89.

76. Ibid.

77. Mittelstadt, *From Welfare to Workfare*, 14; Bell, *Aid to Dependent Children*, 57–60.

78. Brown, *Race, Money, and the American Welfare State*, 167; Mittelstadt, *From Welfare to Workfare*, 58. See also California State Department of Education, "Rehabilitation of Disabled Parents in the Aid to Needy Children Program: An Experiment in Co-Operative Relations," *Bulletin of the California State Department of Education* 23 (Aug. 1954): 23, 60; Harry Friedman in "Senate Interim Committee on Social Welfare Public Hearings on Child Care Centers, Los Angeles, Oct. 4–5, 1954," 209–13, Joint Legislative Budget Committee, Transcripts of the Senate Interim Committee on Social Welfare, 1955–62, CSA, Sacramento.

79. "Keeping of Child Care Centers Urged," *San Francisco Chronicle*, Oct. 2, 1954. See also Mary Young to Betty Bachman, Oct. 1, 1954, MY Papers, author's possession.

80. "Statement on the Child Care Program," Joint Executive Board of Culinary Workers, Bartenders and Hotel Service Workers, box 8/1, Organizations, Calif. Senate Interim Committee on Social Welfare folder, 1954–55, TSM Papers, POCP.

81. Ibid.; *Legislative Bulletin 2*, NCANE, Oct. 1, 1954, box 8/1, TSM Papers, POCP. For a discussion of the role of the San Francisco Waitresses Local 48 in state and local child care struggles, see Cobble, "Recapturing the Working-Class Feminism," 72, and Cobble, *Dishing It Out*, 134. For the UAW on the national level see UAW-CIO Women's Bureau, Solidarity House, *Women Then and Now*, Sept. 1954, box 125B:97, Dorothy M. Healey Papers, California State University at Long Beach, and Cobble, *The Other Women's Movement*, 135–39.

82. "Senate Interim Committee on Social Welfare Public Hearing on Child Care Centers, Los Angeles, Oct. 4–5, 1954, 90–91,Transcripts of Senate Interim Committee of Social Welfare, 1955–62, Joint Legislative Budget Committee files, CSA, Sacramento.

83. McGirr, *Suburban Warriors*, 31, 43–44, 49.

84. *Legislative Bulletin 2*, NCANE, box 8/1, TSM Papers, POCP.

85. *Report of the Senate Interim Committee on Social Welfare*, 48–49. For more on Murdy see Maxine Murdy Trotter interview by Maureen McClintock Rischard, Aug. 28–29, 2001, OH 2933, transcript, Family Life in Early Orange County, Orange County Pioneer Council and Fullerton Oral History Program.

86. "Senate Interim Committee on Social Welfare, Public Hearings on Child Care,"

Oct., 1, 1954, San Francisco, California, Transcripts of Senate Interim Committee of Social Welfare, 1955–62, Joint Legislative Budget Committee Files, CSA, Sacramento.

87. "Child Care Hearings End on a Note of Disagreement," *Los Angeles Times,* Oct. 6, 1954.

88. *Report of the Senate Interim Committee on Social Welfare,* 1955, 8.

89. "Child Care Centers Left Out of Budget," *San Francisco Examiner,* Jan. 12, 1955; "Little Hope Held for Child Care Centers," *San Francisco Chronicle,* Jan. 13, 1955; "Stiff Fight Due on Child Care Centers," *San Francisco Chronicle,* Jan. 17, 1955.

90. "Strength in unity" from Theresa S. Mahler, *Legislative Report 3,* Jan. 11, 1955, box 4/1, LHD, CC, 1955, TSM Papers, POCP; Theresa S. Mahler, *Legislative Bulletin 4,* March 22, 1955, box 4/1, LHD, CC, 1955, TSM Papers, POCP.

91. Loretta Juhas remembers that Mahler "knew somebody in all the papers and she used to write editorials." Loretta Juhas interview with author.

92. Mary E. Young to Editor, "Child Care Centers," *San Francisco Chronicle,* Jan. 14, 1955.

93. "Letters to the Editor," *San Francisco Chronicle,* Jan. 19, 1955; "Letters to the Editor," *San Francisco Chronicle,* Jan. 21, 1955; "Child Care Centers," *San Francisco Examiner,* Jan. 22, 29, 1955. A similar phenomenon took place in southern California; see "Child Care," *Los Angeles Times,* Jan. 15, 1955.

94. Feldstein, *Motherhood,* 2–3.

95. "Child Care Center Program in Peril," *Los Angeles Mirror and Daily News,* March 11, 1955, box 5/1, Child Care Centers, Pamphlets and Convention Programs, 1948–62, TSM Papers, POCP.

96. Lawrence Arnstein interview with Edna Daniel, 125–30; Frank Wright, "Child Care Centers Come of Age," Oct. 15, 1955, box 2/1, miscellaneous notes, papers, TSM Papers, POCP; Lawrence Arnstein to Richard Pourade, *San Diego Union,* April 1, 1955, box 4/1, LHD, CC, 1955. On rural support see "Continue Child Care Centers," *Stockton Record,* March 5, 1955, box 6/1. Scrapbooks 1949–59, legislative clippings, 1954–55; "Homemaking Students Get Experience in Child Care," *Fresno Bee,* June 15, 1955, box 5/1, clippings, 1955; Theresa Mahler to Ernest Geddes, April 20, 1955, box 4/1, LHD, CC, 1955, TSM Papers, POCP.

97. Ernest Geddes to Theresa Mahler, Jan. 29, 1954, box 4/1, LHD, CC, 1954, TSM Papers, POCP.

98. Theresa Mahler to Ernest Geddes, Feb. 2, 1954, box 4/1, LHC, CC, 1954, TSM Papers, POCP.

99. Mahler, *Legislative Bulletin 4,* March 22, 1955, LHD, CC, 1955, TSM Papers, POCP.

100. California Parents' Association for Child Care Centers, *California Child Care Centers;* Young to Ernest Geddes, March 2, 1955, and Theresa Mahler to Ernest Geddes, March 23, 1955, miscellaneous files, both in MY Papers, author's possession.

101. Story to Theresa Mahler, Feb. 18, 1955, box 4/1, LHD, CC, 1955, TSM Papers, POCP.

102. League of Women Voters of California, Working Papers on Platform Reappraisal, 1954–55, box 17, Folder 84B, SFLWV Papers, CHS, San Francisco. By Parent Teacher Association, they meant CPACC.

103. Minutes, Non-Partisan Round Table, March 7, 1953, box 24, folder 162, League of Women Voters of California [CALWV] Papers, CHS, San Francisco.

104. "Strategy," *Legislative Bulletin 4*, March 22, 1955, box 4/1, LHD, CC, 1955; "Knight Backs Child Care Centers Bill: Tells Why He Left Out Fund Request in His Budget," *San Francisco Examiner*, Jan. 19, 1955, box 7/1, clippings-general, 1950–58, TSM Papers, POCP.

105. Theresa Mahler reported that "someone in Berkeley heard from an authoritative source that Hulse says he isn't opposed to a two-year bill!" Theresa Mahler to Ernest Geddes, March 23, 1955, MY Papers, author's possession; Theresa Mahler to Ernest Geddes, April 20, 1955, box 4/1, LHD, CC, 1955, TSM Papers, POCP.

106. Louis Sutton to Mary E. Young, May 11, 1955, miscellaneous file, MY Papers, author's possession.

107. "Child Care Bill Passes," *San Francisco Examiner*, June 8, 1955, box 6/1, legislative clippings, 1955, TSM Papers, POCP.

108. "Obituary," *Los Angeles Times*, Oct. 21, 1955.

109. Emilie Stolzfus points out the Mahler took a two-month vacation to Europe during the 1956 budget session, indicating she must have been confident about the program's future. Stolzfus, *Citizen, Mother, Worker*, 193n183.

110. *San Francisco Chronicle*, Jan. 5, 1957.

111. "Senate Interim Committee on Social Welfare, Public Hearings on Child Care," Los Angeles, 174.

Chapter 5. "We Do Not Consider Ourselves Welfare Cases"

1. Theresa Mahler, *Legislative Report*, Oct. 10, 1962, box 4/1, Legislative Historical Data [hereafter LHD], Children's Centers [hereafter CC], 1962, Theresa S. Mahler [hereafter TSM] Papers, Pacific Oaks College at Pasadena [hereafter POCP]. For more on labor force participation, see Filene, *Him/Her/Self*, 161, and Weiner, *From Working Girl*, 6.

2. U.S. Department of Labor, Women's Bureau, *Working Mothers and the Need for Child Care Services* (Washington, D.C.: U.S. Government Printing Office, 1965), 6; U.S. Bureau of the Census, *U.S. Census of Population 1960, vol. 1: Characteristic of the Population*, part 6, California, 66; Solinger, *Wake Up Little Susie*, 13; Patterson, *America's Struggle against Poverty*, 101–4. Mimi Abramovitz discusses this general trend in relation to the change in ADC clients in the 1950s in *Regulating the Lives of Women*, 321.

3. On the historical development of equating "welfare" with AFDC, see Gordon, *Pitied but Not Entitled*.

4. Mink, *Welfare's End*, 47.

5. Nelson, "The Origins of the Two-Channel Welfare State," esp. 145; Brown, *Race, Money, and the American Welfare State*.

6. Kessler-Harris, *In Pursuit of Equity*, 131.

7. Gordon, *Pitied but Not Entitled*, esp. 289–99.

8. U.S. Congress, *Handbook of Public Income Transfer Programs: 1975*, 170. It is un-

clear from the table produced in this report whether the figures on the cost of ADC are adjusted for inflation.

9. Lemann, *The Promised Land*; Mittelstadt, *From Welfare to Workfare*; Orleck, *Storming Caesar's Palace*.

10. California Legislature, *Technical Staff Report, 365*; Kurtz, *Day Care Needs and Resources*, 6.

11. California State Department of Education, *Survey of Families Requesting Service*, 19.

12. Theresa Mahler, Statement before the Interim Assembly Education Subcommittee on Special Education, Sept. 21, 1962, box 4/1, LHD, CC, 1962,TSM Papers, POCP.

13. Barbara Gach interview with the author, July 2, 1998, Belvedere, Calif.

14. Ibid.

15. Ellen Hall Mitchell interview with author, Feb. 8, 2006, Long Beach, Calif.

16. Ibid.

17. Rose, *A Mother's Job*, 198–210.

18. Self, *American Babylon*.

19. Letters to the Editor, *San Francisco Chronicle*, July 4, 1957, box 6/1, Scrapbooks, 1948–59, and other miscellaneous Letters to the Editor, legislative clippings, 1954–55, TSM Papers, POCP.

20. "Child Centers Are No Luxury," *San Francisco Call-Bulletin*, Feb. 5, 1958, box 7/1, clippings-general, 1950–58, TSM Papers, POCP.

21. "Spears Urges Cut in Child Care Centers," *San Francisco Examiner*, May 11, 1958; "Spears Talks of Cuts in Child Care," *San Francisco Chronicle*, May 11, 1958; Joan Salit Fernandez, "San Francisco Report to California State Association for Child Care Centers," Annual Convention, Nov. 15, 1958, City Council Activities, in folder: Marcus Whitman, Child Care 1958: A San Francisco View [hereafter Whitman, Child Care 1958], Mary E. Young [hereafter MY] Papers, author's possession.

22. San Francisco Unified School District, Office of the Superintendent, "Superintendent's Survey of the Child Care Program," May 12, 1958, Whitman, Child Care 1958, MY Papers, author's possession.

23. Ibid.

24. "Letters to the Editor," *San Francisco Call-Bulletin*, Feb. 10, 1958, box 5/1: folder, Child Care Centers, Analysis, Reports, Meetings, *Legislative Reports*, 1950–61, TSM Papers, POCP.

25. Tebb, *Thoughtful Reflections*, 25–26.

26. All biographical information on Young comes from Nyda Young, "Where's Nyda? An Illustrated Autobiography," in Karl Young's possession. Young began the autobiography in 1994 but did not complete it before she died in 1997.

27. San Francisco Parents' Association for Child Care, *Save Child Care*, May 1958, Whitman, Child Care 1958, MY Papers, author's possession.

28. Fernandez, "San Francisco Report to California State Association for Child Care Centers," Whitman, Child Care 1958.

29. Debbie Young, Mary Young's daughter, remembers nights spent stuffing envelopes

and going to parents' meetings with her mother. Deborah Young interview with author, Dec. 15, 1998, Fairfax, Calif.

30. Fernandez, "San Francisco Report to California State Association for Child Care Centers."

31. Barbara Gach interview with author.

32. "Labor Assails Cut in Child Care Funds," *San Francisco Chronicle*, May 24, 1958.

33. Statement reprinted in San Francisco League of Women Voters, Minutes of Membership Meeting, May 21, 1958, box 1, folder 1, League of Women Voters of San Francisco Papers, California Historical Society, San Francisco.

34. Statement of Child Care Parents' Association of San Francisco, Board of Education meeting, May 20, 1958, City Council Activities, Whitman, Child Care 1958, MY Papers, author's possession.

35. In San Francisco, the average enrollment in child care centers was fifty-three children. Superintendent's Survey of Child Care Program, May 12, 1958,Whitman, Child Care 1958, MY Papers, author's possession.

36. Ibid.; Statement of Nancy Koehler, past president of the Child Care Centers Parents' Association of San Francisco, May 20, 1958, City Council Activities,Whitman, Child Care 1958, MY Papers, author's possession; Minutes, San Francisco Board of Education, May 20, 1948, Spears MSS., Manuscripts Department, Lilly Library, Indiana University, Bloomington.

37. "Petition to the San Francisco School Board Supporting the Child Care Program," May 20, 1958, Whitman, Child Care 1958, MY Papers, author's possession.

38. "School Board Orders Cut in Child Care," *San Francisco Chronicle*, May 21, 1958; Fernandez, "San Francisco Report to California State Association for Child Care Centers," Whitman, Child Care 1958.

39. "Spears Drops Plan to Shut Care Centers, *San Francisco Chronicle*, June 7, 1958; "Spears Moves to Keep Open S.F. Child Centers," *San Francisco Call-Bulletin*, June 6, 1958; "Child Care Centers Stay Spears Rules," *San Francisco News*, June 6, 1958.

40. Barbara Gach interview with author.

41. Fernandez, "San Francisco Report to California State Association for Child Care Centers," Whitman, Child Care 1958.

42. Mary Young, California Parents' Association for Child Care Centers, Thirteenth Annual Conference, Nov. 11, 1961, MY Papers, author's possession.

43. CPACC, "Tips on Organizing Parent Meetings," Governor of California folder, MY Papers, author's possession.

44. Young, CPACC, Thirteenth Annual Conference, Nov. 11, 1961.

45. Theresa Mahler, "The Individual as an Activator in Legislation," 1959, box 2/1, Speeches-Statements, 1951–64, TSM Papers, POCP.

46. Ibid.

47. On voluntary associations as sites that "nurtured the development and exchange of women's ideas about a range of important ideas," see Perry, "The Women's Voluntary Association," 39–44.

48. U.S. Children's Bureau, "Licensed Day Care Facilities for Children," preliminary report prepared by Seth Low, October 1960, in U.S. Congress, House of Representatives,

Public Welfare Amendments of 1962: Hearings before the Committee on Ways and Means, 87th Cong., 2d sess., Feb. 7, 9, 13, 1962, 193, 212.

49. For an excellent discussion of this national movement for child care, see Michel, *Children's Interests/Mothers' Rights,* 192–235.

50. On public preschool programs see Beatty, *Preschool Education in America;* Greenblatt, *Responsibility for Child Care;* and Steiner, *The Children's Cause.*

51. As quoted in Michel, *Children's Interests/Mothers' Rights,* 235.

52. Theresa Mahler, *Legislative Report,* Oct. 10, 1962, box 4/1, LHD CC, 1962, TSM Papers, POCP.

53. Kurtz, *Day Care Needs and Resources,* 3.

54. California Legislature, Assembly, *Report on the Child Care Program by the Assembly Interim Committee on Social Welfare,* 24; see also California Legislature, Assembly, *Child Care Center Operations under the Geddes-Kraft Child Care Center Act,* 8.

55. "A History of Major Legislation Affecting Child Care and Preschool Funding," *On the Capitol Doorstep,* 1994, and California State Board of Agriculture, Resolution, re: Child Care Centers, box 4/2, LHD, CC, 1964, TSM Papers, POCP.

56. Emma Gunterman interview with Jacqueline S. Reinier, *Emma Gunterman: Lobbyist and Advocate for Consumers, Children, and Seniors, 1967–1986,* 86.

57. Dymally succeeded longtime child care center advocate Augustus Hawkins when Hawkins was elected to the U.S Congress in 1962. Haskins, *Distinguished African American Political and Governmental Leaders,* 74–75.

58. Mervyn M. Dymally, Memorandum, "Child Care and Pre-school Centers: AB 1423," box 8, folder 23: Child Care Centers, Mervyn M. Dymally [hereafter MD] Papers, John F. Kennedy Library [hereafter JFKL], California State University at Los Angeles [hereafter CSULA].

59. Ibid.

60. Mary Young, *Legislative Report,* California Parents' Association for Childrens' Centers Seventeenth Annual Conference, Nov. 29, 1965, miscellaneous files, MY Papers, author's possession.

61. SCANE *News and Views,* Legislative Committee Report, Aug. 1961, box 10–6, Newsletter SCANE, 1953–68, Southern California Association for the Education of Young Children Papers, Urban Archives, California State University at Northridge, Northridge; Theresa Mahler to Mervyn M. Dymally, March 20, 1963, and Mrs. Barbara Betzenderfer, legislative advocate, CAAAUW to Mervyn M. Dymally, April 2, 1963, both in box 8, folder 24, MD Papers, JFKL, CSULA.

62. Mervyn M. Dymally, "Analysis of Assembly Bill 265," box 8, folder 22: Child Care Centers, 1965, MD Papers, JFKL, CSULA.

63. Mervyn M. Dymally, Memorandum, "Child Care and Pre-school Centers: AB 1423."

64. "Unruh Bill Hit: Periled Image of Kindergarten," *San Francisco Chronicle,* April 8, 1965.

65. Ibid.

66. Linda Gordon and other historians have identified "superior" and "inferior" tracks in the U.S. welfare system, observing the substantial differences between "social insurance and public assistance, federal and state/local, contributory and noncontributory,

contributions or rights-based and needs-based, beneficiaries and dependents, or entitlements and 'welfare.'" Programs in the "inferior" category, such as AFDC, tended to be highly stigmatized. The child care centers, in Mahler's view, at least until 1965, were considered a "superior" program. Gordon, *Pitied but Not Entitled,* 293.

67. Lawrence Arnstein to State Senator George Miller Jr., June 22, 1964, Division of Administration, Division Chief's files, Department of Administration, Child Care/Children's Centers, 1963-66, State Department of Education Records, California State Archives [hereafter CSA], Sacramento.

68. Abramovitz, *Regulating the Lives of Women,* 321; Solinger, *Wake Up Little Susie,* 42–49.

69. Daniel Patrick Moynihan's infamous report, *The Negro Family: The Case for National Action,* came out in March 1965. Although the report was not discussed in public until the summer and fall, Moynihan's conclusions about black families drew on the concerns circulating in the public discourse and in turn reinforced them by confirming the direct connection between black, female-headed families and the rising numbers of families dependent on AFDC. Rainwater and Yancey, *The Moynihan Report,* 51. For the relationship between the attack on welfare and black families, see Abramovitz, *Regulating the Lives of Women,* 319–28.

70. Margaret Pignatelli to Lyndon Johnson, March 29, 1965, box 4/1, LHD, CC, 1965, TSM Papers, POCP.

71. Mary Young, *CPACC Legislative Bulletin 2,* March 15, 1965, box 4/1, LHD, CC, 1965, TSM Papers, POCP.

72. Edith Arrowood to Mervyn M. Dymally, March 31, 1965, box 8, folder 25, Child Care, MD Papers, JFKL, CSULA.

73. Marjorie Hughes to Mervyn M. Dymally, April 8, 1965, box 4/1, LHD, CC, 1965, TSM Papers, POCP.

74. Deborah Young interview with author; Margaret Pignatelli to Mervyn M. Dymally, May 6, 1965, box 8, folder 22, Child Care 1965, MD Papers, JFKL, CSULA; Margaret Pignatelli to Guy Wright, March 29, 1965, LHD, CC, 1965, TSM Papers, POCP.

75. Ibid.

76. Mary Young, *Legislative Report,* CPACC Seventeenth Annual Conference, Nov. 20, 1965, miscellaneous, MY Papers, author's possession.

77. Marjorie Hughes to Mervyn M. Dymally, April 8, 1965, box 4/1, LHD, CC, 1965, TSM Papers, POCP.

78. Ibid. Unfortunately, we will never know whether Johnson replied, for there is no evidence of a response.

79. Theresa Mahler to Leo J. Ryan, April 20, 1965, LHD, CC, 1965, TSM Papers, POCP. For more on the hearings see Young, *Legislative Report,* Nov. 20, 1965.

80. San Francisco Unified School District, Child Care Centers Division, Proceedings at Committee Hearings, April 19, 1965, LHD, CC, 1965, TSM Papers, POCP.

81. Ibid.

82. Theresa Mahler, notes on telephone conversations re: AB1281, Children's Centers Act, May 18, 1965, LHD, CC, 1965, TSM Papers, POCP.

83. Theresa Mahler before San Francisco Child Care Parents' Association, Aug. 19, 1965, as quoted in Stewart, "Preschools and Politics," 198.

84. Theresa Mahler to Leo J. Ryan, April 20, 1965, TSM Papers, POCP.

85. Leo J. Ryan to Theresa Mahler, April 25, 1965, LHD, CC, TSM Papers, POCP.

86. On Mahler's recommendations see Theresa Mahler to Ronald Cox, Oct. 22, 1964, LHD, CC, 1964, TSM Papers, POCP. On changes in legislative intent see Max Rafferty to Edmund Brown, June 30, 1965, Chapter 1717, 1965, Governor's Chapter Bill Files, CSA, Sacramento; Young, *Legislative Report,* Nov. 20, 1965.

87. California Child Care Directors and Supervisors' Association, "Recommendations for Modifications and/or Additions to Chapter 5, Article 1, of the California Education Code," LHD, CC, 1964, TSM Papers, POCP.

Chapter 6. A Different Kind of Welfare State

1. Lynne Monti and Willie Mae Addison to Parents, Aug. 19, 1970, box 8/1, Parents' Association, California, 1970–71, Theresa S. Mahler [hereafter TSM] Papers, Pacific Oaks College at Pasadena [hereafter POCP].

2. Lynne [Monti] Beeson interview with author, May 2, 2006, San Francisco.

3. Deborah Young interview with author, Nov. 25, 2005, Larkspur, Calif.

4. Fay E. [Love] Williams, interview with author, July 12, 2006, Antioch, Calif.; Ellen Hall Mitchell interview with author, Feb. 8, 2006, Long Beach.

5. San Francisco Unified School District, Children's Centers Division, *Legislative Bulletin,* May 10, 1968, box 8/1: Organizations, California Children's Centers, Directors and Supervisors' Association, State Legislative Data, 1968–70, TSM Papers, POCP.

6. Northern Section, California Children's Centers Directors and Supervisors Association, Legislative Committee Meeting, Dec. 28, 1966, box 8/1: Organizations, California Children's Centers Directors and Supervisors' Association, Northern Section, 1966–69, TSM Papers, POCP.

7. Sharon Godske interview with author, March 11, 2006, Berkeley.

8. *California Blue Book,* 1967, 124. Winona Sample also speaks about how critical Vasconcellos was to the child care coalition from the late 1960s forward. Winona Sample interview with author, Nov. 21, 2005, Folsom, Calif.

9. Sharon Godske interview with author.

10. Vinovskis, *The Birth of Head Start,* 150–51; Beatty, *Preschool Education in America,* 194.

11. Theresa S. Mahler, "Legislation—1968—with a Few Glances at 1967," presented at the twenty-fifth annual conference, California Children's Centers Directors and Supervisors' Association, May 4, 1968, box 4/2, LHD, 1968, TSM Papers, POCP.

12. Quadagno, *The Color of Welfare,* 144.

13. Steiner, *The Children's Cause,* 19; Ray H. Johnson, Associate Superintendent of Public Instruction, to District, City, and County Superintendents of Schools Maintaining Children's Centers, memorandum, April 11, 1969, box 8/1: Organization, Children's Centers Directors and Supervisors Association, Northern Section, 1966–69, TSM Papers, POCP.

14. As quoted in Mittelstadt, *From Welfare to Workfare*, 170.

15. Orleck, *Storming Caesar's Palace*, 127.

16. Mittelstadt, *From Welfare to Workfare*, 163. See also Quadagno, *The Color of Welfare*, 144.

17. Cannon, *Governor Reagan*, 350.

18. California State Department of Social Welfare, *Social and Economic Characteristics of Aid to Needy Children Families*, 4.

19. Orleck, *Storming Caesar's Palace*, 128.

20. Niccolaides, *My Blue Heaven*; Self, *American Babylon*.

21. Katz, *The Undeserving Poor*, 68.

22. Cannon, *Governor Reagan*, 5–9; Putnam, "A Half-Century of Conflict," 48–49.

23. Ronald Reagan, Inaugural Address, Jan. 5, 1967, Speeches and Announcements, Governor's Papers, available from http://www.reagan.utexas.edu/archives/speeches/govspeech/01051967a.htm, accessed June 10, 2006; "Reagan Pledges to Squeeze, Cut, and Trim Spending," *Los Angeles Times*, Jan. 6, 1967. See also McGirr, *Suburban Warriors*, 191–210.

24. Self, *American Babylon*, 281–90; Niccolaides, *My Blue Heaven*, 272–80.

25. Quadagno, *The Color of Welfare*, 145–46.

26. Grace J. Angstman to Carley Porter, April 27, 1966, Office Files, Senate Bills, A-C, Assemblymen—Porter, Carley V., Legislature, Assembly, California State Archives [hereafter CSA], Sacramento. See also Betty Moore to John Weber, Aug. 22, 1966, Division of Public Administration, Division Chief's Files, Department Administration, 1963–66, Department of Education, CSA, Sacramento. On backlash against Governor Brown, see Cannon, *Governor Reagan*, 8.

27. Marjorie Caro to Ronald Reagan, July 13, 1967, box 4/2, LHD, re: Children's Centers, 1967, TSM Papers, POCP.

28. Lynne [Monti] Beeson interview with author; Fay [Love] Williams interview with author.

29. The number of Hispanic children enrolled in the state's centers increased throughout the 1960s and 1970s as well; in 1974, they made up 10 percent of the center's children. But there is little evidence of Hispanic parents' political involvement during this period. Legislative Analyst, *Publicly Subsidized Child Care Services in California*, Aug. 23, 1974 (Sacramento: State of California), 74.

30. Fay [Love] Williams interview with author; Self, *American Babylon*, 51.

31. Cohen, *A Consumer's Republic*, 223.

32. Fay Love became Fay Williams when she married Mose Williams in the 1970s. Fay [Love] Williams interview with author.

33. Ibid.; Loretta Juhas interview with author, Jan. 5, 2006, San Francisco.

34. Fay [Love] Williams interview with author.

35. Johnnie Tillmon interview with Sherna Berger Gluck, n.d., Women's History: Welfare Mothers, Welfare Rights, the Virtual Oral/Aural History Archive, California State University, Long Beach, interview 3d segment 4 (10:52–18:19) Segkey: a4812, Aug. 9, 2006, http://www.csulb.edu/voaha.

36. White, *Too Heavy a Load*, 223–26; West, *The National Welfare Rights Movement*,

22, 83. For similar organizing in Las Vegas see Orleck, *Storming Caesar's Palace,* 98–130; for the national scene see Kornbluh, The *Battle for Welfare Rights,* 28.

37. White, *Too Heavy a Load,* 240.

38. Valk, "Mother Power," 49; Orleck, *Storming Caesar's Palace.*

39. As quoted in "Conference Boosts the 'Big Baby Sitter,'" *Los Angeles Times,* May 6, 1969.

40. Ibid; West, *The National Welfare Rights Movement,* 5, 89; Willie Mae Addison, Work History, Jan. 18, 1972, CPACC folder, Lynne Beeson Papers, copy in author's possession.

41. On NAPP in Los Angeles see Tsuchiya, "Race, Class, and Gender in America's War on Poverty," 223–24.

42. "Neighborhood Center Holds 'Outfit the Family' Day," *Long Beach Press Independent,* Feb. 22, 1971; "Disputed Carmelitos Center to Reopen," *Long Beach Press Independent,* April 19, 1972.

43. As quoted in "Neighborhood Center Holds 'Outfit the Family' Day."

44. Mittelstadt, *From Welfare to Workfare,* 136–41.

45. Rosen, *The World Split Open,* 67.

46. Harrison, *On Account of Sex,* 109–14, 157–59.

47. Jensen and Lathrop, *California Women,* 129.

48. Advisory Commission on the Status of Women, *California Women* (1969), 5.

49. Advisory Commission, *California Women* (1967), 30.

50. Ibid., 30, 40.

51. Ibid., 40.

52. Notes of Vern Sturgeon on Memorandum from P. Battaglia, July 5, 1967, box 1967/26, Correspondence Unit, Administrative, Status of Women, June, Gubernatorial Papers, Ronald Reagan Library, Simi Valley, Calif.

53. Advisory Commission on the Status of Women, *Transcript of the Public Hearings on Day Care,* iv.

54. Ibid., 41.

55. Theresa S. Mahler, "The Children's Center and Its Impact on the Community," speech at San Jose State College, Dec. 3, 1966, box 4/1: misc. papers, speeches/statements, 1966–73/74, TSM Papers, POCP.

56. Advisory Commission on the Status of Women, *Transcript of the Public Hearings on Day Care,* 39.

57. White, *Too Heavy a Load,* 231.

58. Espanola Jackson interview with Robert Martin, July 14, 1969, Oral History, Moorland-Spingarn Research Center, Howard University, Washington, D.C.; Crowe, *Prophets of Rage,* 204–8.

59. Espanola Jackson interview with Robert Martin.

60. Ibid., 86.

61. Ibid.; Orleck, *Storming Caesar's Palace,* 98–108.

62. Lynne [Monti] Beeson interview with author.

63. Advisory Commission on the Status of Women, *Transcript of the Public Hearings on Day Care,* 106–7.

64. Espanola Jackson interview with Robert Martin.

65. Alan G. Sieroty oral history interview with Carlos Vasquez, California State University Fullerton, Center for Oral and Public History, State Government Oral History Project, 1989, 1990.

66. The group's statement sits in the files of his children's center construction bill; Neighbors of Watts, Statement, AB 891 files, 1968, Sieroty Papers, CSA, Sacramento. See also "NOW—A Good Neighbor Policy for Beverly Hills," *Los Angeles Times*, May 30, 1968.

67. This child care center opened its doors with great fanfare in 1974. Later it was renamed the Johnnie Tillmon Child Development Center. "Child Care Center Built on Wealth, Welfare," *Los Angeles Times,* Feb. 19, 1974.

68. Theresa S. Mahler to George Miller, April 11, 1968, box 4/2, LHD, Re: Children's Centers, 1968, TSM Papers, POCP.

69. Agatha Cohee, secretary, Southern Section, California Children's Centers Directors and Supervisors Association, to Ronald Reagan, June 5, 1968, AB 891 files, 1968, Sieroty Papers.

70. Theresa Mahler to Caspar Weinberger, April 11, 1968, box4/2, LHD, Re: Children's Centers, 1968, TSM Papers, POCP.

71. Ronald Reagan, Inaugural Address, Jan. 5, 1967, Ronald Reagan Presidential Library, National Archives and Records Administration, accessed Nov. 30, 2010, http://www.reagan.utexas.edu/archives/speeches/govspeech/01051967a.htm; Enrolled Bill Report on SB 39, Health and Welfare Agency, Aug. 15, 1968, chapter 1373, Governor's Chapter Bill Files, CSA, Sacramento.

72. "School Board to Receive Plans for Venice Child Care Center," *Los Angeles Times,* Sept. 26, 1968.

73. Burnett Children's Center Opening, June 23, 1969, box 8/1, Organizations: Children's Centers Parents' Association of San Francisco, 1961–70, TSM Papers, POCP.

74. San Francisco Unified School District, *A Report on Children's Centers,* table 1, March 1973, box 5/1, Children's Center Issues (San Francisco), 1968–74, TSM Papers, POCP.

75. As quoted in Evans, *Tidal Wave,* 24.

76. MacLean, *Freedom Is Not Enough,* 136.

77. Steiner, *The Children's Cause,* 156; Evans, *Tidal Wave,* 55–56. Jill Quadagno observes that federal "child care was never a priority for NOW, and as child-care legislation moved through Congress, no NOW members testified on behalf of the bills." Quadagno, *The Color of Welfare*, 147.

78. Cobble, *The Other Women's Movement,* 197; Evans, *Tidal Wave,* 55.

79. Email correspondence between Aileen Hernandez and Lynne Beeson, May 29, 2006, copy in author's possession.

80. Evans, *Tidal Wave,* 27.

81. *San Francisco Women's Liberation Internal Newsletter,* May 20, Oct. 26, 1970, reel 20, Herstory Microfilm Collection, Women's History Research Center, Berkeley, Calif., 1972. For more examples of women's liberation groups advertising child care services or the forming of child care cooperatives, see the *Berkeley Women's Newsletter,* Oct.–Nov. 2, 1971, issue through March 13–20, 1973, issue, also in the Herstory Microfilm Collection.

82. Gilmore, "The Dynamics of Second-wave Feminist Activism in Memphis," 194; Chappell, "Rethinking Women's Politics in the 1970s," 158.

83. As quoted in Gilmore, "The Dynamics of Second-wave Feminist Activism in Memphis," 194. NOW is not mentioned in transcripts of state legislative hearings on child care from the mid-1960s to 1973 or in the legislative correspondence. The president of the Sacramento Area NOW chapter is quoted in the *California Journal* as supporting child care as "an essential ingredient to bring full equality of opportunity to women in employment and education." "Child Care Services Win Wide Support," *California Journal*, July–Aug. 1971, 202.

84. *The Covenant*, No. 1 (Feb. 1972), Lynne Beeson's personal files, copy in author's possession.

85. Lynne [Monti] Beeson interview with author.

86. Kennedy, *Freedom from Fear*, 196, 198.

87. Jacobs, *Pocketbook Politics*, 226.

88. Lynne [Monti] Beeson interview with author.

89. Most of the information on Beeson's life comes from an interview I conducted with her in 2006; a few additional details are from an interview on January 20, 1980. Transcript, Lynne Beeson's personal files, copy in author's possession.

90. Lynne [Monti] Beeson interview with author.

91. Orleck, *Storming Caesar's Palace*, 83.

92. Gilmore, "The Dynamics of Second-wave Activism in Memphis," 205.

93. Lynne [Monti] Beeson interview with author.

94. Sharon Godske, "A Position Paper on the Legislative Analyst's Recommendations Concerning Children's Centers," California Parents' Association for Children's Centers, 4/2, LHD, re: Children's Centers, 1967–71, TSM Papers, POCP.

95. Theresa Mahler, "A Position Paper Regarding the Legislative Analyst's Proposals Affecting Children's Centers," California Children's Centers Directors and Supervisors' Association, April 28, 1967, 4/2, LHD, re: Children's Centers, 1967, TSM Papers, POCP.

96. Godske, "A Position Paper on the Legislative Analyst's Recommendations."

97. Mahler, "A Position Paper Regarding the Legislative Analyst's Proposals."

98. Docia Zavitkovsky interview with author, July 28, 1998, Los Angeles.

99. Head Start funds had been temporarily cut in 1967 before they were expanded again the following year.

100. Lynne [Monti] Beeson interview with author.

101. "Child Care Services Win Wide Support," 202.

102. State, County and Federal Affairs Committee to the Los Angeles City Council, April 3, 1968, Senate Bill 39, Chapter 1373, Governor's Chapter Bill Files, California CSA, Sacramento.

103. *Children's Centers Are in Jeopardy*, July 18, 1970, box 8/1, CC, Directors and Supervisors Association, State Legislative Data, 1968–70, TSM Papers, POCP; "The Children's Centers," *San Francisco Chronicle*, June 26, 1970; quote from "The Children's Center Should Not Be Cut," *Sacramento Bee*, June 26, 1970. .

104. Fay [Love] Williams interview with author.

105. Lynne [Monti] Beeson interview with author.

106. Fay [Love] Williams interview with author.

107. Jerry Lewis to Ronald Reagan, Sept. 3, 1970, AB 750, Chapter 1619, Governor's Chapter Bill Files, CSA, Sacramento.

108. Theresa Mahler to the Honorable George S. Moscone, Sept. 4, 1970, box 4/2, LHD, Children's Centers, 1970, TSM Papers, POCP.

109. William Roberts, coordinator of children's centers, to Mr. A. Karperos, director of special services, Yuba City Unified School District, October 21, 1971, Division of Public Administration, Division Chief's Files, Department Administration, Development of Child Care/Children's Centers, 1971, Department of Education Records, CSA, Sacramento.

110. Jeanada Nolan interview with author, Dec. 21, 2005, Sacramento.

111. Elizabeth Prescott et. al., *An Institutional Analysis of Day Care Program*, 95; John Weber to Lawrence Arnstein, Dec. 1, 1970, box 1/1, series 1–2, Lawrence Arnstein Correspondence, 1953–73, John R. Weber Papers, POCP.

112. Theresa Mahler to San Francisco Board of Education, March 5, 1971, box 1/1, Personal Papers, Letter to SF Board of Education, TSM Papers, POCP.

113. Lorna Logan to Theresa Mahler, May 18, 1971, box 1/1, Personal Papers, Retirement Cards and Letters, TSM Papers, POCP.

114. John R. Weber, "The Children's Centers Program from the Point of View of the California State Department of Education," Oct. 17, 1968, Compensatory Education, Administrative Files, Preschool Education Programs, Bureau of, 1968–69, Department of Education Records, CSA, Sacramento; California Legislative Analyst, *Publicly Subsidized Child Care Services in California*, vix–x.

115. Sharon Godske interview with author.

Conclusion

1. Thomas M. Jones to Lynne Monti, Nov. 22, 1971, CPACC folder, Lynne [Monti] Beeson [hereafter LB] Papers, copy in author's possession; Pollack, "Schools That Save Families," 82.

2. Farida Melendy, speech at the twenty-third annual conference of the California Parents' Association for Children's Centers, Nov. 12, 1971, CPACC, LB Papers, copy in author's possession.

3. Farida Melendy, To the Parents of Santa Monica Children's Center, Re: Advisory Board Meeting Minutes, Nov. 22, 1971, CPACC, LB Papers, copy in author's possession.

4. Lynne Monti to Yvonne Braithwaite, Dec. 1, 1971, Office Correspondence, Campaign–Child Care, LP 69:19, Yvonne Braithwaite Papers, California State Archives, Sacramento.

5. Lynne Monti to Juliana Hawkes, February 2, 1972, LB Papers, copy in author's possession.

6. Lynne Monti to David Michaelis, [n.d.], CPACC, LB Papers, copy in author's possession. Lynne [Monti] Beeson's letter is a response to Michaelis's November 21, 1971, correspondence.

7. Lynne [Monti] Beeson's papers contain no evidence of correspondence by CPACC after March 1972.

8. "Child Care Crisis Mobilizes Mothers," *Los Angeles Times*, March 16, 1973.

9. "Working Mother's Dilemma: Child Centers or Welfare?" *San Francisco Examiner* and *San Francisco Chronicle*, March 11, 1973; Lynne [Monti] Beeson interview with author, May 2, 2006, San Francisco.

10. As quoted in "Children Join Day Care Cutback Protests," *Los Angeles Times*, March 15, 1973.

11. The *Los Angeles Times* reported that Senator Tunney had received more than six thousand letters and Senator Cranston more than five thousand. Earl Brian, secretary of health and welfare, told a reporter that his office received more than 2,500. "State Welfare Chief's Child Care Stand," unknown newspaper, March 1973, box 158: Research Files (Molly Sturgis Tuthill), Education–Child Care, Governor's Office Files, Ronald Reagan: Gubernatorial Papers, 1966–75, Ronald Reagan Presidential Library, Simi Valley, Calif.

12. As quoted in "Children Join Day Care Cutback Protests."

13. Sharon Godske interview with author, March 11, 2006, Berkeley.

14. Fay [Love] Williams interview with author, July 12, 2006, Antioch, Calif.

15. Ellen Hall Mitchell interview with author, Feb. 8, 2006, Long Beach.

16. Mary Elizabeth [Young] Arnold, interview with author, Oct. 7, 1998, Santa Rosa, Calif.

17. Lynne [Monti] Beeson interview with author, May 2, 2006, San Francisco.

18. Winona Sample interview with author, Nov. 21, 2005, Folsom, Calif.

19. Deborah Young interview with author, Nov. 25, 2005, Larkspur, Calif.

20. Jeanne Miller interview with author, June 16, 1999, Kentfield, Calif.

21. Winona Sample interview with author.

Selected Bibliography

Abramovitz, Mimi. *Regulating the Lives of Women: Social Welfare Policy from Colonial Times to the Present*. Boston: South End Press, 1996.

Acklesberg, Martha. "Communities, Resistance, and Women's Activism: Some Implications for a Democratic Polity." In *Women and the Politics of Empowerment*, ed. Ann Bookman and Sandra Morgan, 297–313. Philadelphia: Temple University Press, 1988.

Anderson, Karen. *Wartime Women: Sex Roles, Family Relations, and the Status of Women During World War II*. Westport: Greenwood Press, 1981.

Anthony, Susan B. *Out of the Kitchen into the War*. New York: Stephen Daye, 1943.

Antler, Joyce. *Lucy Sprague Mitchell: The Making of a Modern Woman*. New Haven: Yale University Press, 1987.

Bakken, Gordon Morris, and Alexandra Kindell. *Encyclopedia of Immigration and Migration in the American West*. Vol. 2. Thousand Oaks: Sage Publications, 2006.

Barrett, Edward L. *The Tenney Committee: Legislative Investigation of Subversive Activities in California*. Ithaca: Cornell University Press, 1951.

Baxandall, Rosalyn. "Re-Visioning the Women's Liberation Movement's Narrative: Early Second Wave African American Feminists." *Feminist Studies* 27 (Spring 2001): 225–45.

Beatty, Barbara. *Preschool Education in America: The Culture of Young Children from the Colonial Era to the Present*. New Haven: Yale University Press, 1995.

Bell, Winifred. *Aid to Dependent Children*. New York: Columbia University Press, 1965.

Berry, Mary Frances. *The Politics of Parenthood: Child Care, Women's Rights, and the Myth of the Good Mother*. New York: Viking Press, 1993.

Bierman, Beatrice. "The Influence of Pressure Groups on Child Care Legislation in California." M.A. thesis, University of California at Berkeley, 1949.

Bookman, Ann, and Sandra Morgan. "Rethinking Women and Politics: An Introductory Essay." In *Women and the Politics of Empowerment*, ed. Ann Bookman and Sandra Morgan, 3–29. Philadelphia: Temple University Press, 1988.

Boris, Eileen. "The Power of Motherhood: Black and White Activist Women Redefine the 'Political.'" In *Mothers of a New World: Maternalist Politics and the Origins of Welfare States,* eds. Seth Koven and Sonya Michel, 213–45. New York: Routledge, 1993.

Bothman, Annette. "Reflections of the Pioneers on the Early History of the Santa Monica Children's Centers and Changing Child-Rearing Philosophies." M.A. thesis, California State University, Northridge, 1976.

Braitman, Jacqueline. "Partisans in Overalls: New Perspectives on Women and Politics in Wartime California." In *The Way We Really Were: The Golden State in the Second Great War,* ed. Roger Lotchin, 215–35. Urbana: University of Illinois Press, 2000.

Brown, Hubert. "The Impact of War Worker Migration on the Public School System of Richmond, California, from 1940–1945." Ph.D. diss., Stanford University, 1973.

Brown, Michael K. *Race, Money, and the American Welfare State.* Ithaca: Cornell University Press, 1999.

Butler, Mary Ellen. *Black Women Stirring the Waters.* Oakland: Marcus Books, 1998.

Cahan, Emily. *A History of U.S. Preschool Care and Education for the Poor, 1920–1965.* New York: National Center for Children in Poverty, Columbia University, 1989.

Campbell, D'Ann. *Women at War with America: Private Lives in a Patriotic Era.* Cambridge: Harvard University Press, 1984.

Cannon, Lou. *Governor Reagan: His Rise to Power.* New York: Public Affairs Books, 2003.

Cantril, Hadley. *Public Opinion, 1935–1946.* Princeton: Princeton University Press, 1951.

Chafe, William. *The American Woman: Her Changing Social, Economic, and Political Roles, 1920–1970.* New York: Oxford University Press, 1972.

Chang, Tse Hua. "Comparative Study of Child Day Care Centers in Los Angeles, California, and Canton, China." Ph.D. diss., Claremont Graduate School, 1949.

Chappell, Marisa. "Rethinking Women's Politics in the 1970s: The League of Women Voters and the National Organization for Women Confront Poverty." *Journal of Women's History* 13 (Winter 2002): 155–79.

Christianson, Helen, Mary M. Rogers, and Blanche A. Ludlum. *The Nursery School: Adventure in Living and Learning.* Boston: Houghton Mifflin, 1961.

Christopher, Maurine. *America's Black Congressman.* New York: Thomas Y. Cromwell, 1971.

Clinton, Ione L. "Migrants' Children Need Daytime Care." *The Child* 10 (Feb. 1946): 125–27.

Close, Kathryn. "Day Care Up to Now." *Survey Midmonthly* 79, no. 7 (1943): 194–97.

Cloward, Richard A., and Frances Fox Piven. *Poor People's Movements: Why They Succeed, How They Fail.* New York: Pantheon Books, 1977.

Cobble, Dorothy Sue. *Dishing It Out: Waitresses and Their Unions in the Twentieth Century.* Urbana: University of Illinois Press, 1991.

———. *The Other Women's Movement: Workplace Justice and Social Rights in Modern America.* Princeton: Princeton University Press, 2004.

———. "Recapturing the Working-Class Feminism: Union Women in the Postwar Era, 1945–60." In *Not June Cleaver: Women and Gender in Postwar America, 1945–1960,* ed. Joanne Meyerowitz, 57–83. Philadelphia: Temple University Press, 1994.

Cohen, Lisabeth. *A Consumer's Republic: The Politics of Mass Consumption in Postwar America.* New York: Vintage Books, 2003.

Coontz, Stephanie. *The Way We Never Were: American Families and the Nostalgia Trap.* New York: Basic Books, 1992.

Cott, Nancy. *The Grounding of Modern Feminism.* New Haven: Yale University Press, 1987.

———. "What's in a Name? The Limits of 'Social Feminism'; or, Expanding the Vocabulary of Women's History." *Journal of American History* 76 (1989): 809–29.

Cray, Ed. *Chief Justice: A Biography of Earl Warren.* New York: Simon and Schuster, 1997.

Crouchett, Lawrence P., Lonnie G. Bunch III, and Martha Kendall Winnacker. *Visions toward Tomorrow: The History of the East Bay Afro-American Community, 1852–1977.* Oakland: Northern California Center for Afro-American Community, 1989.

Crowe, Daniel. *Prophets of Rage: The Black Freedom Struggle in San Francisco, 1945–1969.* New York: Garland Publishing, 2000.

Cunningham, Charles E. and D. Keith Osborne. "A Historical Examination of Blacks in Early Childhood Education." *Young Children* 34, no. 3 (1979): 20–29.

Davis, Martha F. "Welfare Rights and Women's Rights in the 1960s." *Journal of Policy History* 21, no. 1 (1996): 144–65.

Dewitt, Howard. *The California Dream.* Dubuque: Kendall/Hunt Publishing, 1997.

Dratch, Howard. "The Politics of Child Care in the 1940s." *Science and Society* 38 (Summer 1974): 167–204.

DuBois, Ellen. "Eleanor Flexner and the History of American Feminism." *Gender and History* 3 (Spring 1991): 81–90.

Evans, Sara M. *Tidal Wave: How Women Changed America at Century's End.* New York: Free Press, 2003.

———, and Harry C. Boyte. *Free Spaces: The Sources of Democratic Change in America.* New York: Harper and Row, 1986.

Feldstein, Ruth. *Motherhood in Black and White.* Ithaca: Cornell University Press, 2000.

Filene, Peter G. *Him/Her/Self: Gender Identities in Modern America.* Third ed. Baltimore: Johns Hopkins University Press, 1998.

Fousekis, Natalie. "Fighting for Our Children: Women's Activism and the Battle for Child Care in California, 1945–1965." Ph.D. diss., University of North Carolina at Chapel Hill, 2000.

———. "Lois Hayden Meek Stolz." In *Notable American Women: A Biographical Dictionary, Volume 5: Completing the Twentieth Century,* ed. Susan Ware and Stacy Braukman, 617–19. Cambridge: Harvard University Press, 2004.

Fowler, Marion Lyle. "A Study of the Economic Status of Student Veterans of World War II having Children in State-Supported Child Care Centers." M.A. thesis, University of California at Berkeley, 1947.

Frantzich, Stephen. "Citizen Democracy: Political Activist in a Cynical Age." In *People, Passions, and Power: Social Movements, Interest Organizations, and the Political Process,* ed. John C. Green. Lanham, Md.: Rowman and Littlefield, 1999.

———. *Write Your Congressman: Constituent Communications and Representation.* New York: Praeger Publishers, 1986.

Fraser, Nancy. "Rethinking the Public Sphere: A Contribution to the Critique of Actually Existing Democracy." In *Habermas and the Public Sphere,* ed. Craig Calhoun, 109–42. Cambridge: MIT Press, 1992.

———. "The Struggle over Needs: Outline of a Socialist-Feminist Critical Theory of Late Capitalist Political Culture." In *Women, the State, and Welfare,* ed. Linda Gordon, 199–225. Madison: University of Wisconsin Press, 1990.

———. *Unruly Practices: Power, Discourse and Gender in Contemporary Social Theory.* Minneapolis: University of Minnesota Press, 1989.

Fraser, Steve, and Gary Gerstle, eds. *The Rise and Fall of the New Deal Order, 1930–1980.* Princeton: Princeton University Press, 1989.

Freedman, Estelle. *Maternal Justice: Miriam Van Waters and the Female Reform Tradition.* Chicago: University of Chicago Press, 1996.

———. *No Turning Back: The History of Feminism and the Future of Women.* New York: Ballantine Books, 2003.

———. "Separatism Revisited: Women's Institutions, Social Reform, and the Career of Miriam Van Waters." In *U.S. History as Women's History: New Feminist Essays,* ed. Alice Kessler-Harris, Linda K. Kerber, and Kathryn Kish Sklar, 170–88. Chapel Hill: University of North Carolina Press, 1995.

Gabin, Nancy. *Feminism in the Labor Movement: Women and the United Auto Workers, 1935–1975.* Ithaca: Cornell University Press, 1990.

Garrow, David J., ed. *The Montgomery Bus Boycott and the Women Who Started It: The Memoir of Jo Ann Gibson Robinson.* Knoxville: University of Tennessee Press, 1987.

Gerstle, Gary and Steve Fraser, eds. *Rise and Fall of the New Deal Order: 1930–1980.* Princeton: Princeton University Press, 1989.

Gilmore, Glenda. *Gender and Jim Crow: Women and the Politics of White Supremacy in North Carolina, 1896–1920.* Chapel Hill: University of North Carolina Press, 1996.

Gilmore, Stephanie. "The Dynamics of Second-Wave Feminist Activism in Memphis, 1971–1982: Re-Thinking the Liberal/Radical Divide." *NWSA Journal* 15, no. 1 (2003): 94–117.

———, ed. *Feminist Coalitions: Historical Perspectives on Second-wave Feminism in the United States.* Urbana: University of Illinois Press, 2008.

Glenn, Evelyn Nakano. "Social Constructions of Mothering: A Thematic Overview." In *Mothering: Ideology, Experience, and Agency,* ed. Grace Chang, Evelyn Nakano Glenn, and Linda Rennie Forcey, 1–29. New York: Routledge, 1994.

Gluck, Sherna. *Rosie the Riveter Revisited: Women, the War, and Social Change.* Boston: Twayne, 1987.

Goldin, Claudia. *Understanding the Gender Gap: An Economic History of American Women.* New York: Oxford University Press, 1992.

Goodwin, Doris Kearns. *No Ordinary Time: Franklin and Eleanor Roosevelt: The Home Front in World War II.* New York: Simon and Schuster, 1995.

Gordon, Linda. "Black and White Visions of Welfare: Women's Welfare Activism, 1890–1945." *Journal of American History* 78 (1991): 556–90.

———, ed. "The New Feminist Scholarship on the Welfare State." In *Women, the State, and Welfare,* 9–35. Madison: University of Wisconsin Press, 1990.

———. *Pitied but Not Entitled: Single Mothers and the History of Welfare*. New York: Free Press, 1994.

Grant, Julia. "Lois Meek Stolz." In *Women Educators in the United States, 1820–1993: A Bio-Biographical Sourcebook*, ed. Maxine Schwartz Seller, 472–479. Westport, Conn: Greenwood Press, 1994.

———. *Raising Baby by the Book: The Education of American Mothers*. New Haven: Yale University Press, 1998.

Greenblatt, Bernard. *Responsibility for Child Care: The Changing Role of Family and State in Child Development*. San Francisco: Jossey-Bass Publishers, 1977.

Greene, Christina. *Our Separate Ways: Women and the Black Freedom Movement in Durham, North Carolina*. Chapel Hill: University of North Carolina Press, 2005.

Gutherie, Patricia, and Janis Hutchinson. "The Impact of Perceptions on Interpersonal Interactions in an African-American/Asian-American Housing Project." *Journal of Black Studies* 27 (Jan. 1995): 377–95.

Hall, Jacquelyn Dowd. *Revolt against Chivalry: Jessie Daniel Ames and the Women's Campaign against Lynching*. New York: Columbia University Press, 1993.

———, James Leloudis, Robert Korstad, Mary Murphy, Lu Ann Jones, and Christopher B. Daly. *Like a Family: The Making of a Southern Cotton Mill World*. New York: W.W. Norton, 1989.

Halper, Betty Lois. "Recollections of Los Angeles Children's Centers' Early Days." M.A. thesis, California State University, Northridge, 1977.

Harrison, Cynthia. *On Account of Sex: The Politics of Women's Issues, 1945–1968*. Berkeley: University of California Press, 1988.

Hartmann, Susan. *The Homefront and Beyond: American Women in the 1940s*. Boston: Twayne Publishers, 1982.

———. "Women's Employment and the Domestic Ideal in the Early Cold War Years." In *Not June Cleaver: Women and Gender in Postwar America, 1945–1960*, ed. Joanne Meyerowitz, 84–100. Philadelphia: Temple University Press, 1994.

———. "Women's Organizations during World War II: The Interaction of Class, Race, and Feminism." In *Woman's Being, Woman's Place: Female Identity and Vocation in American History*, ed. Mary Kelley, 313–28. Boston: G. K. Hall, 1977.

Haskins, James. *Distinguished African American Political and Governmental Leaders*. Phoenix: Oryx Press, 1999.

Hassan, Amina. "Rosie Re-Riveted in Public Memory: A Rhetorical Study of WWII Shipyard Childcare in Richmond, California, and the 1946–1957 Campaign to Preserve Public Supported Childcare." Ph.D. diss., Ohio University, 2005.

Healey, Dorothy, and Maurice Isserman. *Dorothy Healey Remembers: A Life in the American Communist Party*. New York: Oxford University Press, 1990.

Hewitt, Nancy. *Southern Discomfort: Women's Activism in Tampa, Florida, 1880s–1920s*. Urbana: University of Illinois Press, 2001.

Higginbotham, Evelyn Brooks. *Righteous Discontent: The Women's Movement in the Black Baptist Church, 1880–1920*. Cambridge: Harvard University Press, 1993.

Horowitz, Daniel. *Betty Friedan and the Making of the Feminine Mystique: The Ameri-*

can Left, the Cold War, and Modern Feminism. Amherst: University of Massachusetts Press, 1998.

Hymes, James. *Living History Interviews, book 2: Care of the Children of Working Mothers*. Carmel, Calif.: Hacienda Press, 1978.

Jacobs, Meg. *Pocketbook Politics: Economic Citizenship in Twentieth-Century America*. Princeton: Princeton University Press, 2005.

Jensen, Joan M., and Gloria Ricci Lathrop. *California Women: A History*. Sparks, Nev.: Material for Today's Learning, 1988.

Jetter, Alexis, Annelise Orleck, and Diana Taylor, eds. *The Politics of Motherhood: Activist Voices from Left to Right*. Hanover: University Press of New England, 1997.

Johnson, Glenna. "What Mothers Think about Day Care." *The Child* 10 (Jan. 1946): 103–6.

Johnson, Marilynn S. *The Second Gold Rush: Oakland and the East Bay in World War II*. Berkeley: University of California Press, 1993.

Jones, Elizabeth, and Elizabeth Prescott. *An Institutional Analysis of Day Care Program, part 2: Group Day Care: The Growth of an Institution*. Pasadena: Pacific Oaks College, 1970.

Kaledin, Eugenia. *Mothers and More: American Women in the 1950s*. Boston: Twayne Publishers, 1984.

Kaplan, Temma. *Crazy for Democracy: Women in Grassroots Movements*. New York: Routledge, 1997.

———. "Female Consciousness and Collective Action: The Case for Barcelona, 1910–1918." *Signs* 7 (Spring 1982): 546–66.

Katcher, Leo. *Earl Warren: A Political Biography*. New York: McGraw-Hill, 1967.

Katz, Michael B. *The Undeserving Poor : From the War on Poverty to the War on Welfare*. New York: Pantheon Books, 1989.

———. "The Urban 'Underclass' as a Metaphor for Social Transformation." In *The "Underclass" Debate: Views from History*, ed. Michael B. Katz, 3–24. Princeton: Princeton University Press, 1993.

Kelley, Edna Ewing. "Uncle Sam's Nursery Schools." *Parent's Magazine*, March 1936, 24–25.

Kennedy, David M. *Freedom from Fear: The American People in Depression and War*. New York: Oxford University Press, 1999.

Kerber, Linda. "A Constitutional Right to Be Treated Like American Ladies: Women and the Obligations of Citizenship." In *U.S. History as Women's History: New Feminist Essays*, ed. Alice Kessler-Harris, Linda K. Kerber, and Kathryn Kish Sklar, 17–35. Chapel Hill: University of North Carolina Press, 1995.

———. "The Meanings of Citizenship." *Journal of American History* 84 (Dec. 1997): 833–54.

Kesselman, Amy. *Fleeting Opportunities: Women Shipyard Workers in Portland and Vancouver during World War II and Reconversion*. Albany: State University of New York Press, 1990.

Kessler-Harris, Alice. *Out to Work : A History of Wage-Earning Women in the United States*. New York: Oxford University Press, 1982.

———. *In Pursuit of Equity: Women, Men, and the Quest for Economic Citizenship in Twentieth-Century America.* New York: Oxford University Press, 2001.

———. *A Woman's Wage.* Lexington: University Press of Kentucky, 1990.

Kornbluh, Felicia A. *The Battle for Welfare Rights: Politics and Poverty in Modern America.* Philadelphia: University of Pennsylvania Press, 2007.

———. "To Fulfill Their 'Rightly Needs': Consumerism and the National Welfare Rights Movement." *Radical History Review* 69 (1997): 76–113.

———. "The New Literature on Gender and the Welfare State: The U.S. Case." *Feminist Studies* 22 (Spring 1996): 171–97.

Korstad, Robert Rodgers. *Civil Rights Unionism: Tobacco Workers and the Struggle for Democracy in the Mid-Twentieth-Century South.* Chapel Hill: University of North Carolina Press, 2003.

———, and Nelson Lichtenstein. "Opportunities Found and Lost: Labor, Radicals, and the Early Civil Rights Movement." *Journal of American History* 75 (Dec. 1988): 786–811.

Koshuk, Ruth Pierson. "Developmental Records of Five Hundred Nursery School Children." *Journal of Experimental Education* 16 (Dec. 1947): 134–48.

Kunzel, Regina. *Fallen Women, Problem Girls: Unmarried Women and the Professionalization of Social Work, 1890–1945.* New Haven: Yale University Press, 1993.

———. "White Neurosis, Black Pathology: Constructing Out-of-Wedlock Pregnancy in the Wartime and Postwar United States." In *Not June Cleaver: Women and Gender in Postwar America, 1945–1960,* ed. Joanne Meyerowitz, 304–31. Philadelphia: Temple University Press, 1994.

Kurtz, Dorothy M. *Day Care Needs and Resources.* Sacramento: State Department of Social Welfare, November, 1962.

Lachantere, Diana. "Interview with Katherine Stewart Flippin." In *Black Women Oral History Project: From the Arthur and Elizabeth Schlesinger Library on the History of Women in America,* ed. Ruth Edmonds Hill. Westport: Meckler, 1991.

Ladd-Taylor, Molly. *Mother-Work: Women, Child Welfare, and the State, 1890–1930.* Urbana: University of Illinois Press, 1994.

Lazerson, Marvin, and W. Norton Grubb. "Child Care, Government Financing, and the Public Schools: Lessons from the California Children's Centers." *School Review* 86 (Nov. 1977): 5–37.

Lebsock, Suzanne, and Nancy A. Hewitt, eds. *Visible Women: New Essays on American Activism.* Urbana: University of Illinois Press, 1993.

Lemann, Nicholas. *The Promised Land: The Great Black Migration and How It Changed America.* (New York: Vintage Books, 1992).

Lemke-Santangelo, Gretchen. *Abiding Courage: African American Migrant Women and the East Bay Community.* Chapel Hill: University of North Carolina Press, 1996.

Lemons, Stanley. *The Woman Citizen: Social Feminism in the 1920s.* Charlottesville: University of Virginia Press, 1990.

Lerner, Gerda. *Fireweed: A Political Autobiography.* Philadelphia: Temple University Press, 2002.

Levenstein, Lisa. *A Movement without Marches: African American Women and the Politics of Poverty in Postwar Philadelphia.* Chapel Hill: University of North Carolina Press, 2009.

Lichtenstein, Nelson. *Labor's War at Home: The CIO in World War II.* New York: Cambridge University Press, 1982.

Lichtman, Sheila. "Women at Work, 1941–1945: Wartime Employment in the San Francisco Bay Area." Ph.D. diss., University of California at Davis, 1981.

Lotchin, Roger. *The Bad City in the Good War: San Francisco, Los Angeles, Oakland, and San Diego.* Bloomington: Indiana University Press, 2003.

———. *Fortress California, 1910–1961: From Warfare to Welfare.* New York: Oxford University Press, 1992.

———, ed. *The Way We Really Were: The Golden State in the Second Great War.* Urbana: University of Illinois Press, 2000.

Low, Ann Marie. *Dust Bowl Diary.* Lincoln: University of Nebraska Press, 1984.

Lundberg, Emma. "Ascertaining Day-Care Needs." *The Child* 7 (July 1942): 6–8.

———. "A Community Program of Day Care for Children of Mothers Employed in Defense Areas." *The Child* 6 (Jan. 1942): 152–61.

———. "State and Local Committees Planning Day-Care Programs." *The Child* 7 (July 1942): 8–9.

Lynn, Susan. *Progressive Women in Conservative Times: Racial Justice, Peace, and Feminism, 1945 to the 1960s.* New Brunswick: Rutgers University Press, 1994.

MacLean, Nancy. *Freedom Is Not Enough: The Opening of the American Workplace.* Cambridge: Harvard University Press, 2006.

———. "The Hidden History of Affirmative Action: Working Women's Struggles in the 1970s and the Gender of Class." *Feminist Studies* 25 (Spring 1999): 43–78.

Margolis, Maxine. *Mothers and Such: Views of American Women and Why They Changed.* Berkeley: University of California Press, 1984.

May, Elaine Tyler. *Homeward Bound: American Families in the Cold War Era.* New York: Basic Books, 1999.

McEnaney, Laura. "Nightmares on Elm Street: Demobilizing in Chicago, 1945–1953." *Journal of American History* 92 (March 2006): 1265–91.

McGirr, Lisa. *Suburban Warriors: The Origins of the New American Right.* Princeton: Princeton University Press, 2001.

Messer, Lynette. *Who's Who on the Pacific Coast.* Chicago: A. N. Marguis, 1949.

Meyer, Agnes. *Journey through Chaos.* New York: Harcourt, Brace, 1944.

Meyerowitz, Joanne, ed. *Not June Cleaver: Women and Gender in Postwar America, 1945–1960.* Philadelphia: Temple University Press, 1994.

Michel, Sonya. "American Women and the Discourse of the Democratic Family in World War II." In *Behind the Lines: Gender and the Two World Wars,* ed. Jane Jenson, Margaret Randolph Higonnet, Sonya Michel, and Margaret Collins Weitz, 154–67. New Haven: Yale University Press, 1987.

———. *Children's Interests/Mothers' Rights: The Shaping of America's Child Care Policy.* New Haven: Yale University Press, 1999.

———. "The Limits of Maternalism: Policies toward American Wage-Earning Mothers during the Progressive Era." In *Mothers of a New World: Maternalist Politics and the Origins of Welfare States,* ed. Seth Koven and Sonya Michel, 277–320. New York: Routledge, 1993.

——— and Seth Koven. "Introduction: 'Mother Worlds.'" In *Mothers of a New World: Maternalist Politics and the Origins of Welfare States,* eds. Seth Koven and Sonya Michel, 1–42. New York: Routledge, 1993.

Mink, Gwendolyn. *Welfare's End.* Ithaca: Cornell University Press, 2002.

Mittelstadt, Jennifer. *From Welfare to Workfare: The Unitended Consequences of Liberal Reform.* Chapel Hill: University of North Carolina Press, 2005.

Mobil Travel Guide: California and the West. New York: Rand McNally, 1975.

Mouffe, Chantal. *The Democratic Paradox.* New York: Verso Press, 2000.

Muncy, Robyn. "Cooperative Motherhood and Democratic Civic Culture in Postwar Suburbia, 1940–1965." *Journal of Social History* 38, no. 2 (2004): 285–310.

———. *Creating a Female Dominion in American Reform, 1890–1935.* New York: Oxford University Press, 1991.

Murray, Sylvie. *The Progressive Housewife: Community Activism in Suburban Queens, 1945–1965.* Philadelphia: University of Pennsylvania Press, 2003.

Nadasen, Premilla. "Expanding the Boundaries of the Women's Movement: Black Feminism and the Struggle for Welfare Rights." *Feminist Studies* 28 (Summer 2002): 271–301.

Naples, Nancy. *Grassroots Warriors: Activist Mothering, Community Work, and the War on Poverty.* New York: Routledge, 1998.

Nash, Gerald. *The American West Transformed: The Impact of the Second World War.* Bloomington: Indiana University Press, 1985.

Nasstrom, Kathryn L. "Down to Now: Memory, Narrative, and Women's Leadership in the Civil Rights Movement in Atlanta, Georgia." *Gender and History* 11 (April 1999): 113–44.

Navasky, Victor S. *Naming Names.* New York: Penguin Books, 1991.

Nelson, Barbara J. "The Origins of the Two-Channel Welfare State: Workmen's Compensation and Mother's Aid." In *Women, the State, and Welfare,* ed. Linda Gordon, 123–51. Madison: University of Wisconsin Press, 1990.

Niccolaides, Becky. *My Blue Heaven: Life and Politics in the Working-class Suburbs of Los Angeles, 1920–1965.* Chicago: University of Chicago Press, 2002.

Nickerson, Michelle. "The Power of a Morally Indignant Woman." *Journal of the West* 42 (Summer 2003): 35–43.

———. "Women, Domesticity, and Postwar Conservatism." *OAH Magazine of History* 17 (Jan. 2003): 17–21.

Orleck, Annelise. *Common Sense and a Little Fire: Women and Working-Class Politics in the United States, 1900–1965.* Chapel Hill: University of North Carolina Press, 1995.

———. "'If It Wasn't for You I'd Have Shoes for My Children': The Political Education of Las Vegas Welfare Mothers." In *The Politics of Motherhood: Activist Voices from Left to Right,* ed. Annelise Orleck, Alexis Jetter, and Diana Taylor, 102–88. Hanover: University Press of New England, 1997.

———. *Storming Caesar's Palace: How Black Mothers Fought Their Own War on Poverty.* Boston: Beacon Press, 2005.

———. "Tradition Unbound: Radical Mothers in International Perspective." In *The Politics of Motherhood: Activist Voices from Left to Right,* ed. Annelise Orleck, Alexis Jetter, and Diana Taylor, 3–20. Hanover: University Press of New England, 1997.

Parker, Zelma. "Strangers in Town." *Survey Midmonthly* 79 (July 1943): 170–71.

Parson, Don. *Making a Better World: Public Housing, the Red Scare, and the Direction of Modern Los Angeles*. Minneapolis: University of Minneapolis Press, 2005.

Pateman, Carole. "The Patriarchal Welfare State." In *Democracy and the Welfare State*, ed. Amy Gutman, 231–60. Princeton: Princeton University Press, 1988.

Patterson, James T. *America's Struggle against Poverty, 1900–1985*. Cambridge: Harvard University Press, 1986.

Perry, Elisabeth Israels. "The Women's Voluntary Association as a Source for Women's Intellectual History." *Intellectual History Newsletter* 15 (1993): 39–44.

Pittman, Tarea Hall. "The Operation of State and County Residence Requirements under the California Indigent Aid Law in Contra Costa County." M.A. thesis, University of California at Berkeley, 1946.

Pollack, Jack Harrison. "Schools That Save Families." *Nation's Business* (Sept. 1952).

Prescott, Elizabeth, Elizabeth Jones, Ellen Marshall, and Cynthia Milich. *An Institutional Analysis of Day Care Program*, part 2: *Group Day Care: The Growth of an Institution*. Pasadena: Pacific Oaks College, 1970.

———, Cynthia Milich, and Elizabeth Jones. *The "Politics" of Day Care*. Washington, D.C.: National Association for the Education of Young Children, 1972.

Pritchard, Robert. "California Un-American Activities Investigations: Subversion on the Right." *California Historical Society Quarterly* 49 (Dec. 1970): 309–27.

Putnam, Jackson K. "A Half-Century of Conflict: The Rise and Fall of Liberalism in California Politics, 1943–1993." In *Politics in the American West*, ed. Richard Lowitt. Norman: University of Oklahoma Press, 1995.

———. "The Progressive Legacy in California: Fifty Years of Politics, 1917–1967." In *California Progressivism Revisited*, ed. William Deverell and Tom Sitton, 247–68. Berkeley: University of California Press, 1994.

Putnam, Robert D. *Bowling Alone: The Collapse and Revival of American Community*. New York: Simon and Schuster, 2001.

———. "The Prosperous Community: Social Capital and Public Life." *American Prospect*, no. 13 (Spring): 35–42.

Quadagno, Jill. *The Color of Welfare: How Racism Undermined the War on Poverty*. New York: Oxford University Press, 1994.

Raftery, Judith. "Los Angeles Clubwomen and Progressive Reform." In *California Progressivism Revisited*, ed. Willliam Deverell and Tom Sitton, 144–74. Berkeley: University of California Press, 1994.

Rainwater, Lee, and William L. Yancey. *The Moynihan Report and the Politics of Controversy*. Cambridge: M.I.T. Press, 1967.

Rawls, James J., and Walton Bean. *California: An Interpretive History*. Fourth ed. New York: McGraw-Hill, 1983.

Reese, Ellen. "Maternalism and Political Mobilization: How California's Postwar Child Care Campaign Was Won." *Gender and Society* 10 (Oct.1996): 566–89.

Reese, M. Lisle. *South Dakota: A Guide to the State*. New York: Hastings House, 1952.

Reeves, Nancy. "California: Child Care Centers." *Frontier* 6 (May 1955): 11–12.

Riley, Susan. "Caring for Rosie's Children: Child Care, American Women and the Federal Government in the World War II Era." Ph.D. diss., University of California at Berkeley, 1996.

Roland, Carol Marie. "The California Kindergarten Movement: A Study in Class and Social Feminism." Ph.D. diss., University of California at Riverside, 1980.

Rose, Elizabeth. *A Mother's Job: The History of Day Care, 1890–1960*. New York: Oxford University Press, 1999.

Rosen, Ruth. *The World Split Open: How the Modern Women's Movement Changed America*. New York: Penguin Books, 2000.

Ruderman, Florence. *Child Care and Working Mothers: A Study of Arrangements Made for Day Time Care of Children*. New York: Child Welfare League of America, 1968.

Ruiz, Vicki L. *Cannery Women, Cannery Lives: Mexican Women, Unionization, and the California Food Processing Industry, 1930–1950*. Albuquerque: University of New Mexico Press, 1987.

———. *From Out of the Shadows: Mexican Women in Twentieth-Century America*. New York: Oxford University Press, 1998.

Rupp, Leila J., and Verta Taylor. *Survival in the Doldrums: The American Women's Rights Movement, 1945 to the 1960s*. New York: Oxford University Press, 1987.

Sale, June Solnit. "Implementation of a Head Start Preschool Education Program: Los Angeles, 1965–1967." In *Project Head Start: A Legacy of the War on Poverty*, ed. Edward Zigler and Jeanette Valentine, 175–94. New York: Free Press, 1979.

Scales, Janola. "A Study of the Development of the Los Angeles Unified School District Children's Centers." Ed.D. diss., Pepperdine University, 1983.

Schlup, Leonard C., and Donald W. Whisenhunt, eds. *It Seems to Me: Selected Letters of Eleanor Roosevelt*. Lexington: University Press of Kentucky, 2005.

Self, Robert. *American Babylon: Race and the Struggle for Postwar Oakland*. Princeton: Princeton University Press, 2003.

Shapiro, Virginia. "The Gender Basis of American Social Policy." In *Women, the State, and Welfare*, ed. Linda Gordon, 36–54. Madison: University of Wisconsin Press, 1991.

Sides, Josh. *L.A. City Limits: African American Los Angeles from the Great Depression to the Present*. Berkeley: University of California Press, 2003.

Sklar, Kathryn Kish. *Florence Kelly and the Nation's Work: The Rise of Women's Political Culture, 1830–1900*. New Haven: Yale University Press, 1995.

———. "Hull-House in the 1890s: A Community of Women Reformers." *Signs: The Journal of Women in Culture and Society* 10 (Summer 1985): 658–77.

Skocpol, Theda, and Morris P. Fiorina. "Making Sense of the Civic Engagement Debate." In *Civic Engagement in American Democracy*, ed. Theda Skocpol and Morris P. Fiorina, 1–20. New York: Russell Sage Foundation, 1999.

Smith, Jessie Carney, ed. *Notable Black American Men*. Detroit: Gale Research, 1999.

Solinger, Rickie. *Wake Up Little Susie: Single Pregnancy and Race before Roe v. Wade*. New York: Routledge, 1992.

Sparks, Holloway. "Dissident Citizenship: Democratic Theory, Political Courage, and Activist Women." *Hypatia* 12 (Fall 1997): 75–110.

———. "Dissident Citizenship: Lessons on Democracy and Political Courage." Ph.D. diss., University of North Carolina at Chapel Hill, 1999.

Stack, Carol. *Call to Home: African Americans Reclaim the Rural South.* New York: Basic Books, 1996.

Starr, Kevin. *Embattled Dreams: California in War and Peace, 1940–1950.* New York: Oxford University Press, 2002.

———. *Endangered Dreams: The Great Depression in California.* New York: Oxford University Press, 1996.

———. *Inventing the Dream: California through the Progressive Era.* New York: Oxford University Press, 1985.

———. *Material Dreams: Southern California through the 1920s.* New York: Oxford University Press, 1990.

Staub, Michael. "Labor Activism and the Postwar Politics of Motherhood: Tillie Olsen in the People's World." In *The Critical Response to Tillie Olsen*, ed. Hoyle Nelson and Nancy Hulse, 104–9. New York: Greenwood Press, 1994.

Steiner, Gilbert Y. *The Children's Cause.* Washington, D.C.: Brookings Institute, 1976.

Steinfels, Margaret O'Brien. *Who's Minding the Children? The History and Politics of Day Care in America.* New York: Simon and Schuster, 1973.

Stevenson, Louise L. "Women's Intellectual History: A New Direction." *Intellectual History Newsletter* 15 (1993): 32–38.

Stewart, Dorothy Jean. "Preschools and Politics: A History of Early Childhood Education in California." Ed.D. diss., University of California at Berkeley, 1990.

Stock, Catherine McNicol. *Main Street in Crisis: The Great Depression and the Old Middle Class on the Northern Plains.* Chapel Hill: University of North Carolina Press, 1992.

Stolz, Lois Meek. "Effects of Maternal Employment on Children: Evidence from Research." *Child Development* 31 (1960): 749–82.

Stolzfus, Emilie. *Citizen, Mother, Worker: Debating Public Responsibility for Child Care after the Second World War.* Chapel Hill: University of North Carolina Press, 2003.

Storrs, Landon. *Civilizing Capitalism: The National Consumers' League, Women's Activism, and Labor Standards in the New Deal Era.* Chapel Hill: University of North Carolina Press, 2000.

———. "Red Scare Politics and the Suppression of Popular Front Feminism: The Loyalty Investigation of Mary Dublin Keyserling." *Journal of American History* 90 (Sept. 2003): 491–524.

Straub, Eleanor. "Government Policy toward Civilian Women during World War II." Ph.D. diss., Emory University, 1973.

Sussman, Leila. *Letters to FDR: A Study of Political Letter Writing.* Totowa: Bedminster Press, 1963.

Swerdlow, Amy. "The Congress of American Women: Left-Feminist Peace Politics in the Cold War." In *U.S. History as Women's History: New Feminist Essays,* ed. Alice Kessler-Harris, Linda K. Kerber, and Kathryn Kish Sklar, 296–312. Chapel Hill: University of North Carolina Press, 1995.

———. *Women Strike for Peace: Traditional Motherhood and Radical Politics in the 1960s.* Chicago: University of Chicago Press, 1993.

Tebb, Kathleen Phillips. *Thoughtful Reflections for Future Directions: The Los Angeles*

County Child Care Oral History. Los Angeles: Los Angeles County Child Care Advisory Board, 1998.

Thelen, David. *Becoming Citizens in the Age of Television: How Americans Challenged the Media and Seized Political Initiative during the Iran-Contra Debate.* Chicago: University of Chicago Press, 1996.

Tilly, Charles. "From Interaction to Outcomes in Social Movements." In *How Social Movements Matter,* ed. Marco Giugni, Doug McAdam, and Charles Tilly. Minneapolis: University of Minnesota Press, 1999.

Tobias, Sheila, and Lisa Anderson. *What Really Happened to Rosie the Riveter? Demobilization and the Female Labor Force, 1944–47.* New York: MSS Modular Publications, 1974.

Tsuchiya, Kazuyo. "Race, Class, and Gender in America's War on Poverty: The Case of Opal C. Jones in Los Angeles, 1964–1968." *Japanese Journal of American Studies,* no. 15 (2004): 213–36.

Valk, Anne. "'Mother Power': The Movement for Welfare Rights in Washington, DC, 1966–1972." *Journal of Women's History* 11, no. 4 (2000): 34–58.

———. *Radical Sisters: Second-Wave Feminism and Black Liberation in Washington, D.C.* Urbana: University of Illinois Press, 2008.

Verge, Arthur. *Paradise Transformed: Los Angeles during the Second World War.* Dubuque: Kendall/Hunt Publishing, 1993.

Vinovskis, Maris. *The Birth of Head Start: Preschool Education Policies in the Kennedy and Johnson Administrations.* Chicago: University of Chicago Press, 2005.

Ware, Susan. "American Women in the 1950s: Nonpartisan Politics and Women's Politicization." In *Women, Politics, and Change,* ed. Louise A. Tilly and Patricia Gurin, 281–299. New York: Russell Sage Foundation, 1990.

———. *Partner and I: Molly Dewson, Feminism, and New Deal Politics.* New Haven: Yale University Press, 1987.

Warren, Earl. *The Memoirs of Earl Warren.* New York: Doubleday, 1977.

Weigand, Kathleen. *Red Feminism: American Communism and the Making of Women's Liberation.* Baltimore: Johns Hopkins University Press, 2001.

Weiner, Lynn. *From Working Girl to Working Mother: The Female Labor Force in the United States, 1820–1980.* Chapel Hill: University of North Carolina Press, 1985.

West, Guida. *The National Welfare Rights Movement: The Social Protest of Poor Women.* New York: Praeger, 1981.

Westbrook, Robert. *John Dewey and American Democracy.* Ithaca: Cornell University Press, 1991.

———. "'I Want a Girl, Just Like the Girl that Married Harry James': American Women and Problem of Political Obligation in World War II." *American Quarterly* 42 (Dec. 1990): 587–614.

White, Deborah Gray. *Too Heavy a Load: Black Women in Defense of Themselves, 1894–1994.* New York: W.W. Norton, 1999.

White, Lucie E. "Listening across the Race Line: Conversations with Women in Project Head Start." Unpublished manuscript, Dec. 1999.

———. "No Exit: Rethinking 'Welfare Dependency' from a Different Ground." *George-town Law Journal* 81 (June 1993): 1961–2002.

Wild, Mark. *Street Meeting: Multiethnic Neighborhoods in Early-Twentieth-Century Los Angeles*. Berkeley: University of California Press, 2005.

Woods, Elizabeth. "A Community Plans a Nursery School." *Childhood Education* 27 (May 1951): 415–19.

Youcha, Geraldine. *Minding the Children: Child Care in America from Colonial Times to the Present*. New York: Scribner, 1995.

Young, Iris Marion. "Gender as Seriality: Thinking about Women as a Social Collective." *Signs: Journal of Women in Culture and Society* 19 (Spring 1994): 713–38.

Young, Mary. *Descendents of Josiah Bull, Jr. (1738–1813) of Dutchess County New York and His Ancestry*. Vol. 1. Baltimore: Gateway Press, 1992.

Zeiger, Robert. *The CIO, 1935–1955*. Chapel Hill: University of North Carolina Press, 1995.

Government Documents

California Advisory Commission on the Status of Women. *California Women*. Sacramento: State of California, 1967.

———. *California Women*. Sacramento: State of California, 1969.

———. *Transcript of the Public Hearings on Day Care*. Sacramento: State of California, 1968.

California Legislative Analyst. *Publicly Subsidized Child Care Services in California*, Aug. 23, 1974. Sacramento: State of California, 1974.

California Legislature. *Technical Staff Report to the Joint Committee on Preschool and Primary Training*. Sacramento, Jan. 17, 1947.

California Legislature, Assembly. *Child Care Center Operations under the Geddes-Kraft Child Care Center Act*. Sacramento, March 1952.

———. *Report on the Child Care Program by the Assembly Interim Committee on Social Welfare*. Sacramento, Jan. 1951.

California Legislature, Senate Interim Committee on Economic Planning.1943 Regular Session. *Report of the Senate Committee to Investigate the Establishment of Nursery Schools and Child Care Centers*. Sacramento, 1943.

California Senate 1943 Regular Session. *Report of Senate Fact-Finding Committee: Care of Children and Aged in California*. Sacramento, 1943.

California Senate Interim Committee on Social Welfare. *Report of the Senate Interim Committee on Social Welfare, part 6, The Child Care Center Program*. Sacramento, 1955.

———. *A Report on the Care of Children in War Time*. Sacramento: Curtis Publishing, 1942.

California State Department of Education. *California Program for the Care of Children of Working Parents*. Sacramento, Aug. 1943.

———. *Child Care by California School Districts*. Sacramento, Dec. 1945.

———. *Report of Child Care Centers Administered and Operated by California School Districts*. Sacramento, March 1948.

———. *Survey of Families Requesting Service or Enrolling Children in Child Care Centers.* Sacramento: State Department of Education, 1955.

California State Department of Social Welfare. *Social and Economic Characteristics of Aid to Needy Children Families, March 1960.* Research Series Report 17. Sacramento: State Department of Social Welfare, 1961.

Public Papers of the Presidents of the United States: Lyndon B. Johnson, 1965–69. Washington, D.C.: U.S. Government Printing Office, 1969.

U.S. Bureau of the Census. *Fifteenth Census of the United States: 1930, Population.* Vol. 3, part 2. Washington, D.C.: U.S. Government Printing Office, 1932.

———. *Historical Statistics of the United States: Colonial Times to 1970,* part 1, *Bicentennial Edition.* Washington, D.C.: U.S. Government Printing Office, 1975.

———. *U.S. Census of Population: 1950,* vol. 2: *Characteristics of the Population,* part 5, *California.* Washington, D.C.: U.S. Government Printing Office, 1952.

———. *U.S. Census of Population: 1960,* vol. 1: *Characteristics of the Population,* part 6, *California.* Washington, D.C.: U.S. Government Printing Office, 1963.

U.S. Children's Bureau. *Child Care Arrangements of Working Mothers.* Report by Henry Lajewski, No. 378. Washington, D.C.: U.S. Government Printing Office, 1959.

U.S. Congress. House Committee on Naval Affairs, Subcommittee of the Committee on Naval Affairs. *Investigation of Congested Areas.* 78th Cong., 1st sess., 1943.

———. Joint Economic Committee Subcommittee on Fiscal Policy. *Handbook of Public Income Transfer Programs: 1975: A Staff Study Prepared for the Use of the Subcommittee on Fiscal Policy of the Joint Economic Committee, Congress of the United States.* Washington, D.C.: U.S. Government Printing Office, 1974.

———. Senate. *Wartime Care and Protection of Children of Employed Mothers: Hearing before the Committee on Education and Labor.* 78th Cong., 1st sess., June 8, 1943.

U.S. Department of Labor, Women's Bureau. *Working Mothers and the Need for Child Care Services.* Washington, D.C.: U.S. Government Printing Office, 1965.

———. "Women Workers in Ten War Production Areas and Their Postwar Employment Plans." *Bulletin of the Women's Bureau,* No. 209. Washington, D.C.: U.S. Government Printing Office, 1946.

U.S. Federal Security Agency, U.S. Public Health Service. *Vital Statistics of the United States,* part 1, *Illegitimate Births by Race: Birth Registration Area, 1917–1946.* Washington, D.C.: U.S. Government Printing Office, 1948.

U.S. Women's Bureau. *Employed Mothers and Child Care.* Bulletin 246. Washington, D.C.: U.S. Government Printing Office, 1955.

———. *Women Workers in Ten War Production Areas and Their Postwar Employment Plans.* Bulletin 209. Washington, D.C.: U.S. Government Printing Office, 1946.

Oral Histories

Albrier, Frances Mary. *Frances Mary Albrier: Determined Advocate for Racial Equality.* Interview by Malca Chall. Women in Politics Oral History Project, Black Women Oral History Project, Bancroft Library, Schlesinger Library, 1977–78.

Arnstein, Lawrence. *Community Service in California Public Health and Social Welfare.*

Interview by Edna T. Daniel. Transcript, Regional Oral History Office (formerly Regional Cultural History Project), Bancroft Library, University of California at Berkeley, 1964.

Debs, Ernest. *Oral History Interview with Ernest E. Debs*. Interview by Carlos Vasquez. Oral History Program, University of California, Los Angeles, for the State Government Oral History Program, 1987.

Eliel, Harriet (Mrs. Paul). League of Women Voters Oral History Interview by Carol Farley. Transcript, California Historical Society, 1973.

Geddes, Ernest R. *California Assemblyman*. Interview by Enid Douglas. Transcript, Oral History Program, Claremont Graduate School, Claremont, Calif., 1976.

Gunterman, Emma. *Emma Gunterman: Lobbyist and Advocate for Consumers, Children, and Seniors, 1967–1986*. Interview by Jacqueline S. Reinier. Transcript, California State Archives, State Government Oral History Program, 1989–90.

Hawkins, Augustus F. *Black Leadership in Los Angeles: Augustus F. Hawkins*. Interview by Clyde Woods. UCLA Oral History Department, 1995. Department of Special Collections, Charles E. Young Research Library, University of California, Los Angeles.

———. Oral History Interview by Carlos Vásquez, 1988. UCLA Oral History Program. California State Archives, State Government Oral History Program.

Kaross, Sonia Baltrun. *Women in California Collection: Trade Unionists and Left Wing Women*. Interview by Lucy Kendall. Transcript, California Historical Society, 1977.

Lambert, Louise Todd. *Women in California Collection*. Interview by Lucy Kendall. Transcript, California Historical Society, 1976.

MacGregor, Helen. *Helen MacGregor: A Career in Public Service with Earl Warren*. Interview by Amelia Fry, June Hogan, and Gabrielle Morris. Transcript, University of California, Regional Oral History Program, Earl Warren Oral History Program, 1973.

Orr, Violet. *Women in California Collection: Trade Unionists and Left Wing Women*. Interview by Lucy Kendall. Transcript, California Historical Society, 1976, 1977.

Pittman, Tarea Hall. *Tarea Hall Pittman: NAACP Official and Civil Rights Worker*. Interview by Joyce Henderson. Transcript, University of California, Regional Oral History Program, Earl Warren Oral History Program, Bancroft Library, University of California at Berkeley, 1974.

Stolz, Lois Meek. *An American Child Development Pioneer*. Interview by Ruby Takaneshi. Transcript, UCLA Academic Senate Research Committee; copy in Special Collections, Milbank Memorial Library, Teachers College, Columbia University, 1977.

———. *Interviews with Leaders in the Child Guidance and Clinic Movement*. Interview by Milton J. E. Senn. History of Science and Technology Collection, Bancroft Library, University of California at Berkeley, 1968.

———. *Lois Meek Stolz: An Interview by Margo Davis*. Stanford Oral History Project, University Archives, Stanford University, 1983.

Tenney, Jack. *California Legislator*. Interview by Donald Schippers. Transcript, Oral History Program, University of California, Los Angeles, 1965–66.

Oral Interviews

Arnold, Mary Elizabeth [Young]. Interview by author, Oct. 7, 1998. Tape recording, Santa Rosa.

Beeson, Lynne [Monti]. Interview by author, May 2, 2006. Transcribed tape recording, San Francisco.

Gach, Barbara. Interview by author, July 2, 1998. Tape recording, Belvedere, Calif.

Godske, Sharon. Interview by author, March 11, 2006. Transcribed tape recording, Berkeley.

Juhas, Loretta. Interview by author, Jan. 3, 2006. Transcribed tape recording, San Francisco.

Miller, Jeanne. Interview by author, June 16, 1999. Transcribed tape recording, Kentfield, Calif.

Mitchell, Ellen Hall. Interview by author, Feb. 8, 2006. Transcribed tape recording, Long Beach.

Nolan, Jeanada. Interview by author, Dec. 21, 2005. Transcribed tape recording, Sacramento.

Rall, Elizabeth. Interview by author, Nov. 18, 1997. Tape recording, Mill Valley.

Rose, Virginia. Interview by author, May 28, 1998. Tape recording, Oakland.

Sample, Winona. Interview by author, Nov. 21, 2005. Transcribed tape recording, Folsom, Calif.

Young, Deborah. Interview by author, Dec. 15, 1998. Tape recording, Fairfax, Calif.; Interview by author transcribed tape recording, Nov 25, 2005, Larkspur, Calif.

Williams, Fay E. [Love]. Interview by author, July 12, 2006. Transcribed tape recording, Antioch, Calif.

Zavitkovsky, Docia. Interview by author, July 28, 1998. Transcribed tape recording, Los Angeles.

Newspapers

Berkeley Gazette
California Eagle
CIO News
Daily People's World
Humboldt Times
Labor Herald
Los Angeles Mirror
Los Angeles Sentinel
Los Angeles Times
Oakland Tribune
Sacramento Bee
San Francisco Call-Bulletin
San Francisco Chronicle
San Francisco Daily News
San Francisco Examiner
San Francisco News

Archival Collections

AFRICAN-AMERICAN MUSEUM AND LIBRARY AT OAKLAND

Colored Women's Clubs Association Collection
Vertical Files—Frances Albrier

BANCROFT LIBRARY, UNIVERSITY OF CALIFORNIA AT BERKELEY

Berkeley Day Nursery Records
Helen MacGregor Papers
Lawrence Arnstein Papers
League of Women Voters of Berkeley Papers
Robert W. Kenny Papers
San Francisco Council of Industrial Organizations Records
San Francisco Labor Council Records

CALIFORNIA HISTORICAL SOCIETY, SAN FRANCISCO

League of Women Voters of San Francisco, 1916–63
League of Women Voters of California, 1934–79
Muriel Shoesmith Papers, 1919–73

CALIFORNIA STATE ARCHIVES

Alan Sieroty Papers
California State War Council Records
Carley V. Porter Papers
Department of Social Welfare Records
Earl Warren Papers
Goodwin Knight Papers
Governor's Chapter Bill Files
Joint Legislative Budget Committee Files
Office of Economic Opportunity Papers
Robert Moretti Papers
State Department of Education Papers
Yvonne Braithwaite Papers

CONGRESSIONAL ARCHIVES, UNIVERSITY OF OKLAHOMA, NORMAN

Helen Gahagan Douglas Papers

DEPARTMENT OF SPECIAL COLLECTIONS, STANFORD UNIVERSITY

Goodwin J. Knight Papers
Tillie Olsen Papers

GOLDEN GATE KINDERGARTEN ASSOCIATION, PHOEBE A. HEARST PRESCHOOL LEARNING CENTER, SAN FRANCISCO

Golden Gate Kindergarten Association Papers
Rhoda Kellogg Papers

MARIANNE WOLMAN ARCHIVES, PACIFIC OAKS COLLEGE, PASADENA

Docia Zavitovsky Papers
John Weber Papers
Theresa S. Mahler Papers

NATIONAL ARCHIVES AND RECORDS ADMINISTRATION (NARA), PACIFIC REGION (SAN FRANCISCO), SAN BRUNO

RG 12, Office of Education
RG 171, Office of Civilian Defense
RG 211, War Manpower Commission

NARA, COLLEGE PARK, MD.

RG171, Office of Civilian Defense
RG 211, War Manpower Commission
RG 215, Office of Community War Service

OAKLAND HISTORY ROOM, OAKLAND PUBLIC LIBRARY, OAKLAND

Oakland History Collection

OTHER

Lynne Beeson Papers, in Lynne Beeson's possession
Mary Young Papers, in author's possession

RONALD REAGAN PRESIDENTIAL LIBRARY, SIMI VALLEY, CALIF.

Ronald Reagan Gubernatorial Papers

SOUTHERN CALIFORNIA LIBRARY FOR SOCIAL STUDIES AND RESEARCH

Communist Party Subject Files
Women's Subject Files

SPECIAL COLLECTIONS, UNIVERSITY OF CALIFORNIA, LOS ANGELES

Augustus F. Hawkins Papers

SPECIAL COLLECTIONS, JOHN F. KENNEDY MEMORIAL LIBRARY, CALIFORNIA STATE UNIVERSITY, LOS ANGELES

Ernest E. Debs Papers
Mervyn M. Dymally Papers

UNIVERSITY ARCHIVES, CALIFORNIA STATE UNIVERSITY, LONG BEACH

Dorothy Healey Collection

URBAN ARCHIVES CENTER, CALIFORNIA STATE UNIVERSITY, NORTHRIDGE, CALIF.

California Association for the Education of Young Children Collection
League of Women Voters of Los Angeles
Los Angeles County Federation of Labor, AFL-CIO
Rosalie M. Blau Papers

Index

AAUW (American Association of University Women), 26–27, 135
abortion rights, 159
Abshire, F. Presley, 114
activism: of African Americans, 45–46, 193n39; of Blau, 48, 69–70, 73; of educators, 69–72; grassroots, 20, 42–48, 67–69, 107, 151; of Mahler, 84, 93–96, 100–109, 114–18, 157; parental, 40, 42–48, 73–74, 125, 130–31, 171–74; of women, 2, 40, 42–48, 94–96; of Woods, 33–35, 60, 69–70, 116; of working mothers, 67–69, 72–88, 94–96, 125, 128–31; of Young, Mary, 93–100, 104–8, 114–18, 171–74. *See also* women: politicization of
ADC. *See* Aid to Dependent Children
Addison, Willie Mae, 141, 144, 152, 158
Advisory Committee of Preschool Educational Programs, 169
AFDC, 112, 146
AFL (American Federation of Labor), 22
African Americans: activism of, 45–46, 193n39; California Council of Negro Women, 81; employment opportunities for women, 37; and letter-writing campaigns, 75; migration of, 21, 123; *The Negro Family: The Case for National Action* (Moynihan), 208n69; and public child care centers, 19–20, 149, 184n24; and welfare, 6, 111, 123, 136–37, 163; welfare statistics, 146. *See also* racial tensions; racism
Aid to Dependent Children (ADC): anti-welfare movement, 5–6; economic benefits

of, 112; and means tests, 51–52; recipient statistics, 123; and stigma of welfare, 123; supervision and moral judgments of, 6, 57, 121–23; and working mothers, 79–80. *See also* Aid to Families with Dependent Children
Aid to Families with Dependent Children (AFDC), 112, 146
Aid to Needy Children (ANC), 111–12, 151. *See also* Aid to Dependent Children
Aid to Needy Children Mothers Anonymous, 151
Alameda County Welfare Commission, 25
Alpha Kappa Alpha, 19
American Association of University Women (AAUW), 26–27, 135
American Federation of Labor (AFL), 22
American Women (President's Commission on the Status of Women), 153
ANC (Aid to Needy Children), 111–12, 151
ANC Mothers Anonymous of Watts, 157
Angstman, Grace J., 148
anticommunist movement, 61–63, 68, 84, 94
anti-war movement, 148
anti-welfare movement, 5–6, 147–48
Arnstein, Lawrence, 103–7, 112–13, 115–17, 136
Avalon Child Care Guild, 46

Bachman, Betty L., 99, 106, 110–12, 116–18
Baldwin, Mrs. Harris, 27
Baruch, Dorothy, 29
Bass, Carlotta, 46

NATALIE M. FOUSEKIS is an associate professor of history and the director of the Center for Oral and Public History at California State University, Fullerton.

The University of Illinois Press
is a founding member of the
Association of American University Presses.

Designed by Jim Proefrock
Composed in 10.5/13 Minion Pro Regular
with Scala Sans Pro display
by Celia Shapland
at the University of Illinois Press
Manufactured by Sheridan Books, Inc.

University of Illinois Press
1325 South Oak Street
Champaign, IL 61820-6903
www.press.uillinois.edu